FATWA

To Mohandes Akbar Taheri, without
whose generous support I could hardly have
accomplished my studies at Tehran University,
many years ago

and

to all writers, thinkers, journalists and artists,
victims of repression and intolerance.

Mehdi Mozaffari

FATWA

Violence & Discourtesy

AARHUS UNIVERSITY PRESS

Copyright: Aarhus University Press, 1998
Printed on permanent paper conforming to ANSI
standard Z39.48-1984 by The Alden Press, Oxford, England
Cover photograph: Ole Woldbye/The David Collection, Copenhagen
ISBN 87 7288 776 1

AARHUS UNIVERSITY PRESS
Building 170
University of Aarhus
DK-8000 Aarhus C, Denmark
Fax + 45 86 19 84 33

73 Lime Walk,
Headington, Oxford OX3 7AD
Fax (+44) 1865 750 079

Box 511,
Oakville, Conn. 06779
Fax (+ 1) 860 945 9468

Contents

Illustrations

Introduction

The *fatwa* is the central theme of this book. The word 'fatwa' became known worldwide in February 1989 when Ayatollah Khomeini delivered a death sentence against Salman Rushdie and the distributors of *The Satanic Verses*. Before this event, Muslims of course knew the word 'fatwa', but otherwise only specialists in Islamic studies and maybe a few erudites were familiar with it. Now, 'fatwa' belongs to our new universal vocabulary. When CNN, BBC and other international media use it, everybody knows what it is. Yet, the question remains: What is a fatwa? The fact is that most people think it is equivalent to 'death sentence,' to 'violent and arbitrary action,' and to 'terrorism.' However, this is not at all the real meaning of fatwa.

As we will see in the first chapter, the fatwa is originally and essentially an Islamic version of the Roman *jus respondi*, which during history has been transformed into various versions. I am Muslim by birth, so I knew that a fatwa is not only about violence and death sentences. As a student of political science at Tehran University and as a political activist in Iran in the 1960s, I became familiar with this and other Islamic terms. It was during these years that Khomeini became leader of the rebellion against the Shah's regime and delivered his famous fatwa prohibiting the practice of *taqiyya*, which roughly means 'dissimulation of political opinion'. This fatwa played a decisive role in the open struggle against the Shah's regime. My knowledge of Islamic terminology broadened when in Paris I started research on *La Conception Shi'ite du Pouvoir*, my doctoral thesis at Sorbonne (February 1971). Many years later, when Ayatollah Khomeini delivered his fatwa on Rushdie, I — like everyone else — first took it to be a fatwa, without questioning its adherence to Islamic rules for valid, genuine fatwas. The reason for the general acceptance must be found in Khomeini's well-known theological competence. Just as in previous instances, he fulfilled all requirements for delivering a fatwa, so there was no reason to doubt the validity of this particular fatwa. Likewise, nobody questioned whether Khomeini's fatwa conformed to the existing law of the Islamic regime, established by Khomeini himself. It was not until I seriously began to study fatwas in general and Khomeini's fatwa in particular that I discovered several deviant and abnormal aspects of his fatwa on Rushdie. These abnormalities are so fundamental that the entire validity of this particular fatwa must be questioned.

The fact that Khomeini's fatwa does not conform to Islamic rules and that it contradicts Iranian law is crucial, because this evidence will erode the Iranian government's argument that 'this is a fatwa and nobody can change it'! Of course, I do not mean to say that if Khomeini had delivered a valid fatwa, it would have been right and justified. Absolutely not. But had it conformed to these rules, we would at least have been dealing with a formally and legally valid act. This is not the case, because when Khomeini delivered his fatwa, he broke his own rules, in fact violated his own laws. This makes a huge difference, because in addition to breaking his own rules, his fatwa also contradicts all basic rules of civil social behaviour and freedom of speech.

This book is also about *toleration*, or more precisely about the *lack of toleration*. Therefore it is important to emphasize from the start, that this book is neither for or against Islam, nor is it for or against Salman Rushdie. My intention is to present a more accurate picture of the history of the fatwa and its many consequences, some of them tragic. The content of Khomeini's fatwa is in itself horrible. A number of people have already been killed because of it, among them the Italian and the Japanese translators of *The Satanic Verses*. Others were killed *before* the fatwa, during demonstrations against Rushdie's book in Pakistan and elsewhere. The astonishing thing is that there are still millions of people who obviously support this fatwa, and some of them are ready to kill Rushdie. An Iranian ambassador volunteered to kill Rushdie with his own hands! It is evident that those who value the freedom and dignity of human beings clearly distance themselves from such primitive behaviour and unconditionally condemn censorship and repression. I also vigorously condemn Khomeini's fatwa and support Rushdie as a writer, but this position does not necessarily force me to accept the contents and the substance of *The Satanic Verses*. In my view, it is quite possible and even healthy to defend a writer in the name of freedom of speech and at the same time criticize him. This position is generally called Voltairian. Voltaire said that: 'I do not agree with what you say, but I defend to the death your right to say it.' Of course, I do not think of Rushdie as my enemy, but I am not sure that what he wrote was innocent. Innocence, in the Voltairian sense, means respecting the beliefs, the symbols, and the dignity of other people. Everybody, including your enemies. Generally, we are all tolerant of people with whom we share opinions and beliefs. Real toleration means giving space to people with whom we *do not* share opinions and beliefs. In this respect, I intend — as much as possible — to see the 'case' from both sides without prejudice, and leave everybody to draw their own conclusions. Therefore, I intentionally leave out my own conclusion.

The book is divided into six chapters which I call 'Sura'. Sura is the name of the different chapters in the Koran. I find this name original and beautiful, and therefore I use it instead of 'chapter'. There is no Koranic prohibition against this practice, and it is only in an aesthetic and exotic spirit that I use 'Sura', and absolutely not for any polemic or provocative reason. *Sura I* is a condensed review of the birth and evolution of the concept and the institution of fatwa under various Islamic empires. *Sura II* demonstrates the false character of Khomeini's fatwa as well as its fallacies, and describes Khomeini's cognitive map and his necrophiliac personality. Furthermore, a part of *Sura II* studies different stages of Shi'a violence before and after the Islamic revolution. We will see that Rushdie has not been the first and only writer to receive a death sentence from Khomeini and his cohorts. Other writers have been assassinated by Islamists for the same 'crime'. Shi'a violence is a rather new phenomenon, at least in the Imâmi branch which

Khomeini represents. I argue that this violence was not exclusively a result of one man's will and decisions, but that it was (and is) structural as well. To illustrate this aspect, I will argue that the violence, especially in its revolutionary form, emerged because of the economic interests of a specific social group, the *Bazar*. This argument contrasts the dominant opinion that the Islamic revolution was merely a *religious* revolution. My argument is that although religion, and especially the Shi'a priesthood, played an important role in this revolution, the role of the Bazar was just as important. After the victory of the sacrosanct Bazar-Ulama alliance, the Shi'a violence, which until then had been sporadic and conjectural, became systematic and structured. All these questions are discussed in *Sura III*, while *Sura IV* focuses on *blasphemy* in Judaism, Christianity and Islam (Sunni and Shi'a). The discussion will proceed to a study of secular regimes' position on blasphemy and related issues. *Sura IV* will also discuss Salman Rushdie's position in the Universe of Islam, and I will, in the Voltairian spirit, formulate a brief criticism of Rushdie. I will argue that Rushdie did not show Muslims the proper respect and courtesy. Khomeini's fatwa provoked (and still does) extraordinary international reactions. This is the subject of *Sura V*, where the reactions of different states and organizations (Western and Islamic) as well as the reactions of Muslim and non-Muslim intellectuals and writers are systematically reviewed. In the last chapter, *Sura VI*, I will argue that religion in general, and Islam in particular, are unfamiliar with freedom of speech. Religion has promised human beings *salvation*, but not freedom of speech or democracy. Therefore, it is too much to expect religion to also guarantee freedom and to offer favourable conditions for democracy.

The Man in the Black Mantle

Nothing indicated that February 14, 1989 was destined to be a special day. Tehran was calm, cold and sad. Tehranis were going about their daily business. Women in chador, men with beards, some of them with a rosary in their hands. Their eyes were empty of light and their feet were tired from moving their bodies to another 'millioni' demonstration in glory of new martyrs.

February is a dreary month, also in Tehran. Especially in Tehran. It was only two weeks ego that they celebrated the 10th anniversary of the Revolution. On this day they were searching for the shortest queue for rice, bread and detergent. In February the days are short; since February 1979, they had become twice as short.

Since then, Iranians have only two words for colour: black and red. Red is the noble colour, the colour of martyrs. Black is the common colour: men, women, children, and priests wear black. Not because it is the colour of oil, the wealth of the country; but because of mourning. The Shi'a still mourn the death of Husayn who was assassinated in Karbala in AD 680. Everybody will give his life for Husayn; everybody loves Husayn and cries over his tragic death. After his death, Husayn was elevated to the status of The Lord of Martyrs. In Paradise, his lordship has even more souls than today's China. From Iran alone, two million people recently joined his 'China Town'. Two blocks to the right of 'China Town' you find 'Q8 City'. It is the name that one million Iraqis who were killed from 1980 to 1988 have given to this oasis in Paradise. Between them is the UN's Safe Haven. Kurds and Bosnians live there. The

People of Grozny still do not have a designated spot. They camp on the hill. The flag in 'China Town' is red.

On this dark day of February 14, the only white colour visible to Tehranis was the snow on the peak of the majestic Damavand, the Iranian Mont Blanc. For years, many Tehranis didn't look at Damavand. It stands there as always, but nobody would pay much attention to it. Or, deliberately, they wouldn't look in that direction. An Old Man lives there, not far from the mountain. In Jamaran. The Old Man has a black turban and a black mantle. His face looks noble with a long, white beard, a nice nose and healthy teeth. He certainly has eyes also. But nobody has ever seen them. He is looking steadily at nowhere. Perhaps those who are the Spirit of God look like that. Ruh Allah (Spirit of God) is the name of the Old Man.

Last night, Ruh Allah watched TV together with his son Ahmad. So, he has eyes and he can see. Ahmad is also in black and always looks melancholy. People have given him a nickname: 'Crying Ahmad.' Ahmad served *chai* from the Caspian Sea region and gave some heart pills to his father. Ruh Allah has a heart disease, but the doctors couldn't find any heart in his body. They told him that the Spirit of God is created of pure 'spirit' without a heart. But he can get heart disease from solidarity with the martyrs' mothers. Ahmad asked The Spirit if he would like to see a video which Sadegh — Ahmad's brother-in-law — had recently brought back from his trip to Germany. It was a gift from Germany's Foreign Minister, Hans-Dietrich Genscher. The Spirit asked, 'what is it about?' 'Animal life', answered Ahmad. 'Oh, turn the TV on', said The Spirit. On the *glass wool* (Iranian post-revolutionary term for TV screen) a bearded man in black appeared who announced the tragic events which had happened the day before in our brother country, Pakistan. It was a violent demonstration in which six persons were killed and a great number injured by the police. The demonstrators were crying in Urdu.

The Spirit who was lying in his bed, got up slowly and sat cross-legged. He understood what was going on, but not completely. 'Damn it! Who is Rushdie?' screamed Ruh Allah. 'He is a man of Bombay, like us!' said Ahmad without raising his voice. 'I don't know any animal with this name', said The Spirit furiously. 'Me neither, father. He wasn't on Genscher's video which I saw over at Sadegh's place', murmured Ahmad and gently turned the TV off. Now, The Spirit was walking in his modest room, softly, still looking nowhere. He looked tired and went back to bed without asking for more pills. When Ahmad was about to leave the room, The Spirit said, 'Baba! We are from Kashmir, not Bombay. Don't forget this!' Ahmad left the room after switching off the electric lamp.

Ahmad's house was connected to his father's place. Ahmad's house was always full of people. Ministers, military staff, ayatollahs, governors, revolutionary guards, from 7 a.m. to 7 p.m. After that, Ahmad's private life began. This evening he was with his old friends from his former football club. The menu was *chello kabab-e soltani*, the same as the previous evening. They talked about everything between heaven and earth. The good old days, when they played football together, and went to *hammam* together. Everyone still had his own idol. Ja'far was for Pele, Taqi for Beckenbauer, and Mohsen for Cruyff. Ahmad did not change his idol either. He was still a fan of the Briton, Chelston. Mohsen, who is now a prosperous businessman, said that Chelston was no longer in England. He had become a trainer for a German club. He also talked a lot about the British hooligans and the hard criticism of them that he heard during his stay in London. But this stuff was no longer the centre of discussion in England. Now, everybody everywhere was talking about a book. He couldn't remember the title: 'Satanic ... something'. Mohsen told his comrades — who were now listening to him intently — what he had seen on TV in his hotel room in Kensington. Clashes between police and Bengali Moslems who burned the book of a Pakistani writer, Rushdie. Ahmad said that Rushdie was from Bombay, not Pakistan, and told them what he and his father had seen on TV that evening.

When his comrades left his place, Ahmad opened the window

for some fresh air. Through the heavy smoke flowing out of the room, Ahmad noticed light in the room of The Spirit. It was 3 o'clock on the morning. Too early for morning prayer. He quickly went to his father's room, without making any noise. The Spirit was praying. Non-mandatory 'night' prayer. *Assallamu alaykum va rahmatullah va barakatuhu*. The Spirit turned his head first to the right, then to the left, touching his face with two hands from the top of his forehead to the end of his beard. It was the end of the prayer. 'Salaam', said Ahmad respectfully. 'Salaam, Ahmad! ... You know I had a strange dream tonight. I saw a tall man with a black turban, bigger than mine. He was beautifully draped in a black mantle. I couldn't see his face, I only heard his angry voice telling me, 'Your power is mine, your power is mine', and then it disappeared. But the voice was there; and I heard the same voice again and again, like an echo'. Ahmad, staring at his father's mouth, said to himself, 'Who could it be? ... The Shah maybe'.

The Spirit raised his right hand, pointed to Ahmad and said: '*Ahmagh* (Stupid!) The Shah is dead. Dead, you understand!' 'You are right, father. The damned Shah hated both turbans and beards.' 'Of course!' Ruh Allah said triumphantly. 'Of course! The *Aghâ* I saw tonight is the Hidden Imam. It is not the first time that I see the *Aghâ*. Last time was the night that I decided to continue the war against Saddam. The *Aghâ* was laughing.' The Spirit was totally convinced that the man in the black mantle was the Hidden Imam who was unhappy with him. He couldn't understand the reason. Thousands and thousands of enemies of Islam are now eliminated or in prison. Two million impure escaped the country. No longer a drop of alcohol is drunk under Islamic rule, no music, no song, no dance. Islam is everywhere now. Why should the *Aghâ* be angry. 'Aahh ... I know why.' Ahmad could see his father's eyes were beginning to smile. Maliciously. He knew what that smile meant. A new victory for Islam was on the way. A big decision was made. 'This animal ... Rushdie, he has made the *Aghâ* so unhappy. He must go to Hell!' The joy was clearly apparent in his voice when Ruh Allah ordered Ahmad to write ...'*Bismihi ta'âla*. I would like to inform all the intrepid Muslims in the world that the author of the book entitled *The Satanic Verses* which has been compiled, printed and published against Islam, the Prophet and the Koran, as well as those publishers who were aware of its contents, have been sentenced to death...'

It was 8 a.m. when Tehran radio announced the sentence. Tehran was calm, cold and sad. The Man in the black mantle was laughing! ...

What is and What is not a Fatwa?

Definition of Fatwa

The problem with the term *fatwa* is that it has been used to describe different things simultaneously. Therefore, during the long history of Islam, *fatwa* has become more and more complex and also more and more vague and imprecise. We will try here to clarify the concept of *fatwa* by 'liberating' it from other concepts with which it has been confused.

First of all, we can say that a *fatwa* is not a *judiciary verdict* (*hukma al-qadâ*) which is issued by a competent trial. A *fatwa*, a fortiori, is not a *law* (*qânûn/shar'*) or an *act of law* (*hukm al-qânûn /hukm al-shar'*). Furthermore, a *fatwa* is not an *order* (*Amr/Hukm*) issued by a competent, executory authority.

If *fatwa* is neither a verdict, a law nor an order, what is a *fatwa* then? A fatwa *is the answer which a competent and qualified religious authority gives to a question concerning a point of Islamic law (shari'a).* In this sense, the *fatwa* corresponds to the Roman institution of *jus respondendi*. Henri Laoust, a great specialist in Islam, translated *fatwa* as 'consultations doctrinales' (Laoust, 1970: 278). The *fatwa* must obviously have an *object*, i.e. a *question* on which the *fatwa* has been issued.

In this respect, there are two kinds of objects. The first consists of voicing an opinion on a *single* point of law in which the competent and qualified authority has been asked. This is the original and regular kind of *fatwa*. The second type is applying the *fatwa*, by metaphor, to a series of questions that have not been asked — not directly anyway — but the 'answers' are delivered on the *fatwa* giver's own initiative. The *Fatawi-al Kubra* (plural of *fatwa*) of Ibn Taymiyya (d. 855) are examples of the partial, metaphorical application of *fatwa* to a book (generally in many volumes) containing the author's opinion on different issues of *shari'a*. It must also to be said that a number of Ibn Taymiyya's *fatwas* are real *fatwas*, i.e., the questions were raised with him by specific *fatwa* callers (an individual or a group). Contemporary examples of this kind of *fatwa* are the fatwas of Shaykh Mhmud Shaltut (1893-1963) who became Shaykh al-Azhar (in 1958) and, his fatwas are collected under the subtitle: 'A study of contemporary problems which arise in a Muslim's everyday life' (Zebiri, 1991: 109). There is also a significant difference between the Shi'a and Sunni use of the word *fatwa*. While the Sunni fatwa(s) apply to both the first and second categories described above; the Shi'a generally use the fatwa adhering to the first meaning; the second category is called *Risâla 'Amaliyya* (Book of Religion's Practice) The fatwa of the first and the second categories are valid only on the *Subsidiary Principles (Forû')*. Nobody is allowed to follow (*taqlid*) on the matters which are connected with the *Princpal Principles (Usûl)* — (Golpayegani 'Ayatollah', 1986: 4). In this study, we will follow the regular and normal *fatwa*, the first type.

Origins of Fatwa

The word *'fatwa'* as such does not figure in the Koran. On the other hand, derivatives of the word *'fatwa'* have been used in the Koran (9 times: S. IV, v. 127 and 176, S. XII, v. 41, 43 and 46, S. XXIII, v. 32 and S. XXXII, v. 10 and 149) in different contexts and concerning different questions. The common feature of all of them is that the derivatives always indicate *questioning, pronouncing an opinion*, and never a verdict, an act of law, or an order. For example, 'They will ask thee for a pronouncement concerning women ...' (S.IV, v. 127.) or 'Joseph, thou true man, pronounce to us ...' (S. XII, v. 46).

Historically, the institution of *fatwa* was unknown during Mohammad's lifetime and also during the whole period of the

Rightly Guided Vicars (*The Râshidûn*: 632-61), for the simple reason
that there was no need for *fatwa*. Al-Ghazâli (1058-1111), the
prominent theologian affirms this fact; he called the *Râshidûn* 'those
who were *independent* to give *fatwas*' (Ghazâli, 1933: I, 70). In the
context of Ghazâli's observation, there is no doubt that the word
'*fatwa*' has a different meaning depending on its application to the
Râshidûn or to those who came to power after them. It is also worth
mentioning that Al-Ghazâli used the term 'independent' exclusively
for the *Râshidûn* and never for other Muslim rulers or other Ulama.
When the same Ghazâli excludes the power holders in general as
qualified *fatwa* givers, it seems clear that applying the term *fatwa* to
Râshidûn indicated only their theological/jurisdictional *competence*
to deliver the *fatwa*, but not their *ability* to do it, because their office
as power holders is not compatible with the function as *fatwa*-giver.
What is valid for *Râshidûn*, is also *a fortiori* true for the Prophet
himself. It seems unthinkable that the Prophet would ask somebody
else to give him their opinion on Islamic law when he himself was
building it up and formulating it! He asked for advice, but never
for a *fatwa*! Furthermore, the Prophet's words had nothing to do
with *fatwa*, because they were incorporated in the Koran either as
God's words or as *sunna* (the Prophet's verbal expression besides
his practical expression). His also gave orders to his immediate
followers, but not *fatwa*. The *fatwa* was not practiced after his death
either. His four direct companions who came to power successively
had enough knowledge about the Koran and other matters related
to political and social life and events that they did not feel any
need to ask for *fatwa*. With the disappearance of the first generation
of the Prophet's Companions, the institution of a vast administration and an immense empire, the need for *fatwa* increased at the
same speed as the emergence of new cases, new problems, and new
questions. In this connection, one can say that the institution of
fatwa originally was motivated by *political and administrative* needs
rather than purely *religious* imperatives. But since the formal bases
of the new empire were religious, the people who were considered
competent to give their qualified opinion on a point of law were

persons who knew the Koran and *sunna* well. These persons were later labelled Ulama, *Mufti, Mujtahid,* etc.

In his impressive work on the history of Islamic jurisdictional organization, Émile Tyan arrived at the conclusion that *fatwa* giving appeared spontaneously in early Islamic history. Faced with a new set of norms and rules embodied in a new religion, Muslims, especially the new converts, needed to know how to deal with their new religion in daily life. Therefore, they asked for advice from those who were most learned in the still infant Islamic law. The demands for *fatwa* initially came from private persons and not from the administrative authorities. For example, in the first century of *hijir* (the Islamic calendar), the famous Hassan al-Basri (a prominent figure of the Mu'tazili school) used to deliver *fatwa* to individuals without having been appointed to this charge. Similarly, in the beginning of the 2nd century, Yazid ibn al-Habib came from Iraq to Egypt and acted as 'consultant' to the local population. There are other similar examples from the following centuries. Slowly and progressively, the spontaneous and private character of *fatwa* changed into an official position and a public function (Tyan, 1960: 219-22).

It is not clear when the first *fatwa* — *stricto sensu* — was delivered and by whom. A qualified guess would be the so-called *'fatwa'* that Shurayh gave at the request of Yazid, the second caliph of The Umayyad dynasty (d. AD 683). Shurayh had previously been appointed by Omar (the Second Rightly Guided Caliph) as judge (*qâdi*), and he remained in office also under Yazid. The Shurayh's *'fatwa'* was motivated by Husayn's rebellion against Yazid, accusing him of being a usurper. Husayan (assassinated in Karbala in 680) was the second son of Ali and the third Shi'a Imam. Shurayh, in terms of a *fatwa*, condemned Husayn's action. It seems that the so-called Shurayh's *'fatwa'* falls under the category of judicial acts without having any consultative characteristics. But the fatwa institution really flourished during the Abbasids dynasty (750-1258). During this long period, the Islamic administration expanded vastly and the immense empire became a huge agglomerate of different nations, cultures, and ethnic groups living together in the huge empire. One can imagine the extraordinary number of problems (administration, taxation, arbitrage, etc.) which could arise in such a heteroclite society. Add to this the different kinds of wars that the empire was confronted with (both internally and externally). The central administration had to come up with answers to all these problems. If answers could not directly and indisputably be found either in the Koran or in *Sunna*, the Ulama (jurisconsults) were asked to resolve the problems by using analogy (*qiyâs*) or to form a consensus (*ijmâ'*), if one did not already exist on the point in dispute. This was the regular and normal way to make new laws. Again only by metaphor, the codification of the juridical opinions of a specific mujtahid/mufti or even a judge (*qâdi*). These kinds of collections are usually a mixture of true *fatwa*s (based on a specific question asked of the mujtahids), and the mujtahid's opinions (*ra'y/ârâ'*) initiated by himself in absence of the 'asking' procedure. At the same time, there are many examples that regular and normal *fatwa* giving worked under the Abbasids as well as under the Saljuqs (1038-1194), and later on under the Ottomans (1281-1922). In all these examples, one thing remained predominant: the public character of *fatwa*. That means that the *fatwa* was generally asked by the Caliph or Sultan himself, or by the judges or administrators for the purpose of their functions. Private persons or groups rarely asked for *fatwa* until sometime in the 19th century. This fact has two explanations: Firstly, individuals as such did not have enough importance/ influence under Islamic regimes; and secondly, in the Mujtahids' eyes it was uninteresting to deliver *fatwa* to a private person, because such an act would not give them prestige or more influence.

So far, we have mostly discussed *fatwa* in a genuine Islamic system, dominated by Sunni. The use of *fatwa* in Shi'a (= Imâmi /Twelvers) occurred relatively late. This can be explained by two things: First, the Shi'a as opposed to Sunni never seized power, except in some local dynasties. At the time of the Safavids (1501-1732) in Iran, the Shi'a were recognized as an official sect, and by virtue of that, the Shi'a Ulama exercised some tangible influence. Second, the Shi'a believe in twelve imams of which the last disappeared in 868. During the lifetime and physical presence of the Twelfth Imam, the question of *fatwa* could not have been posed, because the imams, like the Prophet, were recognized as infallible, and as such their words were considered to be the indisputable truth. It was only after the disappearance of the Twelfth Imam, and especially after the institution of Safavids, that the Shi'a Ulama began to deliver *fatwa*.

The Constitutive Elements of Fatwa

A qualified *fatwa* has three different constitutive elements: 1) a *fatwa-giver (Mufti)*, 2) a *fatwa-caller (Mustafti)*, and 3) a specific *object/question*. Although it is not a constitutive element, the physical form of *fatwa* is also important.

The Fatwa-giver (Mufti/Mujtahid)

Unlike Christianity, Islam has neither churches nor monasteries. The non-institutionalized character of Islam's religious personnel and authorities has resulted in the *diffusion* of religious authorities. By 'diffusion,' we mean the absence of a centralized and hierarchical institution in religious matters equivalent to the Vatican. In the very first period (the period of Mohammad himself and then the period of the *Râshidûn*), the question was not raised concerning the specification and separation of 'political matters' on the one hand, and 'religious matters' on the other. Both matters were incorporated in one and the same person: the Prophet and his immediate (Four) Vicars. They decided everything, sometimes even in detail, and had enough power and legitimacy to enforce their decisions. They not only led the wars and decided on peace, but they also led prayers and issued decrees on all religious questions. Sometimes, they delegated some of their responsibilities to their close companions and 'colleagues'. The Prophet had appointed Abu Bakr (d. 634, who later became his immediate successor) to lead prayer *by delegation*. Omar (the second caliph, d. 644) had also appointed a limited number of persons as judges, though by delegation. The religious authority always remained in the hands of one single person: the Caliph. Consequently, the words, decrees, and other acts that emanated from the Prophet and the *Râshidûn* were not the expression of their *opinion (fatwa)*, but the illustration of their *will*, followed by a decision which must be obeyed and executed by everyone. More correctly, they gave *orders (amr)*, not *advice*.

Under the Umayyads and Abbasids, the expansion of the Islamic empire and the complexity of its administration led to the expansion of the Caliph's religious delegation to the Ulama. During this long period, a caliph had never given a *fatwa*. The reason is quite simple: delivery of a *fatwa* was foreign to the Caliphate institution. This institution was designed to rule an empire and to be a 'consulting firm'. If the Caliphs, the Sultans or the judges needed qualified advice related to Islamic law (*shari'a*), they asked the Ulama who possessed deep knowledge on these matters. Generally, the Ulama's opinions — when they were asked for — were published by the Caliph or Sultan's offices; because generally, the Ulama's opinions (*fatwa*) were in accordance with the government's will and interest. The *fatwa* was somehow a justification and legitimization for an action that the government had already accomplished, or an action that it would undertake in the future.

For instance, Al-Ghazâli, one of the most influential religious authorities during the Abbasids' reign, delivered a number of important *fatwa*. One of them was on the request of Ibn Tashfîn with the purpose of justifying his war against the Muslim rebels. Al-Ghazâli satisfied the Ruler's demand and gave the requested *fatwa* (1086). In this way, the Ulama gradually became *fatwa*-givers. Subtle relations were woven between them and the government. The more powerful the Caliph/Sultan, the higher the degree of the Ulama's docility and the fewer the number of *fatwa*. A weak Caliph/Sultan risked confronting stronger Ulama and facing an increase in the quantity of *fatwa*; sometimes he even had to live with some *fatwa* criticizing his person or his administration.

It is true that during the Umayyad, the Abbasid, and later during the Ottoman reign, the Ulama succeeded in establishing themselves as a powerful group which was more or less institutionalized. Depending on the prestige and influence of each *mufti /mujtahid* among his colleagues and also among the population, he was nominated to a higher or lower ministry. For example, the position of Chancellor of Nizamiyya in Baghdad (the Abbasid capital) was incomparably more important and prestigious than other positions. Under the Ottomans, the position of the *fatwa*-giver (*mufti*) suffered some deterioration and also some elevation. Deterioration in the sense that the *mufti* label became a title for the genuine clergymen:

However, as the orderly administration of the rapidly expanding empire was seen to demand a unified system of legal practice, such authority was gradually confined to few individuals of public position. But this too was unsatisfactory as it seemed to secularize the divine law and make it an instrument of the ruler's will; therefore, sometime during the reign of Murad II (1421-51) the right to issue [*fatwas*] was vested exclusively in an individual known as the *shaykh ul-Islam* who was appointed by the Sultan. (Walsh, 1960: 866-67).

Under Mehmed II (1451-81), the rules regarding the organization of the Ulama were formalized in the so-called *Kanunname (Acts of Law)*. R.C. Repp describes the procedure of the Islamic learning process under Mehmed II as follows:

The principal provisions pertaining to the structure of the learned profession lay down that a candidate for office, a *mulâzim* — [literally 'one who is assiduous, constant in attendance'] — shall first teach at a 20-akce medrese [theological school], that is one at which the stipulated salary of the *müderris* [teacher in Islamic law] is twenty akce daily, and shall then proceed to advance by 5-akce stages ... until he reaches the 50-akce medreses of which there are three classes: *khârij* [external], *dâkhil* [internal], and the *Sahn* [public lecturing]. The last of these classes consists of the famous eight medreses which Mehmed II had built round his mosque in Istanbul. ... After the *Sahn*, the highest of the 50-akce medrese, the scholar may become a 500-akce *qâdi* [judge] and thence *kazasker* [Literally the 'Judge of military tribunal]. (Repp, 1986: 32)

The *Mufti* of Istanbul, or the *Shaykh ul-Islam* (= *Seyhülislâm*), was the most prestigious figure among the Ulama. He was often likened to the Pope, and had 'unquestionably become comparable in prestige, perhaps even, in some respects, in authority, to the Grand Vizir, the sultan's "absolute deputy"' (Repp: xix). The *Mufti* of the capital was 'Chief of the Ulama' and was therefore in charge of giving *fatwas* to the people. However, the Sultan took *fatwas* on matters of public policy from a number of the Ulama and not from the *Mufti* of Istanbul alone. While the *Muftis* of 'the early period [15th century] held office for life and were not subject to dismissal from office, ... from the beginning of the seventeenth century dismissal from office was very much the rule rather the exception' (Repp: 303).

It becomes clear that the *Muftis*, under the Ottoman empire, were appointed by the Sultan who paid them a salary. As a result, the *Mufti* of Istanbul as well as other empire *muftis* did not have much autonomy vis-à-vis the political authorities. Therefore, they showed an excess of complacency and softness towards men of the government. The lack of autonomy of religious authorities constitutes a general trend in Sunni regimes. The Shi'a religious authorities always enjoyed more autonomy, even under the Safavids who proclaimed Shi'a the official rite of their kingdom.

After the extinction of the Ottomans and abolition of the office of *shaykh ul-Islam*, the *mufti* of Al-Azhar in Cairo became the highest religious authority for Sunni Muslims. It had however lost some of its lustre, partially because of Egypt's political decline; but also because of the significant growth in the popularity of Islamic fundamentalism in this country. Among the factors which contributed to the degradation of the authority of the *shaykh al-Azhar*, we have to add the fact that this function became (under President Nasser) a public position; Egypt's president nominated the *mufti* of al-Azhar. Among the *fatwa*s delivered by al-Azhar, the condemnation of some writings of Nobel Prize winner Najib Mahfuz, as well as the incompatibility of *Arabian Nights* with Islamic morality, are worth mentioning. It is also noteworthy that the former *mufti*, Gadel Hag Ali Gadel Haq, declared that seizing power by violent means is not in concordance with Islam (*Le Monde*, April 11, 1995). Is this a *fatwa* or a simple declaration? It is hard to decide. Besides Egypt, a few countries, for example Saudi Arabia, still have an official *mufti*. Jerusalem actually has two *mufti*s: one appointed by Jordan's King Husayn and the other by PLO's chairman Yasser Arafat. Nowadays, the function of *mufti* is becoming more and more weak and ambiguous.

The required qualities for a *mufti* are more or less the same in all Islamic theological schools and are *grosso modo* as follows: extensive knowledge of Islamic law (*shari'a*) and the history of Islam, high morality and impartiality.

In India, the *fatwa* in general indicates the collections of a specific Muslim authority on various subjects. In this sense, these collections are similar to *risâla*, delivered by the ayatollahs. The *Fatawa-i-Rizvia* is the most important collection of *fatwa*s. It consists of the *fatwa*s issued by the most influential figure among the Indian Ulama — Maulana Ahmad Riza Khân (1856-1921). Some of the practices 'which he allowed, indeed prescribed, were ones which others condemned as vestiges of paganism and polytheism — for instance, observing the anniversaries of *pirs* and "saints"' (Shourie 1995: 5). Another collection is *Kifayat-ul-Mufti*, the work of Mufti Kifayatullah (1872-1952), who was the Mufti of New Delhi and was often addressed as the *Mufti-i-A'zam*, the Grand Mufti. Often, 'he doesn't give a black or white answer; he clears a path in between the contending positions' (ibid: 6). The third collection is the *Fatawa-i Ulema Dar al-Ulum* issued by a group of Ulama, and not by a single Muslim theologian. *Dar al-Ulum* (House of Sciences) was founded in 1866 and often referred to as the Al-Azhar of India. These *fatwa*s are known as being the most reactionary and orthodox ones. The Ulama belonging to this institution advocated against any

innovation, condemning them as *bid'a/heresy*. The fourth collection
called *Fatawa-i-Ahl-i-Hadis* expressed the opinion of the reform
movement. 'They had a large number of followers among the
"aristocracy", they had great influence at courts such as that of
Bhopal; more important, they came in a sense to set the norms'
(ibid: 8). Thus, they did not capture the masses. The fifth and last
collection is *Fatawa-i-Rahimiyyah*, which contains the opinions of
Mufti Sayyed Abdur Rahim Qadri of Rander in Gujarat. As a
number of Indians from Western India went and settled in East and
South Africa, institutions and religious functionaries from places
like Rander came to exercise influence among Indian Muslims in
those countries (ibid: 10). Besides these contemporary collections,
there are of course the Indian classic collections like *fatawa-i-
Alamgiri* (of the 17th century AD), the *Fatawa-i-Qazi Khân* and the
Hidayah (both of the 12th century AD). All these *fatwa*s deal with
almost all aspects and questions related to politics, economy and
generally speaking, to the daily life of Indian Muslims. Some of the
questions presented to the mufti are quite bizarre indeed, revealing
the behaviour of some Muslims. Take for example the following
question and answer:

Question:
Is a pregnant goat which has been used for intercourse *halal* (licit) or
haram (illicit)? Should one wait for her to deliver or should she be killed
and buried without waiting?

Answer:
If there is no ejaculation (inside the animal) its meat and milk are *halal*.
But if there is ejaculation, it is better to kill the animal and bury its
flesh. (Shourie, 1995: 75-76)

In North Africa, *fatwa* delivering flourished in the 19th century.
There were two reasons for this. Firstly, because North Africa faced
a French invasion aiming to colonize this region. Warring against
the new colonizers as well as making peace arrangements with
them needed justification from the Muslim religious authorities. For

instance, when Emir Abd al-Qâdir (1808-83) signed the treaty of
Tafna (1837) with the French Marshal Thomas Bugeaud (1764-1849),
the maternal uncle of Abd al-Qâdir delivered a *fatwa* supporting the
Tafna treaty, arguing that the pursuit of war, when the enemy is in
a position of superior strength, is equivalent 'to exposing oneself to
inexorable peril' (Chater, 1994: 43). In March 1837, 'Abd al-Qâdir,
who had been called upon to impose sanctions and sometimes
death sentences, consulted the Ulama of Egypt and Fez to learn the
position of *shari'a'* (ibid.) Concerning the delicate question of the
legitimacy of the Treaty of Tafna, the *fatwa* (delivered on June 14,
1837) of Ali Ben Abd al-Salam Mdides al-Tassouli of Fez was that
'Truce with the enemy is permissible if the enemy is not in an
offensive mode. Otherwise *jihad* is a personal duty' (Chater: 43).

This raised an important and complicated question which by
analogy has something in common with the Rushdie Affair. In
order to deal with the tribes who had rallied to the side of the
colonial authorities, Abd al-Qâdir consulted the attorney of Fez
before attacking them. 'How should those who have submitted to
the infidel enemy and who have joined his troops be viewed? Are
they apostates? The attorney (*qâdi*) in his *fatwa* of March 5, 1840
'referred to the history of the first caliphs and drew from examples
during the Muslim period in Andalusia, showing that the *fiqh*
schools were not unanimous in considering Muslims who rally to
Christians as apostates' (ibid: 44). He concluded that 'they cannot
be considered infidels'.

If these tribes who allied with the colonial powers could not be
considered 'infidels', the same principle must be applied in our
time to Rushdie.

In connection with the abolition of slavery between 1842 and
1846, Ahmad Bey's letter of January 26, 1846, was a *fatwa* which
pointed out that 'slavery was an object of controversy among the
Ulama; and the *shari'a* actively encouraged manumission'. In
highlighting the liberation agenda of Islam, the author placed himself within the spirit of the law, if not letter' (ibid: 45).

Lastly, in the same spirit, some avant-garde thinkers like Khairal-Din, author of the *Necessary Reforms in the Muslim States* (1867, in Arabic), adopted the methodology of the *fatwa*, advocating the necessity of reforming the Muslim societies, and 'cited European progress founded on justice and the sciences, the necessity of consulting the *shari'a*, the destructive effect of despotism, and man's natural affinity with liberty' (ibid: 45).

So far, we have discussed the position of Sunni *fatwa* givers. Shi'a has a quite different approach to this question. From the outset, it should be emphasized that the term and the title of *mufti* does not exist in Shi'a. Throughout Shi'a history, nobody has been called '*mufti*', nobody has been nominated to this position, and consequently nobody has had the title of *mufti*. This term belongs exclusively to Sunni history and Sunni vocabulary. The reason for the absence of the term *mufti* in Shi'a is clear. As mentioned above, the creation and institutionalization of *mufti* was originally an administrative response to a specific need which comes first and foremost from the Administration itself. By Administration, we mean all forms of government: Caliphate, Sultanate, Emirate, etc. Since the Shi'a have never really been in power and have not governed a large geographical area until the Safavids, the need for one or more *mufti*(s) has not really come up. Hence the lack of the term *mufti* in the rich Shi'a literature. The Shi'a religious dignitaries were almost indiscriminately called *shaykh* (for example, Shaykh al-Mufid (947-1023) or Shaykh al-Tusi (d. 1068) who represent two of the most eminent religious authorities in Shi'a); sometimes they also had the simple title *sayyid* (for example Sayyed al-Murtada (d. 1044), another Shi'a authority). Other common titles were *Mullâ* = Literal (Mullâ Mohsen Feyz in the 16th century), *Mirzâ* = Script (Mirza Hassan Shirazi in the 19th century), or rarely '*Allâma* = Highly Savant ('Allâma Hilli d. 1325). Terms like *Hujjat ul-Islam* = Proof of Islam (i.e. Hujjat ul-Islam Rafsanjani), *Ayatollah* = Sign of Allah (i.e. Ayatollah Khamenei), and *Ayatollah Ozma* = Great Ayatollah (i.e. Ayatollah Ozma Khomeini), became known world-wide through the international media. These titles were in general use during the second half of the 19th century. Historically, the attribution of the *ayatollah* title 'seems to have coincided with crucial moments of influence of Twelver Shiism in Iran. Its first recorded bearer [was] Ibn al-Mutahhar al-Hilli (d. 1325). He was styled *Ayatollah fil-'âlamayn* 'ayatollah in the two words' (Calmard 1995: 162-63). After the Islamic revolution in Iran, the title of *ayatollah* increasingly became subject to the political struggle and to some degree lost its initial religious connotation.

Saying that the term *mufti* did not exist in Shi'a does not mean that Shi'a is unfamiliar with the *fatwa* procedure. The genuine title for fatwa-giver in Shi'a is *mujtahid* (equivalent of *doctor of theology*). A person who wants to become *mujtahid* must follow a number of courses in Arabic language, hadith, Sunna, logic, kalam, theology, and so on and so forth. The study is divided into three phases which are 1) the elementary (*muqaddamât*), 2) the middle range (*sath*), and 3) post-graduate (*khârij*). On average, the whole study takes 20 years. Thus, successful completion of the study is not enough in itself to gain access to the dignity of *mujtahid*. The candidate must obtain an authorization (*ijâza*) from at least one of the great *mujtahids*. Generally, the authority who gives *ijaza* is the candidate's mentor, who has taught him during the study. The *ijâza* can be *general* or *partial*. A *general ijâza* authorizes the candidate to make pronouncements on all questions related to *shari'a*. Since the partial or sectorial authorization is limited to some specific domains, the *ijâza* is always delivered in written form, signed and sealed by the *ijâza*-giver. Once the *ijâza* is obtained, the candidate is recognized as *mujtahid*. However, all *mujtahids* are not equal. The majority of them continue as *bookless mujtahid*. Only a few among them proceed to the codification of their own *risâla* which is, in a sense, equivalent to a doctorate thesis. *Risâla* constitutes the *mujtahid's* independent interpretation of *shari'a*, indicating to the believers the paths and the ways in which they can practice their religious duties. The *mujtahid* who has his own *risâla* becomes the 'Source of Emulation' (*Marja'-e Taqlid*). That means that other Muslims are allowed to follow him in his path. Thus, the imitation is not allowed in questions relative to the Shi'as' five fundamental principles which are 1) the unity of God (*tawhid*); 2) the prophecy of Mohammad (*nubuwwat*); 3) Doomsday (*mu'âd*); 4) the Imamate of the Twelve; and 5) Justice (*'adâlat*). Only the *mujtahids* who are the 'Source of Imitation' are recognized as qualified *fatwa*- givers, but not always. In some cases, the 'bookless *mujtahids*' like ayatollah Kashani in the 1950s have also given *fatwa*, or at least pronounced declarations which have been interpreted or been considered *fatwa*. Continuing our voyage into the sophisticated Shi'a system, we have to mention the existence of the highest Shi'a authority which is called the 'Supreme Source of Emulation (SSE)' (*Marj'a Koll-e Taqlid*). We have to keep in mind that the Shi'a have no formalized religious institution. Consequently, nobody can be nominated, co-opted, or elected to the position of SSE. Nevertheless, sometimes (not always), one great *mujtahid* — by virtue of his political, theological, or charismatic influence — gradually becomes the most important and the most powerful *mujtahid*. This is a spontaneous process. In this process, the number of students and followers, as well as the respect that other *mujtahids* demonstrate in his favour, all together play a crucial role. Among the SSE from this century we should mention Ayatollah Isfahani in the 1940s, Ayatollah Burujerdi in the 1950s, and Ayatollah Khomeini in the 1980s.

Finally, it is important to say that in theory, the *mufti* or *mujtahid* are not bound to give a *fatwa* each time they are asked. But in general a *fatwa* will be given, especially if the inquirer is a ruler, judge, or an influential person, normally from the *mufti* or *mujtahid's* own followers. In short, the elementary and necessary conditions for a qualified *fatwa*-giver are as follows: 1) to be Muslim; 2) to be adult; 3) to be just (*âdil*) in the sense of having a clean (police) record; and 4) to be *mujtahid*. Theoretically, there is nothing that prohibits a Muslim woman from giving a *fatwa*, but in reality there is no evidence that a female *fatwa*-giver has ever existed. Theoretically, also, blindness and deafness do not disqualify a person from becoming a *fatwa*-giver. Some authors have also argued that even a slave could be *fatwa*-giver (Mawardi, 1982: 64). If a person fulfils all the above-mentioned conditions, he is qualified to give *fatwa*. However, under some specific circumstances, a qualified *fatwa*-giver is not necessarily accredited to give *fatwa*.

According to Al-Ghazâli, three categories of people — despite their competence — are excluded from giving *fatwa*. They are: 1) the ruler (*amir*); 2) the executive (of orders — governor, administrator, police, etc., [*ma'mur*]); and 3) someone who has been ordered to give a *fatwa* (*mutakkalif*) (Ghazâli, 1933: 119). This exclusion sounds reasonable and logical, because it is hard to imagine that the ruler and executive's *fatwa*s would be objective and impartial without any temporal interest. The exclusion of the third category seems obvious — perhaps the person concerned could be bribed to do so. When Ghazâli excludes the ruler as a qualified *fatwa*-giver, it confirms our argument that the juridical acts initiated by the *Râshidûn* are not really *fatwa*s, but orders.

Question: Object of Fatwa

The technical term for the act of 'asking' is *istiftâ'* which literally means 'asking for a *fatwa*.' That means that according to the norms, a *fatwa* must be 'asked' and not simply 'given' merely on the initiative of the *fatwa*-giver. The questions are naturally always closely connected with religious (Islamic) matters. The question is like asking for *clarification* (*éclairsissement*), which means that the answer obviously cannot be found anywhere else (in the Koran, in Sunna, or in *ijma'*). Thus, in theory, there is nothing to stop anybody from asking for a *fatwa* on something for which somebody else (generally some centuries ago) has already given a *fatwa*. But in practice, generally the question is new. The domain of *fatwa* is limited to questions arising from the practice of religion (Tyan: 219), and not those which touch on the principles of religion and belief like the unity of God, the prophecy of Mohammad, and Doomsday. In this way, all matters relative to Islam can be subject to *istifta'*. Questions concerning civil law such as matrimonial matters (*e.g.*, marriage, divorce, death, heritage), business law (*mu'âmalât*), or the relationship between Muslims and non-Muslims, etc., can be asked. There is absolutely no limitation or restriction in this matter. However, it is obvious that some questions are of more general interest than others, just as some of them are considered more political than others. For example, a *fatwa* on the subject of war between different fractions of Muslims or between Muslims and non-Muslims gets a lot of attention, because it will have wider implications than a *fatwa* on a private dispute or question.

When the subject of a *fatwa* is war against non-Muslims, the *fatwa* is generally dubbed *jihad*, for example the *fatwa*s which were delivered during the Iranian-Russian war (1808-25). In the same category is the *jihad* declaration (in 1804) issued by Osman ibn Fudi in West Africa against the non-Muslims, and the edict of Sayyed Ahmad Barelwi (d. 1831) which proclaimed most of India a land of non-belief (*dâr ul-kufr*). 'A similar logic was employed during the 1857 mutiny, when a *fatwa* was issued by the 'Ulama of Delhi justifying *jihad* against British rule'. (Dallal, 1995: 15).

Sometimes, the purpose of a *fatwa* is not military war against non-Muslims, but commercial sanctions to prevent their economic domination of Muslims. The best example of this kind of *fatwa* is the *fatwa* delivered by a Shi'a mujtahid in connection with the *Tobacco Rebellion* (1872-92) in Iran. In 1872, Nasser el-din Shah had granted, with far reaching implications, a tobacco concession to a British subject, Baron Julius de Reuter. Since the Iranian tobacco merchants feared that this concession would curtail their activities and profits dramatically, they protested vigorously against the Shah's decision. We should say that tobacco at that time was one of the most important consumer products in Iran. The merchants traditionally represented a social group with very close relations and affinities to the Shi'a Ulama. Their relationship was essentially one of mutual cooperation and rapport. The merchants supported the Ulama financially, and the Ulama supported the merchants morally and politically. This meant that the tobacco concession was perceived by the Shi'a Ulama as an indirect threat to one of their most important financial sources. Consequently, the Ulama not only took a very active role in the anti-concession movement; they also assumed leadership of the protest movement. In this way, a commercial dispute rapidly turned into a religious question, resulting in a *fatwa* delivered by the head of the Shi'a mujtahids, Hajji Mirza Hassan Shirazi, who resided in Samarra (Iraq), stating:

In the name of God the merciful, the Forgiving. Today the use of tobacco in whatever form, is tantamount to war against the Imam of the Age [the Shi'a Twelfth Imam who will appear again by God's decision], may God hasten his glad advent. (Lambton, 1965: 145)

Nowadays, the *istiftâ'* is continuing as before, with the particularity, perhaps, that the public/political aspect of *fatwa* is becoming predominant. This situation is essentially due to the strong progress of *Islamism*. Because of this, even 'innocent' religious questions take on a political character. Also because traditional life, which has been accepted as the normal way of life, now becomes subject to change and transformation. For example, the fact that Muslim women wear veils has never been questioned, but this now becomes a political question when it is confronted with modernity. As a result, a *fatwa* on the veil will today automatically be judged as a political act and a political gesture.

Fatwa Caller: Mustafti

In its authentic sense, a *fatwa* has a caller (*mustafti*). *Fatwas* without an inquirer constitute the expression of personal efforts of a *mujtahid* for the purpose of codification of his opinion (*ra'y*) on different religious matters. The *ra'ys* are not genuine *fatwas*. The only condition for being a qualified caller is to be an adult Muslim. Although the call for *fatwa* theoretically is open to both men and women, we did not find evidence of one single case of a woman asking for *fatwa*. The caller can be the ruler himself (which is rare), a judge, a group of believers, or an individual person. Usually, followers of the *mujtahid* ask for *fatwa*. They are known by the *mujtahid* or at least by his office. Sometimes, the *fatwa* is arranged between the *mufti/mujtahid* and the caller(s), and the subject of *fatwa*, its substance and its modality, has been discussed before the *fatwa* is delivered. This is true especially when the *fatwa's* subject is sensitive or is a political question. It means that in these cases, the substance of the forthcoming *fatwa* is already known by the fatwa-giver and *fatwa* caller(s). Generally, by asking for a *fatwa* the caller is searching for a justification of his own behaviour, case, and/or argument. If the callers are the *mufti's* own followers, particularly if they are supporting the *mufti* financially and morally, the *mufti* comes under moral pressure, depending on the personality and influence of the caller(s).

Forms and Validity of Fatwa

A *fatwa* is always *written*. Usually, the *fatwa* is a *manuscript*, written by the *mufti* himself, or by his secretary if it is a routine matter or if the *fatwa* caller(s) are not that important. In both cases, the *fatwa* is signed, dated, and sometimes sealed by the *mufti*. The text of the *fatwa* always begins with the formula of *basmala* ('In the Name of God, the Merciful, the Compassionate'), or only with 'In the name of God Almighty', and ends with different expressions like 'God knows better' ('*Allahu a'lam*'), or 'Of God I am expecting success' ('*wa minallahi tawfiq*'), and so on.

   Since the *muftis* are generally traditionalists, they do not write their *fatwas* on a typewriter. Furthermore, the handwritten form is considered necessary for other reasons. A handwritten *fatwa* is perceived as having more authority than a typed sheet of paper, because it shows the *mufti's* special attention. As the *fatwa* concerns important issues, especially when it comes from a powerful *mufti* /*ayatollah*, the handwritten form, signed and sealed by the *mufti* himself, makes forgery difficult. For all these reasons, the *fatwa* is handwritten.Generally, the text of a *fatwa* is short; sometimes the question and the answer figures in the same document, especially if the answer is only 'yes' or 'no'. Once a *fatwa* is written, it is sent to the caller(s) and made public either by the caller or the *mufti's*

مبارز سرسخت صهیونیسم و امپریالیسم حضرت آیت‌الله العظمی خمینی مدظله

لزوم پشتیبانی از فدائیان عرب (چریکهای مسلمان فلسطین) را جهت دفاع از

کیان اسلام و آزادی سرزمینهای اسلامی و نابودی سرطان نژادپرست (اشغالگران یهودی) بر عموم

مسلمین اعلام داشتند

بسم الله الرحمن الرحیم

محضر مبارک پیشوای مجاهد و معلم الثان حضرت سلطنه ... آیت‌الله العظمی خمینی ادام الله ...

پیشوای جلیل القدر :

از نظر مبارک پوشیده نیست که مدت‌ها است بین کفار دون یهود و مصداقضی زمینهای اسلامی و دیگر مسلمانان گرفته و سلباً
به گاه آن سابقه دارد آوانه بپا نماید و سود را که در مسطورا استخلاص اماکن مقدسه و استرداد زمینهای اسلامی در مقاورت ساحی
که بنام عملیات فدائی خوانده میشود . چاره این جهت و سنجی شرایط شرعیه او اسلامیان اینکه قوتان اهل سلام مجاهد
داشته اله اینکه چند کلما مال را صاحبین ما رایب معینات اینها خدمت دین سرمی دهند و دفاع از اسلام بکردید ؟ ثانیاً
استکه بنجگی مد مضایای این خطیانان واحد از همین آیام فشته و زمانیات کنارزمینهای اسلام مذهب معاملات
لذا اجامنکند ؟ و مدصوبت وجوب معامات آبرازت از سود و حفظ شرعیت از این زلزله و عمر مرموده مصلح مودن سلطاناً
و زجهت آنان استفاده کرد و خیر ؟ معنی است لقد سباک را مدلین بدی بیان نفهماید . ادام اظلالکم

و مسلرای از خدائیست

بسم الله الرحمن الرحیم

فبلاهم نذرکردار ، ام کد ملت غاسی اسرائیل با مدعا فیک کرارد راه اسلام و مل این سلین خطر
عظیم دله و خودآنست کرآگر مسلین آنها مهلت دهند معت از دست رود و جلوگیری از آنها الله
بدیو نشود و جون احنال خطر منوبه بی اساس اسلام است لازم است بر ولی اسلام و معصوص
و برسایر مسلین همت آکردن این ماذ : خنا دا مهرجمو که امکان ندارد نمایند و از کمک بمدافعان
کوتاهی نکند و معادرات ازمحل ، کوان و سائر مصدقات دراین امر مهم حیانی هزینه نمایند
از خداوند متعال مسئلت مینماید که موجب تنبه و بیداری مسلین و اخرام نمایند
و دفع شراعدا اسلام را ازبلاد مسلین بنماید و السلام علی من اتبع الهدی

A Fatwa issued by Ayatollah Khomeini during his exile in Iraq:
Persian version. Source: Rowhâni, Nehzat-e Emâm Khomeini, p. 886.

office, or both. There is no systematic archive of *fatwas*, since the
muftis, especially those who are independent of a public
administration, do not have registers or filing systems. But the
major *fatwas* are generally known to the public. Under the Ottoman
empire, *fatwa* giving became institutionalized under the name of
Dâr ul-Fatwa (The Office of *Fatwa*), and some *fatwas* from the
Ottoman empire have been archived and preserved. The same
applies to some *fatwas* delivered by Al-Azhar in Cairo. In Iran, the
practice of archiving and publishing the *fatwas* is new — it dates
only from the death of Ayatollah Khomeini (d. 1989). After his
death, his son Ahmad (d. 1995) took the initiative to collect and
publish his father's works, including his *fatwas*. Several volumes
have already been published by the Organization of Cultural
Documents of the Islamic Revolution (*Sâzman-e Madârek-e Farhangui-
e Enghelab-e Eslâmi*).

Is a *fatwa* binding? For whom and for how long? There is no
standard and clear-cut answer to these questions. Two reasons
explain the absence of a clear answer. First, as mentioned before,
Islam does not have a central, religious authority like the Vatican.
Therefore, there are a variety of interpretations, a variety of
practices, and a variety of opinions on this matter. Second, the
question of a *fatwa*'s binding character, its validity and duration
again depends on what one means and how one defines *fatwa*. If
fatwa embraces what an Islamic jurist-theologian has collected in his
risâla, then his opinions are valid for those who belong to his
school, also after the death of the Mufti, but only for the duration
of the lifetime of those followers (*Muqallid*). The new generation of
followers must follow a living Mufti. To be more precise, there are
four different Sunni jurist-theological schools (hanafi, mâliki, shâfi'i
and hanbali). The opinions of the leaders of each of these schools
are only valid for the followers (and justice courts) connected to
that specific school. But, if we are talking about a single *fatwa*, the
dominant tendency among Islamic jurists is that the *fatwa* is not
binding, because the *fatwa* is not a *contract* between *fatwa*-giver and

بسم الله الرحمن الرحيم

ساحه الجبه المجاهد ايه الله العظمى الامام الخمينى ادام الله ظله

سيدنا الجليل

ماهو رأيكم في امر استعارة المسجد الاقصى وديار المسلمين التى اخرجهم منها الكافر اليهودي المحارب ، اذا تعين ذلك بالمقاومه المسلحه وهو ما يسر بالعمل الفدائي فهل يجوز للقادر على هذا السلام من المسلمين او الغني القادر على البذل التخلف عن الانخراط في صفوف او عدم البذل عليها لدرء خطر هذا الكافر و ارجاعه من حيث اخرج المسلمين وهل يجوز صرف الحقوق الشرعيه من الزكاة وغيرها التجهيز امدادها و امدادهم لذلك اتونا مأجورين حفظكم الله .

نفر من الفدائيين

بسم الله الرحمن الرحيم

سبق وان نوهت بما تكنه دولة اسرائيل الغاصبه من النوايا الخبيثة ، كما حذرت المسلمين من هذا الخطر العظيم المحدق بهم وبلادهم ، وهبت بهم ان لا يفسحوا المجال امام العدو كى يتمكن من تنفيذ مخططاته الاجراميه التوسعية ، وان يغتنموا الفرص ويتلافوا الامر قبل ان ينبح الخرق على الراقع . هذا ، وبما ان الخطر يهدد كيان الاسلام فضلى الدول الاسلاميه خاصة وعلى المسلمين عامة يتأكد ان تتوا الدفعه ، وان ينذر وعاف سبيل استنها الدثقى الوسائل الممكنة ، وان لا ينفكوا عن امداد ومعونة المهتمين بالامر و المدافعين عن بيضة الاسلام .

ويجوز ان تصرف الحقوق الشرعيه من الزكوات وسائر الصدقات فى هذا السبيل الحيوى الهام .

واخيرا ابتهل الى الله العلى القدير ان ينبه المسلمين عن سباتهم العميق ويدفع عنهم وعن بلادهم كيد الاعداء و المعتدين والسلام على من اتبع الهدى .

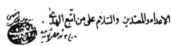

A Fatwa issued by Ayatollah Khomeini during his exile in Iraq:
Arabic version. Source: Rowhâni, Nehzat-e Emâm Khomeini, p. 887.

fatwa caller. It is not an act of allegation either (*bay'a*). Therefore, a man like Hassan al-Turâbi (of Sudan), one of the most prominent figures in Islamism today, thinks that 'the *fatwa* has absolutely no obligatory character. It is merely an expression of a religious opinion' (*Arabies*, May 1995). Almost the same argument has been used by Shaykh Mohammad Sayyed al-Tantawi, the new Shaykh of Al-Azhar (of Cairo), who pronounced against Khomeini's fatwa on Rushdie, despite the fact that, in his opinion, Rushdie should be punished but the punishment should not be death. (AFP and *Le Monde*, 1 November 1997).

Khomeini's Fatwa:
Fallacy and Violence

Political violence is a general phenomenon not exclusive to Shi'a Imâmi. What makes Shi'a violence special is not so much its methods or the way it is organized, but more the way it has evolved from a *quietist* movement into a movement espousing *violence*. Shi'a quietism has lasted for centuries. Therefore, it will be difficult to consider Shi'a quietism an accident or merely an ephemeral phenomenon. The events engulfing Shi'a Imâmi after World War II (first in Iran and later in Lebanon) are accordingly more than a matter of an increase in the degree and intensity of violence and terrorist actions. What has taken place has been nothing less than a *revolutionary* and gradual transformation at all levels. In this respect, Khomeini's fatwa on Rushdie was not an isolated act; this fatwa was a 'logical' consequence and a result of the changing nature of Shi'a from quietist to resurrection and revolution. Ayatollah Khomeini played a crucial role in this substantial transformation of Shi'a. In this chapter, we will first analyze and criticize Khomeini's fatwa and then view it in a larger context.

Khomeini and the Fatwa

Khomeini, one of the most powerful and charismatic world leaders, who succeeded in making one of the most original revolutions in the 20th century, was undeniably a highly complicated and ambivalent person. As a great leader, he possessed the appropriate qualities to hypnotize, manipulate, and mobilize the masses. He

40

Khomeini's Fatwa

was certainly ambitious; he possessed the virtue of patience (not tolerance), but also — and especially — he always exuded an inner peace (*tama'nina*), even under the worst circumstances.

Khomeini literally went through the whole Islamic learning system from beginning to end. He became *mujtahid* in the early 1930s, and received the *ijâza* (permission to deliver qualified opinion on religious matters) from four leading *mujtahids* (Moin, 1994: 68).

This means that Khomeini possessed the necessary qualifications to become a *mujtahid* with the honorific title of 'ayatollah' and then 'great ayatollah'. He had written his own *risâla*, *Tawzih al-Masâ'il* (Explaining the Problems) for the purpose of showing the way to his followers. He also became the 'Source of Emulation' and later, after the 1979 Revolution, he became the 'Supreme Source of Emulation'. Consequently, in accordance with every measure and criteria within the frame of Islamic rules, Khomeini was undoubtedly qualified to deliver a *fatwa*. No question about that.

During his career, Khomeini was either *rebel* or *leader*, and when he was a rebel, he was always the leader of the rebels. His active rebellion started in the beginning of the 1960s, when the Great Ayatollah Burujerdi died and the position of Supreme Source of Emulation became vacant. This period also coincided with the Shah's reform package consisting of land reform, women's voting rights, workers' participation in the benefits of factories, and the nationalization of forests. Already in the beginning of the 1940s, Khomeini was rather unorthodox as a young priest. His first book written in 1943 (see p. 207) indicated his deep engagement and devotion to Islam. His entire life, he demonstrated a venomous hatred against the Pahlavi dynasty. His first book is actually against Reza Shah, and then he deployed and concentrated all his efforts and energy against Mohammad Reza Shah (the son of Reza Shah) finally causing his fall in 1979. From 1945 to 1961, without being directly and personally involved in terrorist actions, Khomeini had close relations with Islamic extremist groups like The Devotees of Islam (*Fadâiyan-e Eslâm*) and religious leaders like Ayatollah

Khomeini reading, c. 1988. Private collection.

Kashani who had played a prominent role in Iraq (between World War I and II) against the British, and in Iran during the movement for the nationalization of oil under the leadership of Dr. Mosaddeq. But, as we said before, Khomeini did not confirm his leadership — politically and religiously — until after the death of Ayatollah Burujerdi in 1961. We have no intention of rehashing Khomeini's entire life here; readers are invited to read Khomeini's biography written by Baqir Moin. During the revolutionary process in Iran in 1978, Khomeini not only became the leader of all Islamic forces, but also the leader of the opposition (all orientations — Socialist, Marxist, Liberals together) against the Shah's regime. After the success of the Islamic Revolution in Iran in 1979, Khomeini became the official Leader of Revolution (*Rahbar-e Enqelâb*) in accordance with the Islamic Constitution, which was shaped by the Assembly of Experts and then approved by plebiscite (December 2-3, 1979). According to official figures, 61.4 percent of eligible voters (13.6 million out of approximately 22 million) participated in the plebiscite, and 99.3 percent of them voted in favour. (Menashri, 1990: 119). According to the Constitution, the Leader who is also called *Valiy-e Faqih* (Jurisconsult) must fulfil the two following conditions:

1) He must have the necessary qualifications (science and virtue) to deliver *fatwa* (*iftâ'*) and act as the 'Source of Emulation';

2) He must be aware of the requirement of the times and be courageous, as well as capable of managing affairs with good sense (Article 109).

After the death of Ayatollah Khomeini, article 109 was revised in such a way that Ali Khamenei could be designated as Leader. However, since he has not been recognized as a 'Source of Emulation' (*Marja'-e Taqlid*), this condition has consequently been dropped from the 1979 Constitution. On the other hand, some new conditions (Justice and Virtue) have been added — conditions judged necessary for 'leading the Umma of Islam'. In such a way, the scope of the competence of the Leader is unilaterally extended to the worldwide Muslim community.

Furthermore, the Constitution gives to the Leader all vital and essential power. He is the Commander-in-Chief of the Armed Forces and appoints and dismisses senior commanders; he establishes the National Defense Council, and is empowered to proclaim general mobilization, declare war and make peace. He appoints the President of the Supreme Court, the President of the High Judicial Council, and the Prosecutor General, confirms the President of the Republic in office, etc., etc. (Articles 107-12).

All these important powers have been given to a person who is not elected, but in the best sense 'recognized' by the population or co-opted by other clergymen. Without opening a constitutional discussion here, we note that not all citizens are eligible for the function of leadership. This option is reserved exclusively for a limited group of clergymen.

In the case of Khomeini himself, he was neither co-opted nor elected, but his authority was recognized spontaneously by virtue of revolutionary legitimacy and 'recognized' by the population. Later on, in terms of his Decree of January 6, 1988, Khomeini reinforced the power of the Leader and the State. The Governance of Jurisconsult (*Velâyat-e Faqih*) which was the 'constitutional' institution since the Revolution, was suddenly transformed into the *Absolute* Governance of Jurisconsult (*Velâyat-e motlaqa-ye Faqih*). According to Khomeini's Decree, 'the Islamic Governance, which stems from the absolute guidance of Prophet Mohammad, is one of the primary injunctions in Islam, taking precedence over all subsidiary precepts, even praying, fasting, and performing the Hajj. The ruler can close the mosques when needed ... the state can on its own abrogate its religiously lawful contract with the people when the contracts are found to be against the interest of the country and Islam.' (Reproduced by Moin 1994: 93; Behrooz 1991: 604).

The Decree of Khomeini leaves no doubt about the authori-

tarian character of his personality, and his very personal interpretation of *shari'a* in relation to the state's 'unlimited' power.
Khomeini was undoubtedly the most powerful man in Iran from
1979 until his death in 1989. It would be no exaggeration to say that
while Khomeini was in power in Iran, his real influence went
beyond Iran's borders; and after his death, he is still powerful to
some degree. Now, the question is how to place Khomeini's *fatwa*
(on Rushdie) in relation to his religious powers and his political
power and responsibilities. It is also very important to emphasize
that giving the title of *imâm* to Khomeini is in complete
contradiction with all Shi'a tradition. In Shi'a, there is only one
exclusive and non-expandable quorum of 12 *imâms*. Nobody else is
entitled to the dignity of *imâm*. Calling another person *imâm* —
except for the specific 12 — is in reality blasphemy according to
Shi'a tradition.

How did Khomeini become *imâm*? To make a long story short,
there is some evidence that while he lived in exile in Iraq, some
Sunni Arab groups, especially the Palestinians, used to call him
imâm (see illustrations, p. 35, and p. 37).

In the Arabic version of Palestinian *Fadâyyin*, Khomeini is called
imâm. In its Persian version, the title *imâm* has been dropped. But
the term *imâm* does not have the same meaning in Sunni and in
Shi'a. In Sunni, almost every clergyman is an *imâm*, but not in Shi'a.
The amazing thing is that Khomeini, who was totally aware of this
incompatibility, nevertheless did not correct the error. He ordered
his fellows to address him by 'Ô, Imâm' (*Yâ Imâm!*) several times
a day. In fact, he seemed to be pleased by this illegitimate
gratification. By this kind of manipulation, he positioned himself in
the same rank as the 12 Shi'a *imâms*. This fact could be considered
pure megalomaniac behaviour. Thus, the question contains some
important juridical implications. The fact is that in Shi'a, the 12
imâms (plus the Prophet and his daughter Fatima) are seen as
infallible. So it is not an exaggeration to say that Khomeini had this
aspect in mind, that some of his followers saw him as infallible and
maybe also as the *13th Imâm*!

تاریخ: ۶۷/۱۱/۲۵

پیام درباره انتشار کتاب کفرآمیز آیات شیطانی

بسمه تعالی

اناالله واناالیه راجعون

به اطلاع مسلمانان غیور سراسر جهان می‌رسانم مؤلف کتاب آیات شیطانی ـ که علیه اسلام و پیامبر و قرآن تنظیم و چاپ و منتشر شده است ـ همچنین ناشرین مطلع از محتوای آن، محکوم بـه اعدام می‌باشند. از مسلمانان غیور می‌خواهم تا در هر نقطه که آنان را یافتند، سریعاً آنها را اعدام نمایند تا دیگر کسی جرأت نکند به مقدسات مسلمین توهین نماید و هرکس در این راه کشته شود، شهید است انشاءالله. ضمناً اگر کسی دسترسی به مؤلف کتاب دارد ولی خود قدرت اعدام او را ندارد، او را به مردم معرفی نماید تا به جزای اعمالش برسد.

والسلام علیکم ورحمةالله و برکاته

روح‌الله الموسوی الخمینی

The Fatwa against Salman Rushdie
Source: Sahifah-e Nur, p. 86

Did Khomeini have the competence to give a fatwa such as the *Rushdie fatwa*? Did he have the ability to do it? Was it a *fatwa* at all? And if it wasn't, what was it then?

Answering these questions is of crucial significance and has important consequences at multiple levels, if, hypothetically, one succeeds in proving that the Rushdie *Fatwa* was not a *fatwa* at all. In this case, the discussion about its juridical validity will consequently fall. Think also of the vital importance of such a discussion for Rushdie's life; on the impact it could have on relations between Iran and the European Union and between Iran and USA. Furthermore, the whole debate on blasphemy would become irrelevant.

We will begin our discussion with the *fatwa* itself: The following is a translation of the entire text of this *fatwa* as it has been published by Khomeini's office:

Date: 67/11/25 (= February 14, 1989) Announcement on the publication of the apostasian book: *Satanic Verses*:

In the name of God Almighty; there is only one God, to whom we shall all return; I would like to inform all the intrepid Muslims in the world that the author of the book entitled *The Satanic Verses* which has been compiled, printed and published against Islam, the Prophet and the Koran, as well as those publishers who were aware of its contents, have been sentenced to death. I call on all zealous Muslims to execute them quickly, wherever They find them, so that no one will dare to insult the Islamic sanctions. Whoever is killed on this path will be regarded as a martyr, God willing. In addition, anyone who has access to the author of the book, but does not possess the power to execute him, should refer him to the people so that he may be punished for his actions. May God's blessing be on you all. (Ruhollah Al-Musavi Al-Khomeini)

Khomeini's *fatwa* invites a number of reflections. First, the Ayatollah considers himself the supreme authority and the most qualified defender of Islam on such matters. Second, the *fatwa* is addressed exclusively to Muslims, as is indeed the rule. Non-Muslims are neither bound nor called upon to carry out the death sentence. Third, Khomeini addresses Muslims throughout the entire world regardless of their nationality and place of residence, including Salman Rushdie himself (born a Muslim, now a British citizen and resident in London) as well as the publishers of *The Satanic Verses*.

Such a *fatwa*, of course, challenges the norms and the rules of international law.

It should be emphasized that shortly after Khomeini's 'fatwa', the Organization of Pânzdah-e Khordâd (which dates back to the rebellion of Khomeinists against the Shah's regime on 5 June 1963) offered a reward of 1 million dollars to any person who would kill Salman Rushdie. In 1998, nine years after the 'fatwa', this Organization is still active, and the reward offered now has increased to 2.5 million dollars. In connection with the ninth anniversary of the 'fatwa', the Iranian government, through its spokesman for the Iranian Foreign Office (Mahmoud Mohammadi), reaffirmed the death sentence against Rushdie (Irna: Islamic Republic News Agency, 16 February 1998). On the same occasion, Shaykh Nateq Nouri, speaker of the Majliss (Iranian Parliament), 'expressed hope that the death sentence on the appostate Salman Rushdie will be executed by Muslims to teach a lesson to those who oppose God and the divine prophets' (Irna, 15 February 1998).

Criticism of Khomeini's Fatwa

If Khomeini had intended to deliver a *fatwa* on Rushdie, did he follow the genuine procedure of *fatwa* deliverance? This is the question we are going to analyze in the following:

1. As stated in Sura I, a *fatwa* is usually a specific answer to a specific question. This procedure was respected by Khomeini himself in his previous *fatwa*s (see p. 35, and 37). In the so-called *Rushdie Fatwa*, Khomeini broke with his own tradition. However, it is not certain that he actually intended to deliver a *fatwa* in the Rushdie Affair. His office, which published it on February 14, 1989,

did not claim that it was a *fatwa*. Why did this *non-fatwa* suddenly become a *fatwa* and who made it a *fatwa*?

It was not the clergy in Iran, nor the Iranians, nor the Muslims, who first called Khomeini's declaration a *fatwa*. According to our research, three great European newspapers (*The Times, The Guardian* and *Le Monde*) used — at least in the beginning — the correct terminology with regard to Khomeini's death sentence. On February 15, 1989 (the day after Khomeini's declaration), *Le Monde* used the following terms: 'Khomeiny *ordonne* l'exécution de ... Rushdie.' Or 'Khomeiny dans un *message* aux musulmans du monde entier...'. *The Times* did the same thing, using the terms 'Khomeini's *order*' and 'Khomeini's *murderous edict*' (February 17). During the following days, *The Times* wrote, 'Ayatollah's *call for the killing*' (February 21), and 'Khomeini's *death threats*' (February 22). *The Guardian* mostly used the term '*death sentence*' (February 16 and 17). Curiously enough, the term '*fatwa*' appeared in *Le Monde* twice, on February 16 and 17. The interesting thing is that while *Le Monde*'s journalists continued to use the correct words, two young French Islamologists introduced the word '*fatwa*' in their writings. First, Olivier Roy wrote 'Mais la *fatwa* "décret" de l'imam Khomeiny ...' (February 17), and then came what could be called the real beginning of the usage of '*fatwa*' with Gilles Kepel's article in *Le Monde* on February 25 (published the day before, as is *Le Monde*'s habit). He began his article with this sentence: 'La *Fatwa* de l'ayatollah Khomeini ... '.

Almost at the same time, Khomeini in his message on 'Strategy for the Future of Revolution', which was issued on February 22, mentioned *en passant* the 'Islamic *fatwa*' followed immediately by the term 'death sentence', which he had delivered on February 14. It is quite astonishing that Khomeini used these two different terms interchangeably. But there is no doubt that in his mind, the term 'death sentence' is predominant; otherwise he would simply use the term '*fatwa*' without any additions. It is also astonishing that when Khomeini talks about other fatwas delivered by his illustrious predecessors to whom he pays great respect and veneration (e.g.

Great Ayatollah Mohammad Taqi Shirazi), he uses the term *'Hukm'* (Order) and not *'fatwa'* (Khomeini, 1971: 172).

Anyway, it seems quite improbable that Kepel had any knowledge about Khomeini's declaration of February 22. Considering the time it takes to write an article and get it published (between February 22 and 23), Kepel had no opportunity to be informed about Khomeini's new message. Nevertheless, it was the first and also the last time that Khomeini used (even yet allusively) the term *'fatwa'* in the Rushdie Affair. Despite this fact, a large number of people, fully convinced that it was a *fatwa*, tried (and continue to try) to cancel it, review it, or execute it. Everybody took part in this play, even ayatollahs in Iran, who also began, though with some moderation, to describe Khomeini's declaration as a *fatwa*.

Furthermore, there is no question about the validity or invalidity of this so-called *fatwa* after Khomeini's death. The real question is whether it is, according to each and every standard which exists within Islamic law on this matter, a *fatwa* at all. It is also surprising that Khomeini on one occasion only (February 22, 1989), referred to his declaration on Rushdie both as an 'Islamic *fatwa*' and a 'death sentence'. Another important thing that obviously did not attract the attention of the experts and observers of the Rushdie Affair, is the fact that during the period immediately following the delivery of the *fatwa* (a few months maybe), nobody in Iran, even the high political or religious authorities who talked about Khomeini's sentence, referred to it as a *'fatwa'*! Iranian newspapers which published articles on this affair the day after the sentence did not use the term *'fatwa'* either. Instead of *'fatwa'*, they used the term 'message' (*payâm*) (*Kayhan*, February 15, 1989). It becomes quite clear that nobody in Iran used the term *'fatwa'* for Khomeini's sentence. Rather it was some western observers who first used this term. A few years before that, some western scholars also invented the term 'fundamentalism' which was unfamiliar to Islamic terminology.

2. We mentioned earlier that a *fatwa* is usually a *handwritten* document (see p. 35, 37, and 45 for an example of Khomeini's *fatwas*). Considering the importance of the Rushdie Affair, which is far more sensitive and delicate if we consider all its implications (internally in Iran and in the world), it seems quite unusual that Khomeini himself did not write it by hand, but left it to another person (presumably his secretary) to type it. Again, this represents a highly unusual behaviour by Khomeini.

3. Yet another highly unusual and irregular thing about this *fatwa* is that the *document is neither signed nor sealed*. Such an insufficiency is also clearly contradictory to both Khomeini's own habits as well as to the old, normal, and regular procedure of *fatwa* delivery. This in itself actually constitutes a violation of normal procedure which brings the validity of the *fatwa* seriously into question. This remark is valid if one considers Khomeini's declaration on Rushdie a *fatwa*, and only a *fatwa*.

4. The list of irregularities in this case is longer than one might expect. To this list we can add the fact that the *fatwa was not requested*. We remember that the original idea of the fatwa institution is based on *istiftâ'* (asking for *fatwa*), which has been and still is one of the essential principles of *fatwa*. *Fatwa* is an answer to a question and it is delivered at the request of somebody else. The critical question is, who asked Khomeini for a *fatwa* on Rushdie? Who is the *mustafti* (*fatwa* caller)? There is absolutely no sign at all that anybody asked Khomeini for a fatwa. One could argue that Khomeini interpreted the anger of millions of Muslims as an *implicit* request and reacted accordingly. There is no doubt that Khomeini in his action was deeply influenced by the tragic events in which a number of anti-Rushdie demonstrators were killed. However, such actions or reactions cannot replace the necessary *asking* procedure. Otherwise, we would have to count all Khomeini's reactions as *fatwas*! Who would subscribe to this?

5. Lastly, even if there was a fatwa caller and all other conditions were fulfilled, the main legal problem remained unchanged; Khomeini as *ruler* did not have the necessary competence to deliver a fatwa. As mentioned above (p. 31), the *Ruler* together with two other categories of persons are — according to shari'a — *ipso facto* disqualified to deliver a fatwa. In the whole Islamic history, there is no single instance where a *ruler* (not even the prophet himself or the Caliphs) has delivered a fatwa while he was in office.

The above points clearly demonstrate that the so-called *fatwa* is defective on more than one fundamental point. There is a *vice de procédure* everywhere within the *fatwa* institution.

If Khomeini's Fatwa is not a Fatwa, What is it?

We have demonstrated that Khomeini's declaration on Rushdie as a *fatwa* leaves us with the task of describing this document and finding an appropriate classification. In this respect, we have to admit that there are only three other possibilities: One is that this document is nothing but a *judicial verdict*, a judicial act. The second possibility is that the document is a governmental act and an *order* issued by a ruler. The third and last possibility is to consider Khomeini's death decree as a Bill of War against the West.

1. *The first possibility: A verdict*

This presupposes that Khomeini acted as a judge (*qâdi*), and Rushdie's condemnation must be considered a judicial act. Such an interpretation brings us to an examination of Khomeini's legal and constitutional powers.

According to the Constitution of the Islamic Republic of Iran, Khomeini as the 'Leader' cannot act as a regular judge, because he is above all the state's institutions. He is not merely the Chief Executive like for example the presidents of the United States or France, who obviously cannot appoint themselves or be appointed by others as judges; Khomeini is more than that. He is also above the Executive Power whose current Chief is the President of the Republic (Article 113 of the Constitution). This means that Khomeini, precisely because of his constitutional powers, has absolutely no right to act as a judge. This remark is only valid, however, if we consider Khomeini as a leader of a modern state, which is perhaps not the case.

Let us now consider him as a leader of a traditional Islamic state like Mohammad, Ali, and others in the same category, with whom Khomeini was always delighted to be compared. It is true that Mohammad himself and his successors frequently acted as judges, rendering judgments on very different issues. It is certain they did, but only after a regular trial (*mahkama*). Trial as an institution and its procedure can be criticized as being rudimentary without any judicial assistance for the accused. Nevertheless, it has always been a trial, just or unjust, but a trial anyway.

In Islamic history, there have been a number of famous trials, especially in connection with blasphemy. Among these trials, the most famous in Sunni were the trials of Al-Hallâj (857-922), of 'Ayn Al-Quzât al-Hamadâni (1098-1131), and Al-Sohrawardi (known a Martyr *shahid*, executed in 1191). In Shi'a, the case of Sayyed Ali Mohammad Shirazi 'Bâb' (1819-50) should be mentioned. Let us look at the first and the last cases mentioned above:

Mansour al-Hallâj, known as Hallâj the Mystic in the 10th century of the Christian calendar, believed in the ontological unity between God and the human being (*vahdat-e vujud*) and proclaimed the 'theopathic phrase': 'I am [God] the Truth' (*An al-Haqq*). He was brought before a court (presided over by the judge Abu Omar) and condemned to death and cruelly executed on March 27, 922. The scene of his execution has been described as follows:

Before an enormous crowd, al-Hallâj, with a crown on his head, was beaten, half killed, and exposed, still alive, on a gibbet. ... The caliph's warrant for his decapitation did not arrive until nightfall, and in fact his final execution was postponed until the next day. ... In the morning, those who had signed his condemnation, grouped around Ibn Mukran, cried out: 'it is for Islam; let this blood be on our heads'. Al-Hallâj's head fell, his body was sprinkled with oil and burned and the ashes thrown into the Tigris from the top of a minaret. (Louis Massignon and Louis Gardet in *Encyclopedia of Islam*, new edition, '*Hallâj*')

The case of Bâb (Sayyed Ali Mohammad Shirâzi) is particularly interesting for our purpose, because it is a case which occurred in the mid-19th century in Iran with a Shi'a trial. Bâb made drastic attacks on corrupt Shi'a *mullas* and *mujtahids*; later on, he claimed to be a gate to the Shi'a *Hidden Imâm* (Al-Mahdi). Then he pretended to be the *Promised Mahdi* in person. At the final stage, he proclaimed himself the latest manifestation of the Primal Will (*Erâdeh-e azali*) and the bearer of a new divine revelation. Bâb was arrested and presented for a trial. The trial was a kind of questioning session by a committee of *mujtahids* in the presence of the Crown Prince of Iran (July 1848) (Tunkâbuni: 61). It was decided to condemn him forthwith. But because of religious riots provoked by his followers, the powerful minister Mirza Taqi Khân considered that the death of Bâb would break up this dangerous movement which continued to attract new adherents. He was put in prison until July 9, 1850, the date of his execution for heresy on the orders of the sovereign, Nasser el-Din Shah (1848-98). The execution took place in the courtyard of the barracks at Tabriz. To avoid any possible disobedience from Muslim soldiers, the Christian regiment was ordered to fire.

In all these cases, the accused were presented at a trial and then executed. In the Rushdie case, such a trial — despite its imperfection and partiality — has never taken place. Hypothetically, if Khomeini had intentions of bringing Rushdie to an Islamic trial, he could possibly make his wish public, inviting Rushdie or his defenders to participate in the trial. And in case Rushdie refused (he would, wouldn't he?), then Khomeini could ask the court to sentence him *in absentia*. But Khomeini did not do that. As a result, Khomeini's act cannot in any way be considered a regular and normal sentence, according to traditional, Islamic judicial custom. Obviously, Khomeini had no intentions of following normal Islamic procedure, because he was furious and wanted to kill Rushdie without a sentence. Also because in Khomeini's eyes, Rushdie was not worthy of being sentenced.

If these presumptions are correct, the facts support them. In this case, Khomeini's gesture was clearly contrary to Islamic tradition from Mohammad to the present time. Islam does not allow anybody to give orders to kill another person without a trial.

2. *The second possibility: An order*

Perhaps the most plausible way to put a name and a category on Khomeini's so-called *fatwa*, is that Khomeini's act can be considered an *order* (*hukm/farmân*). Actually, as the highest authority of the Islamic Republic of Iran, Khomeini had the power to give orders. Even before the establishment of the new regime, Khomeini had given a number of *farmân*, mostly with regard to the appointment of some personalities to elevated functions.

An example, among many others, of this type of *farmân* is Khomeini's act appointing Mehdi Bazargan as the High Authority for the Iranian Oil Industry on December 30, 1978, i.e. before the Shah's departure from Iran. After the adoption of a new Constitution and establishment of the Islamic Republic, Khomeini, who was recognized as Leader with vast powers, could certainly give orders to his subordinates and institutions. Thus, his orders as any other official's orders must be in accordance with the Constitution and within its framework. Only then would the orders be considered legal in an Iranian context, and only then must they be obeyed.

Khomeini, who repeatedly asked people to submit themselves to the lawful government, could not consider himself above the law whose formulation and codification had taken place under his direct guidance. Now let us put this question before any expert of Constitutional Law: Is there anything in the current Iranian Constitution which empowers the Leader to give a *direct* order to kill somebody? The answer to this question is as simple as it is clear. Nothing in this Constitution gives the Leader the power to issue such an order. Moreover, we are talking about an order which has been exclusively initiated and formulated by the Leader himself, without the approval/disapproval of the President of the Republic, without the approval/disapproval of the Prime Minister and his cabinet, without the approval/disapproval of the Parliament, and without the approval/disapproval of the highest judiciary authorities. None of these official persons and institutions were officially consulted on this matter.

Therefore, there is no doubt that Khomeini's decree on Rushdie was, and still is, a *personal, arbitrary and unconstitutional order*. He acted in complete disregard of the Constitution. The legal consequence of an illegal order is naturally that such an order cannot, and must not, be obeyed by anybody (officials or non-officials).

3. The third possibility: A declaration of war

For the sake of objectivity, we will try to find yet another explanation for Khomeini's decree, still within the Constitution. In this respect, it is be possible to interpret this decree as a *bill of war*. There are some reasons in favour of this thesis. Firstly, the tone of Khomeini's decree on Rushdie sounds extremely hostile: 'The author of the book entitled *The Satanic Verses* which has been compiled, printed and published *against Islam*, the Prophet and the Koran, as well as those publishers who were aware of its contents, have been sentenced to death' (emphasis added).

This quote leaves no doubt that Khomeini interpreted Rushdie's book not only as a deliberate act against Islam, the Prophet and the Koran, but as an act of war by Rushdie and the West at large. Khomeini reacted against this act of war by issuing a bill of war: a decree.

The Constitution actually gives the Leader the power to declare war (Article 110, Section e.). Secondly, as we will see later on, Khomeini always perceived the West as an indomitable enemy of Islam in every respect. In his view, which was, by the way, repeatedly confirmed by the numerous statements of other high-ranking Islamist-Iranians, Rushdie was simply an agent of the West whose mission was to destroy Islam. In short, through Rushdie, the West initiated a new type of proxy war against Islam.

Granted, to classify Khomeini's decree as a 'constitutional bill of war' is not unproblematic. Firstly, neither Rushdie nor the West have proclaimed their intention to go to war against Islam or against Iran. According to international law, war must be declared, or at least it must be initiated by actions (i.e. territorial invasion) which clearly indicate the physical beginning of war. In the Rushdie case, there were no such declarations nor any such actions. Secondly, one could maybe argue that *The Satanic Verses* in itself represents a 'declaration of war'; therefore there is no need for a physical action. So this is a matter of interpretation. Individual and subjective interpretations are free as long as they do not lead to violent action. Having an opinion on a question is one thing, the legality of action due to the interpretation is something else. It becomes clear that Khomeini's 'bill of war' was based exclusively on his personal interpretation. Could Khomeini's personal interpretation be considered an act of *ijtihâd*? Yes, if we interpret the *ijtihâd* in its broadest sense, though *ijtihâd* is quite different from the *jihâd* (war action). Even the Prophet had never initiated war before having had intensive consultation with his Companions who represented the different tribes and clans. In Khomeini's case, there is no evidence that he did this. If Mohammad did not do it, how could Khomeini do it? Thirdly, the Constitution allows the Leader to declare war 'on the recommendation of the Supreme National Defense Council'. This Council has never recommended war against Rushdie. Finally, it is absolutely unclear which authority, in accordance with which function, empowered Khomeini to deliver his decree. Did he act as the Leader of the state of Iran? Did he do it as the Leader of all Muslims? Or only as a *mujtahid*? Or even as the three 'offices' altogether? Since he did not specify which authority, all interpretations are plausible.

In the first hypothesis, his decree is valid *only* during the time of his leadership, whilst the second possibility must be rejected because of the absence of evidence that approximately one billion Muslims had ever elected/accepted Khomeini as their leader. The third possibility seems more accurate. The fact is that Khomeini was a recognized *mujtahid*, and by virtue of this, he could proceed to *ijtihâd*. In this condition, we return to our discussion on *fatwa*.

We argued that Khomeini's decree is not a *fatwa*. Another alternative is that it is merely a *mujtahid's* personal opinion. An opinion of this kind cannot be enforced by law (in the present context, Islamic law), unless the Islamic-Iranian parliament had adopted Khomeini's decree as a law. This is not the case.

After reviewing the different aspects of *fatwa* and analyzing the various possibilities in respect to Khomeini's *fatwa*, we can conclude that:

1) Khomeini's so-called *fatwa* is not really a *fatwa*. We demonstrated that nothing in his decree, neither in its form, procedure, nor substance, indicates that it is a *fatwa*. In Khomeini's favour, we could say that he has never claimed to have delivered a *fatwa*, except in a quick allusion, as we mentioned above.

2) We have also argued that Khomeini's decree cannot be considered a judicial act following a judgment.

3) Our discussion on the constitutional aspect of this decree leads us to observe that the current Islamic-Iranian constitution does not allow the Leader to give orders to have someone killed in the absence of trial and judgment.

4) We then tested the possibility of considering it as a *bill of war*. We argued in favour of this possibility, but ran into substantial problems relating to both international law on the proclamation of war and the absence of any concrete action which could be judged as a *war action* from Rushdie's side.

5) Finally, we came to the conclusion that Khomeini's decree on

Rushdie is based only on Khomeini's personal opinion which is outside of *shari'a*. In short, Khomeini had no authority to order Muslims to kill Rushdie. His decree was null and void from the moment it was published.

Khomeini's Motivations

Why did Khomeini deliver his sentence? Did he act for political or religious reasons? Khomeini's motivations are important because they influence the ultimate resolution of the conflict. If he had a political purpose, a political solution might be more plausible than if his motivation was religious, because if he acted solely in the interest of fulfilling his religious duty, the chances of finding a political solution would be close to nil.

Let us begin by assessing the *political* hypothesis. After eight years of an extremely bloody and costly war with Iraq, the Khomeini regime finally accepted a ceasefire (July 1988). At a time when the Iranian armed forces had suffered unprecedented set-backs, and when the morale of the Iranian population was at its lowest, the acceptance was undeniably considered to be a semi-defeat, if indeed not an outright defeat. Khomeini himself said publicly that making such a decision was more painful than 'drinking a glass of poison'. The failure of the regime's military policy, followed by the great disillusionment of the *Pasdaran* (the Revolutionary Guards) after so many promises of a quick and final victory, had unquestionably caused a decline in prestige and credibility, not only in the Iranian population but also in Muslim and international opinion. And to this must be added the great economic and financial difficulties, rampant inflation, shortages, and unemployment. The ceasefire had further deepened dissent within the clerical factions in power. Some influential and respected persons (such as Ayatollah Montazeri, Khomeini's heir apparent, dismissed in April 1989) were at that time expressing their desire for a political opening and liberation. Therefore, all these factors possibly influenced Khomeini. Interpreting these criticisms as a sign of his weakening authority, he reacted in the strongest possible manner, under the influence of anxiety and panic, by increasing pressure on his enemies (for example, several dozen prisoners who had already served their sentences were, without judgment, executed).

In this context, the Rushdie Affair would have been an unprecedented occasion for the Iranian patriarch to regain centre stage and show his authority in the hope of improving his tarnished image, while diverting the attention of Iranians from thorny internal problems and difficulties. Certainly, Khomeini's *fatwa* was immediately exploited politically by different political-clerical factions within Iran as well as by the Ayatollah's immediate entourage and various rival groups. They all hoped to exploit this affair in their own interest. All this seems quite reasonable and politically rational. But the problem of Khomeini's personality remains, as well as the existence of similar precedents which suggest that the Ayatollah's action was motivated first and foremost by religious considerations.

Let us therefore examine the religious hypothesis. There is evidence that Khomeini had a religious purpose. First, he had no political interest in once again thrusting himself into a sensitive international affair, especially so soon after having extricated himself from an extremely costly war. Iran had already begun reconstruction projects which required international loans and credits. To obtain them, the Islamic regime had taken pains to improve diplomatic relations with Western powers. Diplomatic relations with France, after a dramatic break following the Gorji affair (in 1988),[1] had just been normalized, and ambassadors had once again been exchanged. Similarly, after numerous negotiations, diplomatic relations with the United Kingdom had just been re-established, and the diplomatic representative from London had opened his doors in Tehran. Iran had every *political* interest in creating a certain credibility in world opinion, in particular among the Western powers. Thus, as regards foreign policy, level-headedness was dictated in Tehran. Furthermore, in its difficult negotiations with Iraq, Iran needed to acquire as much international support as possible, in particular the support of the two super-powers — or, failing this, at least their neutrality. Consequently it is difficult to understand, from the standpoint of political rationality and a cost-benefit calculation, that Khomeini would have had any interest in shuffling his cards and voluntarily placing his assets at risk.

Khomeini's personal need to defend Islam, a need which sometimes seemed like paranoia and stimulated a lust for destructiveness, indicates that a more detailed picture of his psychology (his 'operational code' or 'cognitive map') would be helpful. Let me point out that such unusual leaders as Hitler, Stalin and Khomeini, who have caused so much death and destruction, cannot be categorized within ordinary psychology. We shall not here enter into a detailed analysis of these topics, but on the basis of a series of observations shall demonstrate that Khomeini in fact behaved in accordance with his religious convictions and general perception of the world.

Research into operational codes and cognitive mapping is well known. Indeed, we shall base our endeavours on a model proposed by Alexander L. George in 1969 in which he modified the model created by Nathan Leites in *On the Study of Bolshevism* (1953). According to George, '[a] political leader's beliefs about the nature of politics and political conflict, his views regarding the extent to which historical developments can be shaped, and his notions of correct strategy and tactics — whether these beliefs be referred to as operational code, *Weltanschauung*, cognitive map, or an elite's political culture — are among the factors influencing that actor's decision' (George, 1969: 197), and 'Political actors have to adapt to and try to cope with these cognitive limits or boundaries to rational decision-making' (ibid: 198). As John Wolger summed up, '[o]pe-rational code analysis proceeds from a basic set of ten questions. Five of these concern philosophical beliefs or fundamental assump-tions about political life. They concentrate on the following areas: Is the political universe essentially one of conflict or harmony; what is the image of opponents; can history be controlled or predicted; is there optimism or pessimism concerning the achievement of political goals; and what is the role of chance?' (Wogler, 1989: 139-40).

We shall now apply this 'menu' to the case of Khomeini. However, keep in mind that this is not meant as a complete analysis of the Ayatollah's operational code, but only an attempt to trace its main contours. We believe the following five characteristics to be the major traits of Khomeini's cognitive map:

1. *Islamomania*

For Khomeini, Islam is the sole existing *verity*. Islam is all. Islam is the answer to every question, of every kind, at all times. 'All the needs of men are expressed in the Koran and (Muslim) tradition ... the Koran explains everything ... All the answers have been given to the totality of human needs from personal, family, and interpersonal problems to regulations concerning war and peace and relations among nations, from penal laws to commercial, industrial, and agrarian law' (Khomeini, 1979: 29).

2. *Politics' absolute dependence on Religion*

Since Islam is everything, politics can only exist within the rigorous framework of religion. The political sphere is non-existent. Politics can neither compete with, be parallel to, nor separate from religion. Politics must thus show absolute obedience to the logic of religion and follow the precepts and directives dictated by religion.

3. *A Manicheist Vision of the World*

The 'terrestrial' world is neatly divided into two: the world of good and the world of evil. Light and darkness. The universe of Islam (*Dâr al-Islam*) and the anti-Islam universe (*Dâr al-Harb*). There is on the one hand the party of God (*Hizb Allah*) and on the other the party of Satan (*Hizb al-Shaytân*). Compromise between the two is impossible. The struggle is permanent, until the first eliminates the second. Thus one must battle for the triumph of Islam. 'Even if one day', said Khomeini, 'I should find myself totally alone against the entire world, I shall not cease to fight in the service of Islam'. In brief, for this man of conviction, only this 'just cause' counted, even if the achievement of the cause would ultimately lead to the annihilation of the entire world: '*Fiat justitia, pereat mundus!*'

4. *Paranoia and Hatred*

An excessive, if not morbid, mistrust characterized Khomeini's behaviour vis-à-vis both the East and the West. In his eyes, the two were continually plotting against Islam, as if the annihilation of Islam was a priority for them. The Ayatollah's suspicion was accentuated by a deep feeling of hatred towards those who held power in the anti-Islam universe. *Vengeance* is the only way to make the powerful suffer the chastisements for their evil actions towards the disinherited masses. Actually, Khomeini was most probably influenced in his paranoia and hatred by old Shi'a history. Throughout Islamic history, Shi'a is represented as a *minority group*. As every other minority, the Shi'a people are suspicious and highly skeptical. They always felt that everybody was against them and that they were permanent victims of conspiracies. The Shi'a invention of *taqiyya* (camouflage) and *kitmân* (dissimulation) in daily life illustrates very well the Shi'a internal fear. This deeply rooted feeling never left the Shi'a spirit, despite the fact that from the start of the Safavid dynasty (1501-1732) until our time, except for short periods, Shi'a became the dominant sect in Iran and the country's official religion. The reason for the perennial fear among Iranians was that Western domination, especially British, succeeded Mongol domination. Between these two dominators, Iran — except for some periods at the beginning of the Safavid period — lived in constant insecurity, war (against the Ottomans and Russia) and crisis. Therefore, the traditional Shi'a paranoia was in reality reinforced by Iranian paranoia vis-à-vis the British.

During many decades, Iranians believed that the British were behind every political, economic and cultural move in Iran. The

Iranian author, Iraj Pezeshkzad, gives a magnificent description of this anti-British paranoia in his famous and popular novel entitled *Uncle Napoleon* (*Dâi jân Nopleon*), which despite its French connotation is about the 'Brit-phobia'. The decline and disintegration of the British Empire reduced this feeling among Iranians, but as a result of American domination, a new paranoia emerged. In this way, Khomeini resumed in himself the different paranoias which prevailed in the Iranian subconscious. In his ferocious attacks on the West and particularly on the USA, Khomeini indicated not only his own feelings, but to some degree he also personified the accumulation of both traditional Shi'a and Iranian (anti-British and anti-American) feelings. Salman Rushdie's citizenship also contributed to the conspiracy theory: A native Muslim who became a British citizen and then published a book 'against Islam' in London — all these factors reinforced Khomeini's inclination to believe in a real conspiracy.

Khomeini's anti-Western paranoia became more obvious in his long message on February 22, 1989, a few days after his '*fatwa*' on Rushdie. Talking about the Rushdie Affair, he indicated explicitly that the anti-Islamic forces (Zionists, British and Americans) were behind Salman Rushdie. These forces were working to destroy Islam and Muslims. In Khomeini's eyes, Rushdie was playing the role of an agent.

Revenge is also a common Shi'a feeling. A very significant part of Shi'a literature and ceremonies evoke the necessity of revenge. The whole story about the re-apparition of the Hidden *Imâm* is also closely connected to this sentiment. According to the rich literature on this matter, when the Hidden *Imâm* announces his re-apparition, he will immediately kill all the persons who are responsible for the martyrdom of the Shi'a *imâms* and other holy figures (Qumi: 537, Corbin 1964: 57, Mufid: 333). In other words, Shi'a is not a religion based on forgiveness. It is a religion of revenge!

Khomeini was a great representative of this Shi'a tradition. During his rule, he never forgave anybody, not even his close colleagues and assistants (Ayatollah Shariatmadari, Sadegh Ghot-

bzadeh) who had helped him seize power. Ayatollah Shariatmadari, one of the most prominent figures of contemporary Shi'a was
deposed as Ayatollah by Khomeini. Ghotbzadeh had served
Khomeini as his assistant and public relations man both in Iraq and
in France. He then served as Minister of Foreign Affairs, but was
later executed by Khomeini. These two cases are not unique.

Everything indicates that throughout his life Khomeini has
always been a person consumed by hate. He was not just *hostile* to
the West, to the Shah and to Rushdie, he *hated* them.

5. *Necrophilia and Narcissism*

In *The Anatomy of Human Destructiveness* (1973), Erich Fromm
presents a gripping analysis of clinical cases of necrophilia, 'love of
the dead,' in general, and more specifically political necrophilia, of
which Adolf Hitler is the most celebrated case. He cites several
elements (taken together) whereby one can identify a necrophiliac.
These are: extreme coldness, a distant attitude, a closed being
incapable of laughing, a sniffer, a magnetic gaze, a belief in the
virtue of violence ('a love of violence' in Augustinian terminology)
as the only means to resolve problems and remove obstacles.

Erich Fromm proceeds to make a distinction between two
different kinds of aggression. One is *benign aggression*, which is
biologically adaptive and life-saving, and the other one is *malignant
aggression*, which is biologically non-adaptive. In Fromm's terms
'what is unique in man is that he can be driven by impulses to kill
and torture, and that he feels lust in doing so; he is the only animal
that can be a killer and destroyer of his own species without any
rational gain, either biological or economic' (Fromm, 1974: 218).
Malignant aggression is divided into two categories: *Sadism* and
necrophilia. Each of them is again divided into *sexual-clinical* and
political categories. Here we will only deal with non-sexual sadism
and necrophilia. Fromm has studied Joseph Stalin and Heinrich
Himmler, chief of the SS, as political sadists. Let us take a brief look
at the case of Stalin. Stalin enjoyed to 'assure people that they were

safe, only to arrest them a day or two later. ... [He] could enjoy the sadistic pleasure of knowing the man's real fate at the same time that he was assuring him of his favour. What greater superiority and control over another person is there?' (ibid: 285). More specifically, Stalin used to arrest the wives and children of some of the highest-ranking Soviet or Party officials (like Molotov, Kalinin, and his own private secretary), and keep them in a labour camp, while their husbands had to do their job and bow and scrape before Stalin without even daring to ask for their release (ibid: 286). Political necrophilia and destructiveness is illustrated by the personality of Adolf Hitler. We do not intend to repeat Fromm's detailed work on Hitler from his childhood until his death, but since there are some similarities (sometimes rather close) between his and Khomeini's personality and behaviour, we will mention here a few points from Fromm's book. Hitler's face betrayed the sniffing expression which is one of necrophilia's characteristics. It was as if he was constantly smelling a bad odor, this is quite apparent from a large number of photographs. His smile was never free, but was a kind of smirk. Another of Hitler's necrophiliac traits was boredom. His conversations at tables are the most drastic manifestation of this form of lifelessness. Hitler's objects of destruction were cities and people. He said once, 'what does it matter if a dozen of our cities on the Rhine and Ruhr are consumed by fire and if a few hundred thousand people lose their lives!' (quoted by E. Hanfstaengel in Fromm: 402). Hitler was also an intense narcissist. He was interested only in himself, his desires, his thoughts, his wishes. The world was interesting only as far as it was the object of his schemes and desires; other people mattered only as far as they served him or could be used (Fromm: 406-7). Nevertheless, the greatest of Hitler's talents was his capacity to influence, impress, and persuade people. He had this ability even as a child. One must first think of what has often been called his *magnetism*, which according to most observers, originated in his eyes (ibid: 413-14). Furthermore, a related factor which facilitated Hitler's influence was his gift for oversimplification. His speeches were not restrained by intellectual or moral scruples. He selected the facts that served his thesis, connected the pieces, and made up plausible arguments, plausible at least for uncritical minds' (ibid: 415). However, the love of death and the desire to destroy remain the dominant and by far the most dangerous characteristics of a necrophiliac.

This portrayal of Hitler differs only slightly from Khomeini's (for instance, Khomeini's speeches usually contained some 'moral recommendations' while Hitler's did not). These two men (a *Führer* and a *Rahbar*) are very similar with regard to their desire for destruction and their love of death.

Without going into detail with Khomeini's rather more intimate traits, it is still possible to pinpoint his indifference and insensitivity to the death and suffering of others. For eight years, he sent Iranians of every category and every age into a war, which according to all observers was totally absurd, especially after 1982 when the Iraqis had been forced to evacuate Iranian territory. Throughout the entire war, death by martyrdom (*shahâda*) became a sublime virtue in post-revolutionary Iran, 'a beatitude reserved only for those selected by God.' From this standpoint, only martyrs enjoy 'eternal life,' for they die for the cause of Allah. As a logical consequence of the sublimation of death, even the term 'long live!' (*zendeh bâd!*) completely disappeared from the post-revolutionary Iranian vocabulary and was replaced by the slogan so often intoned: 'Death to USA! Death to Israel! Death to Liberals!' etc. Another logical consequence was that death was systematically thought of as the pinnacle of bliss and the summit of delight. Offerings of condolences were replaced by offerings of felicitations (*tabrik*) which Khomeini distributed abundantly to the families of the martyrs. His love of death was very clear from the time he returned from exile. His first symbolical gesture was to go directly from Tehran Airport to the city's largest cemetery (*Behesht-e Zahrâ*, Zahra Paradise), where he gave his first public speech. It is noticeable that at that time, this cemetery did not yet contain many hundred thousands martyrs, as it did later on as the result of war and other acts of violence due to the revolutionary events. Blood (*khûn*) and death also became the 'new way of life' of Iranians during Khomeini's rule. A new doctrine was proclaimed — the 'doctrine of blood and martyrdom' (*maktab-e khûn va shahâdat*). Khomeini's blood-thirst was not invented by his opponents; it was real and true. In the cemetery of Zahra Paradise, he erected a huge monument in the honor of blood. This is a macabre fountain which spouts red water symbolizing blood. What happened to this particular cemetery is far from unique. During Khomeini's rule, all cemeteries in Iran became larger and larger, one more macabre than the other.

In brief, in addition to the systematic destruction of the country, death also acquired a place in life under Khomeini. '*Viva la Muerte!*' as the Francoist General Milan Astray exclaimed in the midst of the Spanish Civil War.

As for Khomeini's narcissism, facts and testimonies show in extraordinary agreement that he was a typical narcissist. He believed that he had a mission, exclusively in the service of Islam. Convinced that he alone possessed supreme and authentic Islamic authority, he regarded himself as the truly legitimate and unique successor of the Prophet, and the leader of all Muslims. Most probably, Khomeini's coldness indicated his narcissistic tendencies. Almar D. Volkan, the author of *The Need to have Enemies & Allies* has analyzed Charismatic Narcissistic Leaders. A typical narcissistic leader 'has a rather limited repertoire of feeling. Because he sees others as existing only to adore him and fails to appreciate them as free-standing individuals with lives of their own, he does not exhibit such emotions as concern, sadness, and so on' (Volkan 1994: 200). These characteristics correspond very well to Khomeini's personality. As a person, Khomeini was cold and very distant. He rarely laughed and rarely looked people directly in the eyes. He acted almost timidly. Compared to Hitler who was agitated and had frequent fits of anger, Khomeini was extraordinarily calm, almost as if he had absolutely no feelings. On the plane which brought him from Paris to Tehran, after 15 years of exile, Paul

Balta, *Le Monde's* correspondent asked him what he felt as he was approaching Iran, and he answered laconically 'Nothing!' (*Le Monde*, February 5-6, 1984 and interview with Balta, July 4, 1996). Also, he felt that he was the shepherd (*tchupân* — a frequently used term in his speeches and writings) protecting his herds from the wolves. He had all the places, cities, mosques, and ports which were previously named after the Shah, changed to his name. Moreover, his extraordinary need to be adored was satisfied by deft manipulation of words and titles. He openly allowed people to call him *imâm*, whereas in Shi'a, this title is reserved solely for the 12 designated *Imâms*. And, playing with words, he also liked to be called 'Spirit of God,' which is the literal translation of his own first name Ruhollah, but which in Persian (*Ruh-é Khodâ*), and especially in a political context, has completely different connotations.

In conclusion, Khomeini's death sentence against Rushdie seems to have been determined by his religious beliefs and his idea of his mission. He expressed his tendencies to necrophilia and to narcissism through his deep religious feeling. The *fatwa* on Rushdie could satisfy both his necrophilia, narcissism and his religious beliefs.

Khomeini and Shi'a Violence

The word *assassin(s)* derives directly from Shi'a history. It was the name given to the disciples of Hassan Al-Sabbâh (d. 1124), the Master of Alamut. Alamut is a region in the heart of the Alburz mountains in the Iranian Caspian provinces of Guilan and Mazandaran. Silvestre de Sacy, the great French orientalist of the 19th century and an ardent student of the Assassins, came to the conclusion that the etymology of their name could be traced back to the Arabic word *hashish* (herbage, cannabis, sativa) and other variant forms, such as *hashishi, hashshâshîn* (colloquial plurals, *hashishiyyin* and *hashshâshîn*). In his fascinating book *The Assassins* (first published in 1967; second edition 1985), Bernard Lewis discusses Silvestre de Sacy's thesis but objects that *hashish* is a more modern word and the common term for a hashish taker. While de Sacy did not adopt the opinion held by many later writers that the Assassins had that name because they were addicts, he nevertheless 'explains the name as due to the secret use of hashish by the leaders of the sect, to give their emissaries a foretaste of the delights of paradise that awaited them on the successful completion of their missions' (Lewis, 1985: 12). This explanation may be true, but the phonetic relation between *hashish* in its various forms and *assassin(s)*, seems quite weak, if it exists at all. On the other hand, it is more plausible that the name *assassin(s)* is derived from the name of the *Segnor de Montana*, Hassan Al-Sabbâh, probably called *Al-Hassan* (= Assassin?) by his disciples, for short. This name then later became the collective name for his devotees. Whatever the true etymological background of the Assassins, the fact remains that the Shi'a created a new word for 'murderers' with intimate political connotations. The Assassins were one of the best *organized* terrorist groups, using terrorism systematically in the service of clear, explicitly proclaimed political objectives as expressed in the religious discourse of the time.

     Most of the Assassins were Shi'a and Iranian, but they were not Imâmite Shi'a, which has been Iran's official religion since the 16th century. They were *Isma'ili* Shi'a, who believed only in the first Six of the Twelve Imâms. At the present time, this is the most 'quietist' religious group within Islam, under the leadership of Agha Khân, who spent his efforts promoting and reconstructing Islamic culture, art and architecture. Ironically, even as the contemporary disciples of the old Assassins become advocates of non-violence, a significant number of their semi-coreligionists, the Imâmites (*Ithna 'ashari or Imâmi*), are becoming the New Assassins.

     In comparing *Imâmism* with *Zaidism*, another Shi'a sub-group, it becomes clear that while traditional Zaidism calls for rebellion and insurrection, the Imâmites reject the use of violence and direct confrontation. In fact, the Imâmites have been calm and consistently non-violent throughout their history. The externalization of violence is a relatively new phenomenon in Imâmite Shi'a. Historically, the

choice of non-violence as a tool of survival goes back to the tragic
event in Karbala, where Husayn, the Third Shi'a Imâm was
assassinated together with several of his relatives and followers
(October 680). Since this incident was a result of Husayn's
insurrection and rebellion against the official government (Caliph
Yazid), the Imâmi, traumatized by this massacre, abandoned violent
methods in favour of more peaceful means. Because they had been
a minority for at least a great part of their history, they chose a
two-track strategy as an alternative to violence, namely a systematic
show of conformism outwardly and in public, while retaining for
themselves a deep-down allegiance to their faith. Accordingly, the
Imâmites have devised some useful tactics, such as *taqiyya*, literally
'avoid unnecessary danger', which enabled them to survive,
whereby they even accepted high positions in the administration as
ministers and confidants of a Sunni king or a caliph, while secretly
working against him. The *kitmân* (dissimulation and camouflage) is
another Imâmite tactic. The *taqiyya* and *kitmân* must not be
confused with resignation and submission, which imply passive
behaviour and full acceptance of a perceived unsatisfactory condition. The Imâmi never recognized the legitimacy of the Caliphate,
the Mongol Khâns or anyone else. They would simply not take
unnecessary risks and expose themselves to great danger without
being prepared for it. They were 'waiting' for better times. Indeed,
waiting (intizâr) is an another distinctive Imâmism feature. Since
they believe that justice will be done only with the reappearance of
the Hidden Imâm or the Awaited Imâm (*Imâm al-Muntazar*), they
became more and more accustomed to waiting instead of acting.
The belief in a Saviour who is physically present but living in
hiding has to some extent attenuated the Imâmis' will for revenge
and rebellion. Saying that the Imâmis were placid and peaceful is
not to say that they have never been the source or the initiators of
some confrontation with Sunni sects. Such events, though limited,
are in a sense normal and unavoidable between sects. The main
point is that the Imâmis did renounce violent acts or insurrection
against those in power. The cult of *martyrdom (maktab-e shahâdat)* is

very much present in Shi'a tradition and daily life. Therefore, the introduction of terrorist actions and insurrection into Shi'a =Imâmi) doctrine is a novelty in itself and as such needs explaining.

We must emphasize that the recent Shi'a protest movements, and consequently the terrorist actions, are not part of a *general* trend within Shi'a. Rather, Shi'a representatives and religious authorities had participated in these movements, or these actions emanated from small groups who had labelled their actions 'Islamic'.

They are! In the following, we shall summarize the principal changes and tendencies wrought by these events in certain Shi'a Imâmi groups.

Shi'a move from 'Quietism' To 'Violence'

Historically, Shi'a as a group has always been — or at least seen itself — as a minority among other Muslims. The feeling has never left the Shi'a mind that its legitimacy has been confiscated by the Sunni. This feeling is not new, it is rooted in the beginning of the first period of Islamic history. One could wonder why it was necessary for Shi'a to wait almost fourteen centuries to express its frustration through aggression. The answer to this question does not come from history but from the socio-economic transformations in Iran that started in the second half of the 19th century. In Sura III on *Economic Origins of Shi'a violence*, we attempt to provide the answer to this question.

The Shi'a frustration has been internalized in a such way that Shi'a have become masters in the art of camouflaging real feelings. In general, the Shi'a have not demonstrated their bitterness, frustration and anger in public. They have kept it in their hearts generation after generation, and have become almost schizophrenic. The protest movements from the 19th century up to and beyond the Islamic revolution, provided the Shi'a with the opportunity to publicly expose their accumulated frustration. The origin of the

Shi'a volcanic eruptions in both Iran and Lebanon in the 1980s and 1990s must be found — at least partially — in the sudden externalization of their expression.

The Shi'a had hoped that the Awaited Imâm (al-Mahdi) would, by his apparition, rescue his followers and undo the injustice . He made them wait too long. Therefore, a fraction of Shi'a went into action. The apparition of Khomeini was perceived by many Shi'a as the apparition of al-Mahdi. Some Shi'a really believed that Khomeini was the Imâm they had waited for.

Shi'a is the sect of martyrdom *par excellence*. The whole Shi'a calendar turns around the events related directly (correctly or not) to martyrdom. The rituals, ceremonies, and symbols are shaped for the martyr. The black turban of some Shi'a priests is not only the sign that they are descendants of the Prophet, it is also the symbol of mourning the assassination of Husayn. The cult of martyrs is still strong among the Shi'a believers. What is new is that this has recently been connected to violent actions of revenge. Instead for waiting for the Awaited Imâm to take revenge, the Shi'a in our time went into action themselves with terrorism and kidnappings, etc.

Open struggle replaced the *taqiyya*, which was abolished in 1963 by Khomeini's *fatwa*.[2] The Shi'a must no longer dissimulate their real opinion and must protest publicly against 'injustice' and 'anti-Islamic acts'.

Genuine Shi'a behaviour is masochist in the sense that suffering is considered a value which will be rewarded in the other world. Self-flagellation and cutting the body with knives are some Shi'a rituals. There has also been a change in this area. Khomeini and other Shi'a leaders taught their disciples that the right way is to beat the enemy instead of beating themselves. War, terrorist actions, and especially suicide bomb attacks are the result of the transformed Shi'a behaviour.

After a short review of the Shi'a transformations, we study the stages of Shi'a violence.

Stages of Shi'a Violence

Shi'a violence has appeared in many guises. It has gone from agitation to insurrection, from insurrection to revolution, from revolution to repression, and at the same time, to aggression (war and international terrorism).

The Stage of Agitation (1941-56)

This is one of the most tumultuous periods in Iran's modern history. For all practical purposes, it commenced with the abdication of Reza Shah (September 17, 1941) and ended on January 17, 1956, the day when the main leaders of the terrorist group of Fadâ'iyân-e Eslâm (Devotees of Islam) were executed. This period is of major importance for the search for new sources of contemporary Shi'a violence. Indeed, it was during this period that a new style of Islamist discourse emerged, and the Fadâ'yân was born and began systematically to spread terror among the ruling clique.

The Discourse

At the time, Shi'a, Islamist discourse did not yet have the clarity it would acquire later, especially during the years close to the Islamic revolution. It was still vague and ambiguous, availing itself of foggy and uncertain terms. Its architect was a mullâh, forty years old or so, still with an insignificant rank. This was Ruhollah Khomeini, whose book entitled *Kashf ul-Asrâr* (Discovering the Secrets) would be published in 1943.[3] The book was a disorganized pot-pourri of diverse themes such as pilgrimage to the tombs of the Imâms (p. 66), the problem of intercession (p. 77), and a few themes of current relevance such as the conduct of Pahlavi (Reza Shah) towards the people (p. 239), or the situation of civil servants (p. 251). But all in all, the overall structure of the work gives the impression that the author, despite the outward show of variety, is nonetheless pursuing a specific line and is essentially interested in three principal themes: The first is a refutation of the anticlerical theses put forth at the same time by lay and nationalist writers, such as Ahmad Kasravi and Hakamizâdeh. Kasravi would be assassinated a few years later by the Fadâ'iyân. The second principal theme was that of a deep-seated anti-Pahlavism. When Khomeini criticized Reza Shah, he used very offensive language. It is clear that hatred for Pahlavi was already firmly rooted in the mind of this unique author. The third and last theme consists of a mélange of arguments — albeit primarily religious ones — to justify the supremacy of the role of the Shi'a Ulama in the political affairs of society. It must be admitted that Khomeini's theoretical position at this time was not entirely unoriginal. In a certain sense, it marked a break with traditionalist Shi'a discourse.

Until that time, the most the Ulama had ever demanded was to be granted rights of supervision (*haqq-e nezârat*), especially over legislation.[4] This demand was met by the terms of Article 2 of the Addendum to the Constitution of 1906. However, that article would remain a dead letter until the 1979 Islamic Revolution.

Khomeini, for whom this period was one of out-and-out bitterness, decided to break with the official position of the top-level hierarchy of the Ulama. However, this new requirement was not clearly formulated. It remained latent, but was nonetheless legible in vague terms. He specifies that 'God has ordained the establishment of an Islamic government (*Hukumat-e Eslâmi*) (p. 109). Then, in a quite extensive analysis of the principle of the Imâmate, the *Kashf* author comes to the conclusion that the legitimate wielders of power (*Ulul Amr*), after the Prophet and during the Great Occultation (*Ghaybat al-Kubra*), were neither kings, nor emirs, nor caliphs (p. 110). Who were these ultimate wielders of power? The faqihs, of course.

On this point, although Khomeini presents this *alternative* (in his eyes only) many times, he nonetheless hesitates to directly call for faqih power. He even gives the impression that he has doubts whether such a project could be realized. 'No faqih has ever said or written', he tells us, 'that we should want to become king, or that we should consider royalty (the sultanate) as our right' (p. 186). And he adds that over the course of history, there have been Ulama who supported kings, and now, in our times, some are trying to cause the State to harbour suspicion towards the Ulama (p. 187).[5] The author, apparently conscious of the obstacles standing in the way of the establishment of a faqih government proposes an intermediate solution — not without a touch of pragmatism. While reiterating that power (*hukumat* and *velâyat*) legitimately belongs to the faqih in our era, he introduces a touch of relativism to this postulate by stating that this does not mean that the 'faqih must be king, minister (general), and janitor at one and the same time!' (p. 185). The provisional solution therefore would be for the king to be elected by a Constituent Assembly composed exclusively of authentic mujtahids, who 'have a perfect knowledge of the divine laws, are just, and are free of the temptations of the ego ... and hence whose exclusive concern is to serve the interests of the people and to carry out the divine laws' (p. 185). The chosen person (the king) must be 'just (*'âdil*), obedient to the divine laws, and avoid injustice and oppression' (ibid).

Thus, we see that Khomeini had endeavoured to break with the official and traditional Shi'a discourse since 1943. Still, the break such as it was, was neither clean nor deep. The *Kashf* without a doubt contained the seeds of a radical break, but it took the expulsion of its author from Iran in 1963, followed by the publication of a collection of his courses at Najaf (*Hukumat-e Eslâmi* 1971) for the new discourse to definitively assume its own clear and radical contours. Need it be stated that it was in the name of this new discourse that Khomeini seized power after the Islamic Revolution?

Let us now return to Khomeini's initial discourse, put forth in the *Kashf*, and ask the following question: What was the attitude of Khomeini at that time to the use of violence for the cause of Islam? According to some sources, Khomeini was close to the terrorist circles of the *Fadâ'iyân* and convinced that 'recourse to violence was admissible to defend Islam.'[6] However, there is to this day no irrefutable evidence that he was involved in acts of violence or even incitement to violence in either his writings or his declarations. That leaves only the *Kashf*. However, in that work as well, one will find no direct incitement to violence. True, the tone is very lively and bitter, sometimes straying into the cesspool of cheap insult (e.g., 'syphilitic brains', 'blockheads', 'asses', etc.). Even so, the book generally speaking remains one of refutation and enlightenment. For instance, the author calls upon journalists to read the *Kashf* and make efforts to 'arouse the slumbering people' (p. 333).

But we must not allow such seemingly ingenuous caution to mislead us. The author of the *Kashf* is by no account a pacifist; to convince oneself on that point one needs only to re-read the last page of the book where he refers to three verses of the Koran (Sura Nisâ', verse 137; Sura Mâ'ida, verse 50, and Sura Anfâl, verse 59). These three verses are especially harsh, calling on the faithful to keep their distance from Jews and Christians, even as they encourage them to combat the 'enemies of God'.

Consequently, it would not be wrong to conclude that Khomeini at that time was being careful not to openly incite people to violence. Instead, incitement was couched in soft tones, while the instigator carefully camouflaged himself behind the Koranic verses. Twenty years later, however, Khomeini would make his position clearer by proclaiming the practice of *taqiyya* to be inadmissible, calling for rebellion.

Terrorist Activities

Throughout the entire period of agitation, the exercise of Shi'a violence was the exclusive domain of the Fadâ'iyân-e Eslâm. The Fadâ'iyân organization dates from the years 1944-45, when it was founded by Nawâb Safavi, alias Seyyed Javâd Mir-Lowhi. Nawâb himself is an interesting personality. His origin was among the clergy: his father was initially a cleric, but then later became a barrister-at-law in Tehran — no doubt under the influence of Reza

Shah's secularization policies. He was imprisoned for a time under Pahlavi I. Nawâb himself completed his engineering studies in a German school, after which he went to work at Abadan for the Anglo-Iranian Oil Company.[7] According to some sources, he was dismissed by the Company for his anti-British activities.[8] At that point, he returned to Najaf, a Shi'a city in Iraq, where he studied theology. He returned to Iran only to put an end to the activities, which were judged to be anti-clerical and anti-Shi'a, of the celebrated nationalist writer Ahmad Kasravi, mentioned earlier. Having failed to persuade the latter to abandon his undertakings, Nawâb, now armed with a *fatwa*, hence decided to do away with Kasravi physically.[9] The first attempt, on April 28, 1945, failed, and the victim was only wounded slightly. Nawâb and his accomplice were arrested, but through the intervention of the clergy were promptly released on bail. A bazar merchant paid the bail. Nawâb thereupon lost no time preparing to make a second attempt on the life of the writer, and this time, two of Nawâb's companions succeeded on March 11, 1946 in assassinating Kasravi and his secretary.

The assassination of the anticlerical writer provoked open joy and satisfaction among the Shi'a clergy, and the Shah's impotent government, once again under pressure from clerical circles, did not dare sentence the principal perpetrator (Sayyed Husayn Imâmi) to more than two years' imprisonment.

The war in Palestine caused hundreds of thousands of Palestinians to flee from their native land, and this, followed by the creation of the State of Israel in 1948, was very influential as regards the escalation of Shi'a Islamist activities. At two meetings, organized by the Fadâ'iyân, at the Shah's mosque in the centre of Tehran, on January 11 and May 21, 1948, more than 5,000 volunteers declared themselves ready to depart for Palestine to fight alongside the Palestinian Muslims.[10] A year and a half later, the Fadâ'iyân would resume their terrorist activities: On November 4, 1949, Abdul Husayn Hajir, Minister of the Court and regarded as a member of the Baha'i sect, was assassinated.

However, the real politicization of the Shi'a Islamist movement was brought about by the growth of the movement to nationalize the oil industry. Before that, the Fadâ'iyân had not participated directly in political matters in the strict sense, but were more concerned with peripheral questions such as the repression of the anticlerical movement or the struggle for a Muslim Palestine. Even apart from its breadth and the universal enthusiasm it provoked, the movement to nationalize oil became for all practical purposes by far the most important political movement in Iran, and one in which society as a whole felt itself involved.

The Shi'a Islamists adopted a positive attitude towards this movement, at least in its first phase. Moreover, they contributed to it by assassinating the Prime Minister, General Razmârâ, who was firmly opposed to the project of nationalization. The assassination occurred on March 7, 1951 in a Tehran mosque. The assassin (Khalil Tahmâsbi) was pardoned by a parliamentary decision on November 15, 1952.

The Fadâ'iyân, whose attitude toward this movement was initially positive, changed it to one of implacable hostility towards Mosaddeq, who became Prime Minister after April 30, 1951. They demanded that he immediately apply Islamic Law (Sharî'a), although no responsible political leader was competent to meet such a demand, especially then when the country was experiencing one of its most crucial historical moments and was struggling against one of the most powerful oil companies in the world, the Anglo-Iranian Oil Company, and via this, against the British Empire. Added to this, Mosaddeq as a thorough democrat and believer, who nonetheless was a firm partisan of the separation of state and religion, could not accede to the dictate of the Fadâ'iyân without at the same time disowning his own fundamental political convictions.

Thus, the Fadâ'iyân hostility towards Mosaddeq probably had reasons other than purely religious ones behind it. By virtue of his extraordinary popularity, but also, and especially, because of his protectionist politics — a historical demand of the national bourgeoisie — Mosaddeq had succeeded in seducing bazar circles and thus got his message through to the very heart of the Islamist social bastions. The bazar, traditionally deeply religious (*mazhabi*), had become a nationalist (*melli*) bazar under Mosaddeq's influence. The Fadâ'iyân considered this change of character absolutely impardonable, not only because it made it difficult for them to recruit followers among the bazar strata, but also because it risked cutting them off from the precious financial and logistic sources the bazar provided.

Specifically, to break out of the process of isolation that was becoming irreversible, the Fadâ'iyân passed from verbal attacks on Mosaddeq to physical violence. One of their members, Mehdi 'Abd-e Khodâ'i, only fifteen years old, shot and wounded Husayn Fâtemi, Minister of Foreign Affairs in Mosaddeq's government (February 5, 1952). He would later become a parliamentary deputy after the Islamic Revolution.

Mosaddeq's overthrow in a coup d'état on August 19, 1953 was brought about in part by Islamist agitation and by the Islamists alliance with the Court. Iran's integration into the Western system would accelerate after the coup d'état, and the bonds of dependence on the West would be strengthened. An international consortium would regain control of the oil wealth, and the law nationalizing the oil industry would be de facto abrogated in October 1954. Thereafter, on the resolve of John Foster Dulles, US Secretary of State, Iran would also be integrated into the Western military system. The Baghdad Pact (the future CENTO), comprising Iran, Iraq, Pakistan, Turkey, and Great Britain would make the fait accompli official. The United States chose to remain an observer within the Pact.

It was at this point that the Fadâ'iyân, disillusioned by the turn of events and disappointed in the 'new' regime, made a spectacular comeback, using their usual method, namely terrorism, to do so. On November 19, 1955, Husayn 'Alâ, the Prime Minister, who was preparing to depart for Baghdad to sign the pact, narrowly escaped death from bullets fired by a young worker, thus giving the government a pretext to arrest not only the direct perpetrator of the deed, Mozaffar Ali Zul-Qadr, but also the principal founder of the Fadâ'iyân, Nawâb Safavi, and his lieutenants. Nawâb and three other persons were sentenced to death and executed on January 17, 1956. The execution marked the end of the first stage of activities of the Shi'a Islamists.

The Stage of Insurrection (1962-65)

The principal characteristic of this stage was the fact that, for the first time, the Islamist Shi'a movement not only provoked a popular insurrection against the regime, but also led it. Indeed, from this period onward Shi'a Islamism, henceforth under the aegis of Khomeini, felt strong enough to step onto the political scene as a specific and powerful force. Before that time, the Fadâ'iyân had been distinctly unsuccessful in politicizing their movement, their spectacular terrorist acts notwithstanding. They lived for their cause clandestinely and in isolation.

Khomeini's contribution in this regard was of decisive importance, not because the movement he personified became even more radicalized, but above all because he succeeded in giving it political direction and orientation.

After the execution of the heads of the Fadâ'iyân and then until 1962, the agitational activities of the Islamists were reduced to practically nil. There are several explanations for this setback. In addition to the decapitation of the Fadâ'iyân, a severe blow in itself, there was also the extraordinary repression by the Shah's regime of all oppositional movements. The Baghdad Pact had made Iran an integral part of the system of Western security, and the country's internal stability, i.e., the consolidation of the Shah's regime, was in Western eyes its most important pillar. SAVAK, the Secret Police created in 1957, ensured this security with its repressive activities. The temporary silence of the Islamists throughout these years may therefore be attributed to the combination of repression and the decapitation of the Fadâ'iyân.

The resumption of activities by the Islamists, as well as by the Iranian opposition as a whole, was due exclusively to the fact that the new American administration under President Kennedy had decided on a momentary easing of repression. In addition to allowing certain political freedoms (e.g., women were given the right to vote, and also locally elected officials should henceforth be allowed to be sworn in on the 'heavenly book' of their choice), the new American President insisted that above all the agrarian reform project be finally implemented.

The Shi'a clergy forthwith unanimously rejected this project, and the impact was such that Ayatollah Burujerdi himself, the supreme leader (*marja'-e koll-e taqlid*) of the Shi'as and symbol of quietism par excellence, was quick to openly criticize the agrarian reform in its totality. There was a simple reason for this unanimous negative attitude. The clergy feared, not without reason, that the reform would ultimately deprive them of control over the common lands (*awqâf*) and take valuable financial resources contributed by some land-owners away from them, whether in the form of religious taxes (*khums* and *zakât*) or through various gifts and donations (*sadaqât*). Likewise, they feared that the redistribution of land would end with the annulment of the 'sacred' principle of respecting and safeguarding private property; and, as the aggregate consequence of these factors, that this reform would put a definitive end to their financial autonomy, which they had guarded jealously in the past.[11]

Just when the Shah was announcing his reform projects, a fateful event occurred. Ayatollah Burujerdi died on March 30, 1961. As the *marja'-e koll*, and directly in the tradition of his predecessors, Burujerdi had been in a position to make use of his influence in favour of moderation and the quest for peaceful solutions. His conduct was motivated by a great concern to preserve the cohesion and the survival of the Shi'a community as an autonomous sect. Ayatollah Burujerdi had never believed in the use of violent methods to impose Shi'a principles. When he died, the quietist tradition, personified in the supreme Shi'a authority, vanished with him.[12] The void created in the unified Shi'a authority at first merely benefitted the Shah's power. Since the clergy no longer had a single leader, accepted and respected by all, it could no longer claim to be a representative body — at least in the Shah's eyes — and even less a worthy interlocutor. In fact, the Shah resorted to all kinds of tricks to prevent the installation of a new supreme Shi'a authority in order to make this situation within Ulama circles last as long as possible. Furthermore, if this authority was able to establish itself despite the obstacles, the Shah preferred that it be seated anywhere but in Iran, and that it should be wielded by a non-Iranian Ayatollah.[13] If the absence of a supreme leader had initially reassured the King, it would not be long before that same absence would cause him some grave problems. Specifically, the door was henceforth open to every sort of claim, and each of the Ayatollahs was free to adopt a position on any political question. The resurgence of Khomeini, leader of the extremists, must therefore be seen in this context and understood as the ineluctable consequence of Burujerdi's death.

To return to the crucial question of reforms, the confrontation between the regime and the clergy over this matter was direct and immediate, even in this new situation. Telegrams of protest addressed to the Shah and his Prime Minister (Alam) flowed in. The bazar and the universities were in a state of ferment. To calm people's minds and especially to deepen the division within the clergy, the Shah yielded on the two following points: women's right to vote[14] and the question of oath-taking. In return, the sovereign remained firm on the agrarian reform. Even so, his efforts to divide the Ulama were only partially successful. If the moderate Ulama proved to be satisfied with the annulment of the first two measures, the less moderate among them would become further radicalized and present themselves as another Islamist political alternative.

The Shah's firmness on the agrarian reform was not only due to American pressure but also to his conviction that this reform would enable him to build a new social class made up of 'free peasants' on whose political support he could count. Hence his stubborn perseverance and exceptional determination in this matter. Confronted with this determination, the Shi'a Islamist faction, whose leader was henceforth Ayatollah Khomeini, had but one choice: continue the struggle or give up. It was an irony of fate that, of all possible factors, it was the Shah himself through a tactical mistake who would make the task of the Islamist faction easier. Thus, the Islamists were forced to 'choose' the path of struggle.

Two days before the date set for the referendum on agrarian reform and five other propositions,[15] the Shah on January 25, 1963 in the holy city of Qum, gave a speech of unusual virulence against the Ulama and their allies in the Bazar. Next, stepping up his attack, he continued to bait the radical clergy. Finally, on March 23, 1963, the fateful day arrived. Government troops attacked the Fayziyyah theological school in Qum where a few hundred students (*tullâb*) had gathered to protest against the Shah's anti-religious measures. There were wounded, and according to some sources there were also deaths among the *tullâb*.[16] Without a doubt, the Fayziyyah events provided the Islamists with a pretext to denounce the Shah as an impious person and an enemy of Islam. But such a charge was not in itself new. The Ulama felt that the Pahlavi dynasty from its inception had been downright hostile towards the religion whose principles they upheld. The big novelty in this affair was incontestably the *marginalization of the moderate tendency*, which until that time had had control of the Shi'a movement as a whole. Khomeini then took advantage of the festivities of the *'ashurâ*[17] and in order to set himself apart from his peers, decided to counterattack the Shah. He was arrested on June 4, 1963, but already the following day the Shah was utterly surprised by the extent of the insurrection that Khomeini's arrest had caused. The insurrection on June 5 was cruelly suppressed, and Khomeini was not released until several months later, on April 2, 1964.

At the same time as these events were unfolding, the American penetration into Iranian society assumed an even more concrete

form: numbers of American advisers of every kind would henceforth frequent Iranian soil. To enable them to flaunt national jurisdiction, Washington demanded that the Shah's government
establish a régime of Capitulation. On September 4 and 13, 1964,
the Iranian parliament met this demand. The vote provoked waves
of protest in the population and Khomeini seized this new occasion,
almost totally unexpected, to re-enter the political scene. The new
law was also the target of his first squarely and extraordinarily
virulent anti-American speech. By coincidence, it was given on the
same day as both the Shah's and his own birthday — October 26,
1964.[18] A few days later, Khomeini was arrested again, but this time
he was expelled from the country (November 4). This, however, did
not put an end to the activities of the Shi'a Islamists. According to
information of pro-Khomeini forces published after the Islamic
Revolution,[19] from the time of Khomeini's first arrest in 1963,
various Islamist groups began to organize the harmonizing of their
actions. A new organization was formed, the Organization of
Unified Islamist Groups (UIG) (*Hay'at-hây-e Mo'talafaye-e Eslâmi*),
under the aegis of Khomeini himself. It had a central committee
composed of twelve members[20] and a religious council.[21] After
Khomeini's expulsion to Turkey, the UIG decided, after a pause of
several years, to resort again to terrorist methods. The first victim
was the Prime Minister, Hassan Ali Mansour, assassinated January
21, 1965 in front of the Parliament building by a young bazar
apprentice called Mohammad Bokhârâ'i.[22] This assassination was
followed by the arrest of several members of the UIG, some of
whom were survivors of the Fadâ'iyân. Four of them (including
Bokhârâ'i) were executed on June 16, 1965.[23] Here it is interesting
to note that, again according to the same sources, Hashemi
Rafsanjani, (President of the Islamic Republic from 1989 to 1997),
was a very close collaborator of the 'Bokhârâ'i group' at that time.

Among other Islamist groups attuned at the time to terrorist
action and armed struggle, we should mention the clandestine
organization of the Party of Islamist Peoples (*Hezb-e Melal-e Eslâmi*).
Leaders were Mohammad Javâd Hujatti Kermâni and Mohammad

Kâzem Burujerdi. The organization was discovered and broken up by SAVAK before it was able commit any terrorist actions. Sixty-nine persons were arrested.

These arrests marked the end of the insurrectional phase of the Shi'a Islamist movement and the Islamists thereafter turned their attention to indoctrination and propaganda.

The Revolutionary Stage (1977-79)

A detailed analysis of this period and the period after the revolution, both very eventful, is beyond the scope of this study. The following, therefore, is meant only as an outline.

Between 1965 and 1977, Islamist activities in general, and violent activities in particular, diminished considerably. Indeed, throughout this long period, there were no assassinations or attempted assassinations by Islamist groups. Agitational activities were also reduced to a minimum. At most, a few Khomeinist priests, such as Montazeri and Rafsanjani, who were among those closest to the exiled Ayatollah, were arrested by SAVAK. Two other priests of the same persuasion (Mohammad Reza Sa'idi and Husayn Ghaffâri) were tortured and killed in the Shah's prison in 1970 and 1975, respectively.[24]

However, this pause observed by the Islamists was in no way a faithful reflection of Iranian society of the time. It was certainly not a peaceful and tranquil society, and the severe repression of opposition groups all these years did not prevent the spread of terrorist actions and social turmoil. According to one estimate, there were 124 strike actions in different urban centers and various sectors of the economy in the period from winter 1970 to winter 1977 alone.[25]

At the same time, numerous persons (American advisers, heads of firms, and generals) died at the hands of terrorists. Hence, what is astonishing is not the fact that the Shah's regime had provoked such resistance, but that Islamist groups were completely absent from all these events. Terrorism and agitation during these years were principally the work of the *Mojâhedin-e Khalq*[26] and the *Cherikhây-e Fadâ'i* (independent Marxists).

The Islamists did not re-awaken to resume their activities of former years until close to the Revolution. The fire at the Rex cinema in Abadan on August 18, 1978 was unquestionably the most murderous act (around 400 deaths by burning or asphyxiation) claimed to have been committed by certain Islamist elements.[27] Revolutionary terror, launched in February 1979 after the triumph of the Islamic Revolution, can certainly not be considered a Shi'a specialty. In fact, this form of terror, with all the abuses and tragic excesses it entails, is common to all great revolutions. On the other hand, what distinguishes post-revolution Shi'a violence from the violence of other revolutions is its permanent, systematic and institutionalized character, but also, in particular, the sacred significance attributed to this violence, which has become highly sublimated. That is undoubtedly why the Islamic Revolution has not so far, in this domain, had its Thermidor. Quite contrary, rather than seeking moderation and building a state, this Revolution cultivates violence and aggression. The unnecessary continuation of one of the bloodiest and most destructive wars against Iraq (1980-88), the systematic terrorist actions and kidnappings in Iran and in other countries, which occurred after the Revolution, represent the best evidence of the Islamic regime's violent character. The 'death decree' against Salman Rushdie is only one of many aspects of Islamist structural violence.

Conclusion

We have tried to demonstrate the evolutive character of Shi'a violence. This violence has, with impressive regularity, followed a trajectory from an agitational to an insurrectional phase, and from the latter to a revolutionary phase, finally culminating in institutionalized and expansionist violence (repression, war, and international terrorism). Shi'a violence may therefore be considered 'perfect' violence, although a 'perfection' tainted by a calm that

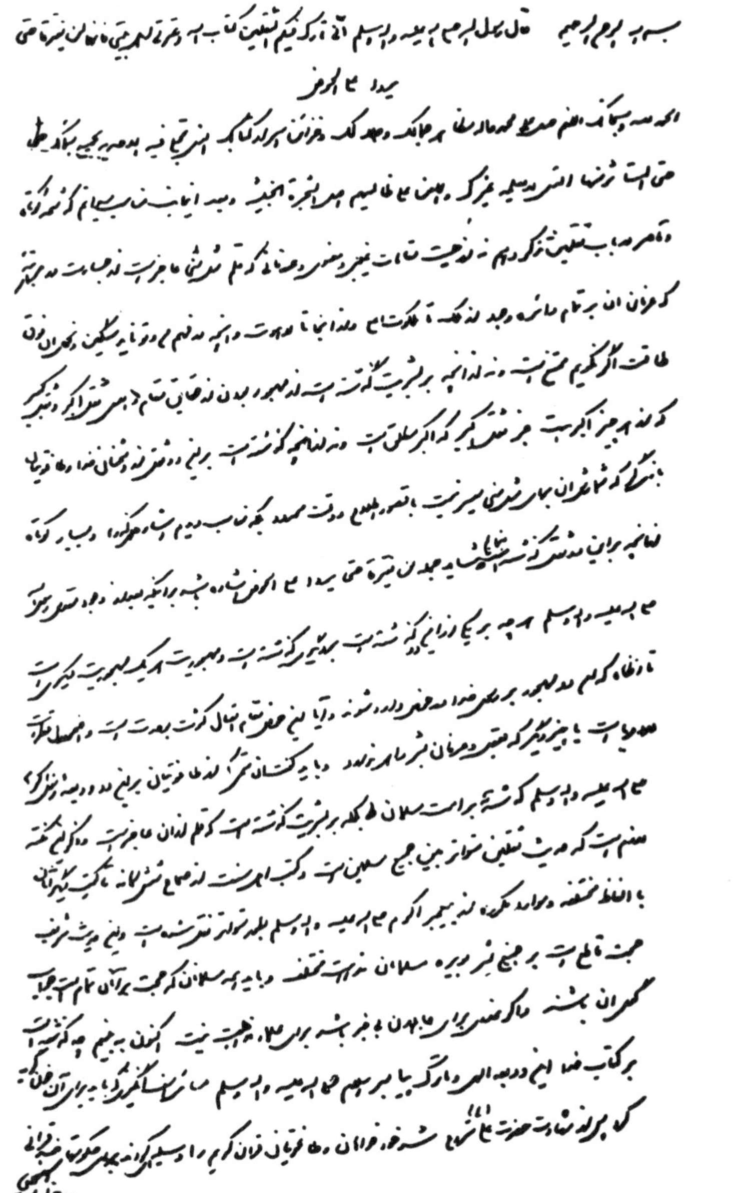
بسم الله الرحمن الرحیم قال رسول الله صلی الله علیه و آله و سلم انی تارک فیکم الثقلین کتاب الله و عترتی اهل بیتی فانهما لن یفترقا حتی
یردا علی الحوض

A page from Khomeini's political testament
Source: Sahifah-e Nur, p. 133

lasted about a dozen years (1965-77) and was due to the socio-economic changes Iranian society was undergoing at the time. An analysis of these changes, however, would go beyond our purposes.

The following conclusions may be drawn concerning the stage of agitation:

1) Shi'a Islamism was originally a reaction to the secularization and anti-clerical policies of Reza Shah. It is what Charles Tilly calls *reactive collective action*. (Tilly, 1975: 502). This was evident in both Islamist discourse and the discourse and activities of the *Fadâ'iyân-e Eslâm* (Table 1);

2) The Shi'a perpetrators of terrorist acts all came from similar social strata. Most were from the middle and poor strata in the Bazar, or from the middle ranks of the clergy. They were all young, around the age of twenty. No women were involved in the Shi'a terrorist activities before the Revolution (Table 2);

3) Shi'a terrorism is an exclusively urban phenomenon. None of the rural population strata has taken part, directly or indirectly;

4) Shi'a agitation has been supported morally, financially and politically by an element of the bazar and an element of the clergy. In contrast, the higher levels of the Shi'a hierarchy have generally been very careful to dissociate themselves from the ideas, and *a fortiori*, from the violent actions of the Shi'a Islamists;

5) Shi'a activism began in a climate of social and political troubles. The weakness of successive governments and their evident lack of will to combat Islamist terrorism has undeniably played a role in intensifying agitation.

Our remarks on the insurrectional stage may be summed up as follows:

a) During this stage, a qualitative change took place in the evolution of Shi'a violence. For the first time, Shi'a Islamists joined
   forces to provoke a wholesale revolt against the Shah's regime
   and to assume leadership over it;

b) This type of violence corresponds to Charles Tilly's *proactive
   collective action* which arises when 'some group carries out an
   action which, under the prevailing rules, lays claim to a
   resource not previously accorded to that group [Ulama and
   Bazar in the Iranian context]; at least one other group inter-
   venes in the action and resists the claim' (Tilly, 1975: 502). After
   the June 5, 1963 uprising, the extremist tendency was diffuse
   and marginalized. It became more and more cohesive, homogeneous and hegemonic;

c) The Islamist tendency was not only able to bring itself to bear
   within the clergy, it also imposed its discourse as an alternative,
   vis-à-vis the discourse of the regime as well as that of all the
   opposition groups together. It was the *Revolution*.

Finally, in the post-revolutionary period, which has been described
elsewhere in this book, it must be conceded that violence in its
most diverse and extreme forms (repression, international terrorism
and war) has become all but the essence of Shi'a Islamism. Only the
future will tell if Shi'a Islamism will be able to extricate itself from
its violence to finally have its own Thermidor or, on the contrary,
if it will remain a prisoner of its own aggressivity, and thus destroy
itself in the end.

Table 1. *Fadâ'iyân-e Eslâm. Terrorist Actions: Dates & Identities of Victims*

Date	Victim	Person/ Function	Political Tendency
April 28, 1945	Ahmad Kasravi (wounded)	Writer	Anti-clerical nationalist
March 11, 1946	Ahmad Kasravi (assassinated)	Writer	Anti-clerical nationalist
Nov. 4, 1949	Abdul Husayn Hajir (assassinated)	Minister of the Court	Accused of sympathizing with Bahai sect
March 7, 1951	Hassan Ali Razmârâ (assassinated)	Prime Minister	Autocrat (general)
Feb. 5, 1952	Husayn Fâtemi (wounded)	Foreign Affairs Minister under Mosaddeq	Nationalist
Nov. 16, 1955	Husayn Ala (wounded)	Prime Minister	Royalist

Table 2. *Fadâ'iyân-e Eslâm. Terrorist Actions: Dates & Identities of Perpetrators*

Date	Aggressor	Profession	Age[1]
April 28, 1945	Nawâb Safavi	Cleric	21
March 11, 1946	Husayn Imâmi[2]	Bazar merchant	21
Nov. 4, 1949	Husayn Imâmi	Bazar merchant	21½
March 7, 1951	Khalil Tahmâsbi	Carpenter	24
Feb. 5, 1952	Mehdi Abd-e Khodâi	No profession	15
Nov. 16, 1955	Mazaffar Ali zol Qadr	Worker	25 (?)

1. At the time of the assassination.
2. He was aided by another disciple of Nawâb Safavi.

Economic Origins Of Shi'a Violence

Qu'est-ce que le Tiers état? — Tout.
Qu'a-t-il été jusqu'à présent dans l'ordre politique? — Rien.
Que demande-t-il? — *A être quelque chose.* Emmanuel Sieyès

Economy belongs to donkey. Ayatollah Khomeini

Issues and Questions

Since the Islamic revolution in Iran, much has been said about the purely religious character of Shi'a violence. This one-sidedness has led to an over-estimation of the role of religion, in this case Shi'a, in the process of violence, and more generally in social evolution and change. Thus, Shi'a has been confused with violence while the decisive role of socio-economic factors in the genesis of violence (though it may be expressed in the idiom of Shiism) has been minimized, if not outright neglected.

The purpose here is to bring some clarity into the issue of the role and the influence of socio-economic factors in the process of Shi'a violence. Of course a thorough and exhaustive analysis of the totality of these factors would go beyond the narrow framework of this chapter. Nonetheless, it is my claim that a study of the Bazar as a specific socio-economic entity and in particular the peripheral position it has held is essential for elucidating the role that non-religious factors have played in setting into motion a very violent movement which refers exclusively to religion, both in its discourse and in the symbols it uses.

From the second half of the 19th century to the Islamic revolution in February 1979, the Bazar was constantly in conflict with the various political regimes in power. It has participated in all anti-state protest movements. The only time that the Bazar refrained from opposing the government was during the government of Mosaddeq (1951-53). But even under Mosaddeq, the Bazar retained its hostility to the Shah, though it may have been an ally of the moment for the government, so there is constancy in the Bazari's antagonistic attitude.

Since the end of the last century, people with origins in the Bazar have assassinated one king, Nasser el-din Shah (1848-96); have contributed largely to the abdication of another, Mohammad Ali Shah (1907-9); and were instrumental in putting an end to the reign of Mohammad Reza Shah (1941-79). *Bazaris* have assassinated two prime ministers (Razmârâ in 1951 and Mansour in 1965), and there have been a significant number of other acts of political violence and political assassinations in which Bazaris were involved. Going further, innumerable strike and protest movements in Iran in this century were either directly instigated by the Bazar or were a product of its activities. And then there are the 'Trois Glorieuses', i.e. the Constitutionalist revolution (*mashrouteh*) at the beginning of this century, the June 5, 1963 insurrection, and finally the Islamic Revolution in 1979. In all these three major events, the Bazar was more than just present — it had in fact given liberally of its political and financial support.

A number of important founders and members of certain extremist organizations such as the *Mojahidin-e Khalq* and the *Cherikhay-e Fadâ'i* stem directly from Bazari social groups or from groups very close to the Bazar.[28]

Since our purpose here is to study relations between the Bazar and Shi'a violence, we shall disregard those groups which are not typically Islamic Shiite.

An unprecedented event occurred after the Islamic Revolution. The Bazar, which heretofore had always been in a state of alert, always ready to initiate strikes and constantly in conflict with those in power, withdrew into itself and ceased to participate in protest movements and violent actions against the regime. Even more, in an abrupt change of attitude, it gave its support to the various forms of violence (terrorism, repression, external war) which the newly established Islamic state had undertaken.

Together, these considerations and circumstances constitute a problem which inspires us to inquire into the causes of conflicts opposing the Bazar's political power, as well as into the motives which impelled the Bazar to resort to violent methods in the present period. Of course, some might object by saying that the above-mentioned acts of violence were the work of Islamic Shiites as such, and that the perpetrators of violence acted as a function of their faith, totally independent of their social affiliation and their professional interests. We do not reject this postulate outright, but should like to pursue the issue further by asking the following questions: Why have the great majority of perpetrators of terrorist acts come from the Bazar? Why is it precisely the Bazar and not other social groups of political forces (with the exception of certain Ulama) which has continually played an instrumental role in the outbreak of movements of protest and insurrection? Why were the *Fadâ' iyân-e Eslâm* (Devotees of the Islam) terrorists freed from prison on bond paid by the Bazaris? Why does the Bazar so easily pass on to acts of protest and opposition, quite often before every other social grouping? The list of questions could continue. Hence, since the postulate of the religious origin of Shi'a violence offers us no clarity on these questions, we should like to consider another, namely that there is a link between two factors: the peripherization of the Bazar and the upsurge of Shi'a violence.

But first we should like to specify what we mean by Shi'a violence. Shi'a violence refers to a group of violent acts which are part of one and the same process, the proclaimed end of which is the restoration of the Medina model of the Umma (Mozaffari, 1987: 23-29). We shall also regard Shi'a violence as a totality, whatever the particular and specific forms in which it is manifested. Thus, protest, agitation, insurrection, revolution, terrorism, repression and foreign war will be regarded as diverse manifestations of the same phenomenon.

Methodology and Hypotheses

Political violence is an extremely varied and widespread phenomenon. It groups under the same heading a series of actions which despite their violent nature are very different in character. These actions vary from agitation, insurrection and repression, to a coup d'état revolution and terrorism.

The diversity and the extent of political violence pose a real theoretical problem. We do not yet have a theory that is capable of embracing the manifold forms in which political violence finds its physical expression. The reason for this lacuna is not hard to find. Often, the various forms have not only different causes but also different consequences. The fact is that no theory in this domain provides a theoretical framework broad enough and precise enough to give a correct explanation of a multitude of forms, causes and consequences transcending time and space. Thus, the existing theories on political violence are actually nothing more than theoretical islands, i.e. partial theories still in need of development. Some of them analyze only one form of violence, generally revolution, which is considered violence par excellence and is hence the preferred study object. Others take up only a particular aspect or only one of the causes of violence, for example psychology, modernization or the economy. The lack of a general theory has made it quite difficult for the scholar who finds himself constantly having to weigh the utility and operationality of this or that theory. He invariably finds that none of them satisfies his needs. Taken separately, they are not able to explicate the problem in all its dimensions and at all its levels. He is therefore compelled to choose among the different theories, if he is to avoid eclecticism, and will select that which seems to have the greatest explanatory power with regard to data.

There are other difficulties which derive from the fact that political violence is influenced by an indeterminate number of factors during the process of its materialization. The causes of violence are never static. They are always in movement, developing and changing, though their substance may remain the same. And since the causes of violence are the product of contradiction, it is essential to know these contradictions which may in turn undergo modifications of their own during the evolution of society.

The first problem is to determine what theoretical framework can best explain the relationship between the peripherization of the Bazar and the upsurge of Shi'a violence. We should state from the outset that we tend to prefer that kind of theory which seeks to discover the origins of political violence in socio-economic structures and relations. But to us the application of historical materialism in its unadulterated form seems far from satisfactory in this particular case. Historical materialism seeks the origins of political violence in conflicts and antagonisms among social classes. Moreover, common Marxism, at least in its original version, considers the state as a part of the social super-structure. But as we shall see further on, the social classes in Iranian society are in a state of diffusion and confusion. Social and political conflicts therefore are *vertical* conflicts instead of *horizontal* conflicts as Marxism tends to imply. This means that the state occupies a select position and pervades the entire political and social arena, to the detriment, moreover, of civil society. According to the basic premise of historical materialism, this can tell us something about the societal nature of conflicts. More explicitly, we use historical materialism as our *methodological* framework which means that we take the fact that social conflicts are engendered by specific societal structures and relations as an invariable. But the social conflicts take different forms in the *process* of their materialization. I believe that the theory of relative deprivation, after necessary modifications are made, can be an operational model in explaining the process of social conflicts in Iranian society, and more specifically, in explaining the process of the Bazaris' frustration and aggression.

The school of collective psychology which takes its inspiration from Dollard's behaviorist thesis (1939) postulates relations of causality between relative deprivation and aggression. Relative deprivation is defined as 'tension that develops from a discrepancy between the 'ought' and the 'is' of collective value satisfaction, and that disposes men to violence' (Gurr, 1977: 23). Between relative deprivation and violence there is *frustration* which as a psychological element, serves as a relay between the intensity of deprivation and the genesis of violence. The values to which Gurr refers are welfare values, power values and interpersonal values.

In this system, political violence has an evolutionary rhythm in three stages. The first is marked by the development of discontent, the second by the politicization of this discontent, and the third and last by the translation of this discontent into violent actions. Gurr's model has a number of weaknesses. First, relative deprivation should, according to Gurr, be perceived and felt, which is to say that deprivation is first and foremost a subjective phenomenon. But Gurr does not explain when and how the perception of deprivation engenders violence. Does this transition take place automatically? That seems quite disputable. In fact, there is no proof that deprivation itself engenders violence for the simple reason that deprivation can also just as well bring about submission, indifference or passivity. It is therefore essential to 'know what forms and intensities of frustration are linked to what forms and intensities of aggression' (Wilkinson, 1979: 57; also Tilly, 1975: 495). Furthermore, Gurr accepts as a given that deprivation is at the origin of violence. But it seems to me that deprivation is itself the reflection and the illustration of something else, i.e. it has its own cause and its own origin. This being the case, we may quote Manus I. Midlarsky:

Certain of these difficulties may be resolved, not by rejecting the frustration/aggression theory, but by modifying it to account for these and other possible criticisms. There exists sufficient empirical evidence confirming the theory, in certain instances, to suggest its retention and application to political science concerns in a somewhat different form. The following framework is proposed as such a modification. Political violence may occur when a unit (group, nation-region or nation-state) has the capability to reduce uncertainty in its environment, but is constrained from doing so, and the uncertainty persists or increases. The unit must be analyzed with regard to its capabilities, and the exercise of these capabilities within its own political context. Thus, for the study of political violence within the nation—state, the group itself must be chosen as the unit of analysis, not the entire nation. (Midlarsky, 1975: 37-38)

Therefore, applying Midlarsky's suggestions, we shall in the present study consider, 1) the Bazar as an analytic unit, 2) situate this unit in its proper political context, and 3) assess the potency of this unit (the Bazar) as an analytic unit.

We shall apply this procedure throughout our study, but we should also say that in our opinion, placing the Bazar in *its proper political context* entails extending that context to include the whole of society and, above all, the state. Only then will we be able to grasp the singularity of the Bazar in all its specificity in employing it as an analytic unit.

Our theoretical approach must also have an appropriate methodology. What shall it be? There are three general methods of analysis and explication. First the method we might call the *multifactorial* method, generally known as the theory of factors. This method is hardly satisfactory in so far as it produces essentially no new knowledge. All the factors play a role and all the factors are equal.

At the opposite extreme is the *unifactorial method*, in which one single factor is posited the cause of a phenomenon or any event. This method is also ill-suited because it is reductionist. Between these two methods there is the *selective multifactorial* method which establishes a hierarchical order between the numerous and diverse factors which were coincidentally together at the genesis of a phenomenon or event.

As Skocpol has explained, coincidence is different from chance (Skocpol 1979/1984). Coincidence (Lenin spoke of 'fusion' with regard to the October Revolution) is the historical moment where principal causes and secondary causes meet. We therefore incline to the selective theory of factors because we think it alone is able to distinguish the important if not determinant factors from those which are not so important.

Having defined our theoretical framework and our methodology, let us begin our study by examining the four following hypotheses to further illuminate the problem:

Hypothesis 1   The nature of authoritarianism in the Iranian state is the cause of violence.

Hypothesis 2   If in earlier periods before the Islamic Revolution the Bazar had been able to maintain a constant opposition to established regimes, and if it has now succeeded in carrying out a revolution in accordance with its own interests, this is because the Bazar is the most homogeneous group in the Iranian society.

Hypothesis 3   The peripherisation of the Bazar has been the principal cause of Shi'a violence.

Hypothesis 4   The integration of the Bazar into the political-economic system of the country has totally changed its violent behaviour with regard to the state.

Now let us examine these four hypotheses in detail.

Hypothesis 1

The nature of authoritarianism in the Iranian state is the cause of violence.

Violence is not the exclusive property of a specific type of society or political regime. It can take place in every kind of society in every type of regime. The only thing which distinguishes democratic pluralist regimes (polyarchies) in this respect from totalitarian and authoritarian regimes is that in polyarchies:

civil liberties, political freedoms, the rule of law, and universal suffrage are recognized and respected, organized opposition and dissent are tolerated, no official ideology limits and confines the boundaries of political discourse and competition decided by the electorate. (Ober-schall, 1973: 69)

The powers that be must therefore be attentive to these discontents and seek adequate remedies for them. Hence opposition movements with access to communication networks, putting them into contact with the establishment, operate in a legitimate and a legal space.

Even totalitarian systems possess channels for surfacing of limited dissent and conflict regulation which provide a safety valve against violent explosion. (Dahrendorf, 1959: 314)

But these channels are such that instead of allowing protest movements to circulate and acquire legitimate expression, they force them to turn back upon themselves and to build up. This is why political and social explosions are rare in this type of regime, but when they do occur, they are extremely violent and destructive. Another difference is that in democratic régimes opposition is a *role* and a state of *transition* (Dahl, 1975: 116). The succession of events is therefore temperate and moderated. In contrast, in totalitarian and authoritarian regimes, opposition is a state of *fact*; far from being a role (interchangeable) it is a *destiny*. Consequently, change takes place only through violent breaks and revolutionary upheavals.

Iranian society is a type of society in which the state has all political power and the source of economic power as well (land or oil, depending on the period). Thus, the power of the state does not derive from the solidity of its structures but is the direct consequence of the segmentation and diffuseness of societal structures. The state is then not 'the locus of strategic organization of the ruling class' (Poulantzas, 1978: 162) or even a mere locus or a centre for the exercise of power without possessing *power in itself* (ibid). The state is power itself, 'power par excellence'. Similarly, the state is not the representative or the instrument of a ruling class, but is *domination itself*. In any case, though Poulantzas' postulate may be applicable to Western societies, it has no credibility with regard to diffuse and segmented societies in which the social classes are practically non-existent or in the best of cases are in a state of gestation and formation. In these types of societies there are only social structures, i.e. the patterns of inequality, whatever they are. Since social classes are non-existant, the very weak relations between the state as such and 'Society' are organically antagonistic relations. Because it has no hold or foothold in the state, society is *against* the state, because the state is against society. These relations are also vertical relations: the state at the summit and the society at the base, and between them a vacuum or a domain where force alone reigns. In other words, the state is *hegemonic*. Hegemonic regimes are non-participatory regimes which:

impose most severe limits on the opportunities available to opponents of the government. Fully hegemonic regimes not only suppress all rival parties or convert into mere appendages of the dominant party, they suppress factions within the dominant party as well. (Dahl, 1975: 126)

Without going back too far into Iran's history, we will note that since the foundation of the Qajar dynasty (1779-1925)[29] up to the present time, this country has experienced three 'States' which are all variants of the traditional Weberian type. To avoid confusion and to avoid using comparisons which often do not fit well with reality, let me name these three 'States' in their chronological order: the *Tribal State*, the *Shah State* and the *Imam State*. All these three states were to different degrees authoritarian and hegemonic. The Tribal State was the product of power relations among the tribes, the most powerful of which became a state (the Khaldounian model), while nonetheless respecting the existence and autonomy of the other tribes which, however, were restricted to specific territories and localities. In other words, whereas military force and superiority were the basis of the Tribal State, the tribal consensus which progressively evolved became the basis of the legitimacy of the Tribal State. In this system, the king was the epicenter of equilibrium as well as the instance for maintaining balance in inter-tribal relations. The rest, i.e. everything outside the tribal system, was considered peripheral and treated as such. The hegemonic characteristics of the state were further reinforced under the Pahlavi regime (1921/25-1979) which we shall here call the Shah State. The Pahlavi State was a sociological orphan, in the sense that it came from nowhere. Unlike the Tribal State, it enjoyed no consensus. Furthermore, its legitimacy was strongly disputed throughout its reign. The Shah State, deprived of any support from the traditional and traditionalist structures and forces (the tribes and the Ulama, in particular), had no choice but to modernize society, i.e. modernize in order to better centralize, and centralize in order to better neutralize traditional structures. To sum up, the Shah State was — especially after the 1953 coup d'état — a totally hegemonic state in Dahl's definition of the term. In this model, the Shah abolished the multi-party regime as it was called in 1975 and decreed a single party regime. In this system, the Shah was the epicenter of disequilibrium and the source of political instability as Easton defines politics, i.e. the 'authoritative allocation of values' (Easton, 1959: 129). The third variant of the traditional type was in the form of what we can call the Imâm State. This state, undergoing its own revolutionary process, is still in a state of inception and awaiting its Thermidor, i.e. its ultimate realization under the aegis of the expected Imâm (Mahdi). This is more a process influx than a State, more a situation than state structures. At first glance it seems intuitively wrong to speak of an Imâm State, when in fact such a state has not yet been formed. But that does not mean that hegemony and authoritarianism are not quite firmly implicated in the actual process of inception of this state. In any case, this state or this process, though of a religious character, is like the Tribal State in the sense that it also benefits from a consensus, a limited and specific consensus, true, but a consensus nonetheless. The regime not only enjoys the support of diverse religious fractions (professional) but also the material support that they bring from the broad strata of the Bazar. In this system, as in the tribal system, the Imâm represents the epicentre of equilibrium and the seat of

arbitration for inter-factional disputes (within the Ulama themselves) but also for any conflicts that might oppose the Bazar's
access to power.

Now that we have outlined these three different types of states,
we may inquire into the relations between the authoritarian state
and violence. Our postulate will be that in an authoritarian regime
everyone resorts to violence. The state is in reality the first and the
most powerful instigator of violence. But the exercise of violence is
not simply one role which the state plays. Violence emanates from
the very structures of the state. Violence is therefore structural (for
example Hitler's Germany, Franco's Spain). In a *non-institutionalized*
authoritarian regime, generally that of Sultanism (Linz, 1975: 179)
the individual is for all practical purposes naked and utterly
unprotected with regard to the state, given the fragmentation of
society and the weakness of associational ties. That does not
prevent the individual from resorting to violence, but this violence
is in general a reaction to structural violence. Individual violence,
which by definition is isolated and sporadic, has no historical scope
and is quickly repressed.

To sum up, insofar as the State has the totality of its power in
its hands, it has the entire society against it. State power is therefore exercised through violence and not consent. In other words,
the state is simultaneously the producer and the illustration of
violence. Arendt described such a situation aptly: 'the extreme form
of power is all against one, the extreme form of violence is one
against all' (Arendt, 1969: 42).

Aside from individuals and the state, there are clearly other
ethnic, confessional, professional groups. These groups are in fact
the only bastions against the abuse of the state and its resultant
violence. The solidity of the group structures varies from one
society to another, and from one group to the other. But only the
most homogeneous social group will be capable of steadily resisting
the state and taking recourse to acts of systematic violence, finally
to bring down the regime in power.

This is what the Bazar did in being the most homogeneous

social group in Iranian society, a remark which brings us to our second hypothesis.

Hypothesis 2

If, in periods before the Islamic Revolution, the Bazar was able to maintain a constant opposition to established regimes, and if it succeeded in carrying out a revolution in accordance with its own interests, this was due first and foremost to the fact that the Bazar is the most homogeneous social group in Iranian society.

The Bazar is a vague and complex term which applies simultaneously to a working place with its souks, serails and boutiques, a specific socio-economic environment, as well as to an ethnic cultural and even professional system.

Traditionally, the Bazar embraces the largest part of the commercial sectors, trade networks, and financial networks. Like any other social system, the Bazar had its stratifications and distinctions, all as a function of the division of labour, material profits and the credibility of each of the groups and individual members of the system. As the Bazar evolved, the upper strata and some of the middle strata of the traditional commercial system separated from it to become part of a bourgeoisie which is difficult to define (import-export business, entrepreneurial, semi-industrial and comprador). Consequently, the term Bazari is today applied only to those socio-occupational strata as co-ops (*asnaf*), craftsmen (*pishehvaran*), small shopkeepers (*kasabah*), wholesalers (*bunakdaran*), exchange agents (*sarrafan*), brokers (*dallalan*), and retail merchants (*furushandehgan*). In addition, their ranks include a certain number of large businessmen (*tujjâr*) who remained a part of the traditional Bazari system (Greenfield, 1906, in Floor, 1976: 126). The Bazar, such as it has just been described, is therefore an essentially urban and petit-bourgeois phenomenon.

The composition of the Bazari strata points out the commercial character of the Bazar. Trade is in fact the essential element linking all these strata to one another. Trade is not simply the material basis of the Bazar, it is also the principal network of communication among the Bazari strata on the one hand, and between the Bazari and the rest of the Iranian society.

Traditionally, commerce in the Bazar has been governed by custom as well as by Shi'a law.[30] In his efforts to laicize the Bazar, Reza Shah established a modern code of commerce as well as a series of laws regulating lending, credit and taxes. These measures, as well as those taken later by Mohammad Reza Shah, were acts applied only partially to the Bazari system. The Bazar endeavoured to elude the state legal system as best it could. It observed legal rules only when it was constrained to do so.

The Bazar also obeys an ethic which has its roots in tradition. The Bazar is traditionalist. A portion of this ethic is written and codified, the rest comes from customary ethical practices. The ethical practice of the Bazaris has social consequences of major import. Ethical practice, elaborated conjointly by the Bazaris and the Ulama, acts in a way to make the Bazar increasingly homogenous, at the same time as it separates itself from the rest of society.[31] Moreover, since the rest of society is unable to produce general ethical norms, and since there are no other social categories which could codify in practice any ethic instead of the Bazar, the ethical norms and rules of the Bazar acquire the status of norms and ethics of the society as a whole. Thus the ethics of the Bazar are a frame of reference not only for the Bazaris themselves, which is obvious; but also, and especially, are a refuge and anchoring point for 'national' identity in periods of social crisis. For this reason, eyes turn towards the Bazar when there is a crisis, every time something basic to society — the collective self — is being sought, and every time society seeks a mirror to reflect its image. In this sense, the Bazar is a kind of 'memory' for the people, the Metro, as André Malraux described it in another context.

The geographic placement of the Bazar likewise reinforces its specificity and autonomy. It occupies the traditional and vital centre of the capital and of the large cities. The Grand Mosque is usually at the centre of the Bazar: At Tehran and Isfahan, the Mosque of the Shah (renamed 'Khomeini's Mosque' after the revolution); at Shiraz the Vakil Mosque; at Mashhad the Gohar Shad Mosque, etc. The relations between the mosque and the Bazar are close, constant and organic. Each has its own function complementing one another in overall harmony. Never in competition, they cooperate and coordinate their common actions. The Bazar is moreover in direct geographical proximity to the Shah's palace and the ministries and administrative offices. In the provinces, the local governors' offices are near the Bazar.

In addition to the geographic element, the Bazar enjoys an autonomy of communication. It has its own signs and symbols which make up a code, the deciphering and comprehension of which remains inaccessible to the uninitiated. All this makes the Bazar an autonomous and exclusive sphere of communication. As a consequence, the *métier* of a Bazari requires not only professional qualifications, but also and especially knowledge of the code of the Bazar, i.e., a set of rituals, ethical rules of behaviour (individual, family and social) and customs. This is why the *métier* of Bazari is essentially a family *métier*, which is passed on from father to son, brother to brother, father-in-law to family, etc.

This is in reality only the description of what is conventionally called the 'core of the Bazar'. In fact, the social and cultural ramifications of the Bazar embrace a large number of social strata which have occupations and professions different from those of the Bazaris. But this does not prevent them from sharing the Bazar ethic, the same morality, and the same political behaviour. Thus in its full extent, the Bazar encompasses middle level administrative cadres, bank employees, a large number of teachers, some lawyers, engineers and students. But this list is not exhaustive, and the boundaries of the periphery of the Bazar are not limited to these groups. It is in fact extremely difficult to draw a clear line of distinction that separates the Bazar and its periphery from the rest of society — above all because of the profound impact of the Bazar culture on the general culture in society. But even so, the Bazar is not one with the rest of Iranian society. The Bazar and its periphery in fact embrace a range of social strata of diverse and varied professions whose social position is roughly equivalent to that of the middle and petty bourgeoisie in the rest of society.

As regards relations between the Bazar and religion, aside from the quite obvious fact that Islam is the religion of the Bazar par excellence, it must be stressed that the Islam of the Bazar is far from being a diffuse Islam, *à la carte* so to speak, which each is free to practice as he chooses. This Islam is a represented, interpreted and visualized Islam. It is represented and interpreted by the Ulama just as it is visualized by a number of rights and moral physical behaviours. A good Bazari, for example, is a person whose physical appearance (beard, closed shirt, and beads in his hand) represents a good, typical Muslim.

The relations between the Bazaris and the Ulama are, however, not hierarchical and vertical. They are based on an interdependence and reciprocity between the two complementary groups. Through his financial contributions (*khums, zakât, sadaqât*) the Bazari is largely the guarantee of the financial independence of the Ulama vis-à-vis the state. In return, the Ulama often interpret Islam to conform to the interests of the Bazaris. This is for example how private property became sacrosanct; the state administration is considered unjust and the agents of the state are considered agents of oppression (*zalama*). Such an interpretation sits well with Bazari businessmen and encourages them not to pay the state taxes or fees.[32]

In addition to their ties based on reciprocal interests, the Bazar and the Ulama are linked together by a number of matrimonial, moral and even culinary links. Bazari and Ulama often intermarry. In other words, the frequency of mixed marriages (Bazari-Ulama) is quite high in terms of marriages outside the group of origin. More concretely, a Bazari would be more disposed to give his daughter in marriage to a member of the clergy than to an administrative worker, a school teacher or a worker, and even less to an army officer. And vice versa. The existence of matrimonial bonds between the Bazar and the Ulama further reinforces the bonds of solidarity between them. We shall come back to this point when we examine the other hypothesis.

The points just explicated under *hypothesis 2* confirm, I would think, the homogeneous character of the Bazar as a social group. As regards the core of the Bazar, this homogeneity appears total. It may be a bit vague and ambivalent in respect of the diverse strata which constitute in one way or other the 'satellites' of the peripheries of the Bazar. The homogeneity of the Bazar might be considered a routine and ordinary fact if there were also other organized homogeneous groups as in Western type societies. This was not the case in Iranian society, not so much because this society is totally devoid of groups, but because the groups that do exist are diffuse (the peasantry) or depend directly on the Prince (the army or the bureaucracy), or because they have no generic social and political message (ethnic and linguistic). But nonetheless, one must not disregard or minimize the importance of the Ulama who also in their totality represent a homogeneous group. But as we have explained, this group depends both financially and socially on the Bazar. Such was the general situation before the Islamic revolution. The Bazar in turn always depends on the Ulama for its political, cultural and ethical needs. These elements are indisputably an integral part of the indispensable ingredients of the Bazar's cohesion.

To better measure the extent of social homogeneity of the Bazar, it must be compared with a number of other socio-professional groups in Iranian society. We have distinguished four different groups among them as representative: the peasantry, the working class, the bureaucracy and the army.

In Iran, the peasantry is still far from being able to represent a homogeneous and powerful social force, if only for ecological reasons, i.e. the considerable distances which separate rural localities, and the lack or inadequacy of the communication networks (Momayezi, 1986: 75-76).[33] Or only as an economy based almost exclusively on agriculture until the end of the 19th century.

In effect, agriculture absorbed between 80 and 85 percent of the total workforce in the 1860s, decreasing only to 70 percent of the total workforce in the first decade of 1900 (Gilbar, 1978: 312). From the second half of the 19th century onward, agricultural economy and the economy in general began to turn increasingly towards trade. The commercialization of the economy took place principally under the influence of two factors, one exogenous and the other endogenous. The exogenous factor was the increasing penetration of foreign powers into the different sectors of Iran's economy. The endogenous factor is best illustrated by the discovery of new sources of wealth and profit for the great merchants (*tujjâr omdeh*). It was under the combined effect of these two factors that the production of non-food farm products (opium, cotton) underwent a spectacular growth as did the production of food, most of which was earmarked for export. Similarly, certain industrial branches, mainly the manufacture of carpets, underwent an unprecedented upswing. The important question was, who profited from this new economic orientation. All available evidence says that the principal beneficiary was a 'small group of Iranian nationals, most of whom were Muslims and big merchants by profession' (Gilbar, 1986: 82; Afshari, 1983: 137). At the political level, the situation meant a growing influence for some of the big merchants, but also and equally, the increased marginalization of the Bazaris. Referring to Persian and European sources, Floor arrives at the conclusion that:

apart from the necessary relationship between the authorities and the merchants, a kind a symbiosis dictated by the need for foreign luxuries, investments, money and financial security, there was within the merchant class an urge towards upward mobility. This aspiration expressed itself amongst other things in a search for government posts and titles.[34] (Floor, 1976: 112)

At the same time they had succeeded in establishing an alliance with high-ranking Ulama. The Constitutionalist revolution, which culminated in 1906 with the establishment of a constitutional monarchy, was to a large extent the direct consequence of this rapprochement. The Bazaris were represented essentially by the corporations (*asnaf*) and the shopkeepers (*kasabah*) and were on the side of the revolutionaries on that account. After the installation of the parliamentary regime, the Bazaris were represented in a respectable number (26 out of 133 seats) in the first legislature (inaugurated on October 7, 1906), but they were eliminated in the next legislature, to enter the Majless (Parliament) again in the third legislature — this time winning only three seats. The absence, or the very weak representation, of the Bazaris in the parliament would remain a political constant up to the Islamic Revolution (Shaji'i, 1966: 176). Control of the 'new regime' very quickly eluded the hands of even the big merchants and the Ulama. Neither of them, either alone or together, had sufficient economic and political power to assume state power and to establish their own regime (Ashraf & Hekmat, 1981: 746; Afshari, 1983: 151).

After the accession of Reza Shah to the throne in 1925, a new era began in the history of the country, an era marked essentially by the establishment of a strong and modernizing regime. Economically, the new sovereign endeavoured to equip the country with economic infrastructures through a policy of import substitution. All aspects of this policy were placed under the direction of the state. The beneficiaries of the policy were once again first and foremost the big merchants who regarded Reza Shah as the person capable of unifying the country, constructing highway networks and communication systems,[35] making the highways safe, as was ardently desired, and finally reducing the power of the tribal chiefs as well as that of the great land-owners. This set of measures, however, could only satisfy the *tujjâr*. In contrast, the Bazaris felt extremely disadvantaged by these measures, for it was they, like the common people anywhere, who had to pay the high price of industrialization (Floor, 1984: 2). In addition, in the pursuit of his policy of statization, Reza Shah sought to extend state control over all social, professional and other types of activities. He felt that such control was necessary to establish order and harmony in the various sectors of society. It was out of this concern for establishing harmony that the first law on the Bazar was published only one year after Reza Shah's coronation. The law of December 11, 1926 would soon be interpreted by the Bazaris as an anti-Bazar law, since it prohibited the heads of corporations (216 in number) from determining the size of the taxes which the corporations had to pay to the state's Treasury. Measures of this type, conjoined above all with those considered to be secularizing (for example the establishment of obligatory military service; Faghfoory, 1987: 425) led the Bazaris and with them certain religious and urban groupings to revolt against Reza Shah. Thus in the years 1926-27, waves of protest and demonstrations (closing of the Bazar, gatherings in the Mosque) extended to a number of cities: Tehran, Qum, Shiraz, Ispahan. Once again in 1935-6, the Bazar joined with the traditionalist forces to organize demonstrations, some of which were rather bloody (Abrahamian, 1982: 152). It is perhaps not uninteresting to say that the big merchants refrained from participating in these movements and, even more, 'when the petty Bazaris demonstrated against the Shah fearing his secularism, the merchants demonstrated in favour of him' (Floor, 1976: 135).

The abdication of Reza Shah in 1941 took place against new political horizons. Lips long sealed, pens in shackles, and forbidden political associations rapidly resurfaced as soon as the founder of the Pahlavi dynasty had left. The Bazaris also lost no time in making their presence known and forcing their demands through. The terrorist actions in which the *Fadâ' iyân-e Eslâm* were engaged, were not only supported by the Bazaris, they even participated actively (Mozaffari, 1988). Even so, the Bazaris had a difficult time defining themselves politically at this time. Indeed after the departure of Reza Shah, four political blocs were formed, one consisting of the big land-owners who at the same time controlled certain sectors of trade (e.g. the Maleks, the Mahdavi and the Qawam), the high aristocracy of the sword (for example, Amir Ahmadi, Yazdanpanah, Arfa'), and the religious aristocracy (Emami, Behbehani, Khorasani); which also included top-level officials in the administration. The second bloc was formed by the Marxists and Socialists. The third was the bloc of Nationalists and Liberals (*azadikhahan*) of every stamp, gathered around Mosaddeq. Finally, the fourth and last bloc comprised the Bazaris as well as middle-level white-collar workers and outsiders (Ayatollah Kashani).[36] There were major frictions within the last three blocs in the wake of the movement for nationalization of the oil industry. Whereas the first bloc conserved its unity, i.e., its implacable hostility to the movement, some elements in the three other blocks were driven into adopting inconsistent attitudes. The Toudeh adopted a critical and later hostile attitude towards Mosaddeq. The Socialists around Khalil Maleki (former member of the Toudeh) rallied around the latter. Ayatollah Kashani and his adherents also initially supported Mosaddeq, but later attacked him ferociously in the last year of his government. Other nationalists such as Dr Baqai and Makki follow-ed Kashani's example. On the whole the Bazar remained loyal to Mosaddeq, but frictions erupted within the Bazar after the break between Mosaddeq and Kashani. There were two reasons for the Bazar's satisfaction (at least before this break) and the support it showed for the Mosaddeq government. The first was the protec-tionist measures Mosaddeq had applied on imports, and the second was that for the Bazaris, and in general for the bourgeoisie, the nationalization of the oil industry fitted naturally among the his-torical battles of the end of the 19th century (the tobacco revolt, the anti-concessionist movement, the Constitutionalist movement, etc).

The coup d'état in August 1953, which brought about Mosad-deq's fall, put a sudden end to this exceptional period. Once again, the Bazar became the object of discrimination and repression, even more than in the past. Indeed, after having regained power, the Shah and his new prime minister, General Zahedi, sought to neutralize every oppositional movement by any means. For reasons we have just mentioned, the Bazar sided with the anti-imperial and anti-imperialist forces throughout the movement for nationalization of the petrol industry. It was thus among the first targets, and among all the Bazars, the Tehran Bazar was the first to suffer the devastation which the tandem Shah-Zahedi inflicted upon the Souk rebels, because of its strategic position and because of the eminent role it played in the protest and opposition movements. General Zahedi quite simply planned to destroy the Tehran Bazar to break its geographical structures, and only lively protests from every quarter prevented the realization of this project. While the buildings in the Tehran Bazar were saved in time, those of the Mashhad Bazar (the first holy city of Iran) were not as fortunate. They were destroyed in 1976-77. Although justified for architectural reasons and the needs of urban planning, the Bazari would hear nothing of such a destruction. For them the matter had a clear and deliberate political character. Serious clashes took place between the forces of order and the merchants during the razing of the Bazar. Several notables of the Mashhad Bazar were arrested and imprisoned. In view of the scope of the movement, it would be no exaggeration to say that the Mashhad events were in a sense precursory signs of a generalized malaise that would end in 1978 with the unleashing of the revolutionary process, now familiar to all.

Retrospectively it can therefore be said that a permanent tension existed in relations between the Bazar and the Shah throughout the entire period following the 1953 coup d'état. This tension was not limited to a specific battle for the simple reason that it was a generalized tension that extended simultaneously over several levels, some simple, others more complicated. For example, when the Bazar obstinately refused to spontaneously celebrate the Shah's anniversary, the Shah in turn did not hesitate to express publicly his animosity for the Bazaris, even going so far as to call them 'a bunch of bearded idiots' (*Yek mosht bâzari-e ahmaq-e rishou*).[37]

This illustrates that despite the sociological isolation to which we have alluded earlier on, the Shah never once dreamed of gaining the sympathy of the Bazari strata. Instead, to break out of his isolation and give his regime a solid social base, the Shah since the early 60s had endeavoured to get to the peasants through the agrarian reform. The agrarian reform did not produce the intended results, and *a fortiori* did not lead to the emergence of an agrarian class. On the contrary, this reform provided the Bazaris with an opportunity to provoke the celebrated insurrection of June 5, 1963. To be sure, this insurrection — which was rife with implications — was not the exclusive product of the Bazar. Islamists, and first and foremost Shiites, henceforth under the aegis of Ayatollah Khomeini, contributed to it. But a study of the declarations and documents published before and after the Islamic Revolution, as well as the sequence of events, show without the least doubt that this insurrection could not have taken place without the support and direct participation of the Bazar.

The failure of the agrarian reform was followed by the industrialization project. Through industrialization, the Shah hoped to achieve two objectives: political and economic. At the political level, the aim was to give rise to an industrial social class of bourgeois character, the bourgeoisie then providing essential support to the regime. The economic objective was the creation of a base industrial sector by a strategy of import substitution (Lonney, 1986: 108-18). The adoption of this strategy coincided with a quadrupling of oil revenues, and that in a period where the Shah's regime was benefiting from a political stability without precedent. Therefore, industrialization got off the ground at an exceptionally favourable time, and the industrial sector enjoyed a serious upswing. For example, the Iranian manufacturing sector chalked up a growth in the period 1963-72 that was twice the average of the other developing countries (Pesaran, 1985: 24). With the precious oil revenue in its hands, the state, through a selective policy, encouraged growth in the private industrial sector . Thus between 1973 and 1975 alone, credits granted to the private sector grew by 289 percent, half of which went to trade and imports. In the same period, the credits which were granted to industrialists were increased by 45 percent per year. Similarly, the volume of credits granted by the Industrial Credit Bank to the private sector increased from 20 million Rials in 1961 to 20,000 million Rials in 1975[38] (Iran Almanac, 1975: 287). Moreover, the control of exchange was eliminated in 1974 with a view to expanding and improving the financial possibilities of the private sector, and importers were henceforth exempted from depositing security with the Central Bank. The number of private commercial banks grew in the period indicated (1971-75) under the effects of the extraordinary stimulus given to the private sector, increasing from 24 to 36, while the volume of transactions increased sixfold. To give a better indication, as well as a better idea of the scope of the private sector's expansion, it need only be pointed out that in Tehran alone, the number of private companies increased from 1700 in 1973 to 2700 in 1975 (Bashiriyeh, 1984: 87-88).

This brings us to the simple, classical question: Who benefitted from this expansion, which was more financial than industrial? The big beneficiaries of oil prosperity came from quite different social and cultural backgrounds. They were first and foremost the members of the imperial family, whose thirst for capital and the acquisition of material goods was insatiable. Their political influence was unbounded and no bank or important financial establishment, no insurance company or construction enterprise escaped their grasp. The other component of the new 'class' was that which Bashiriyeh and others call the 'high bourgeoisie' and which we have called the 'oil bourgeoisie' (Mozaffari, 1981: 31-33; 1984: 55-58). Aside from the terminology, the fact is that the bourgeoisie in question embraced some 150 families most of which derived from the old land aristocracy or the big merchant families, which included a few *'parvenus'*.[39] This bourgeoisie owned 67 percent of the financial establishments and industrial enterprises and was represented in more than 1,000 administrative boards. Similarly, 370 of the 473 most important industrial enterprises belonged to ten families (Bashiriyeh, 1984: 40, and *Tehran Economist*, 28 farvardin 1355 / April 1977). Thus, while the oil bourgeoisie was enjoying an extraordinary affluence offered by the imperial régime, the Bazaris were suffering from the effects of Draconian measures (arbitrary and artificial price fixing, supplementary taxation, legal prosecution) which that same regime had imposed on them. Bashiriyeh describes a situation in which the Bazaris found themselves in the three or four last years of the Pahlavi regime:

From 1975 the petty bourgeoisie of the bazar had been hit by the anti-profiteering campaign and price control. The bazaris particularly disliked the Chamber of Guilds, which was the watchdog of the single party in the bazar. The Chamber had full supervisory powers over all bazar guilds and imposed the guild's regulations and fixed prices. Although in 1977 the anti-profiteering campaign was officially abandoned, the Chamber of Guilds continued to fix the prices in the bazars. In the month of April 1977 alone, the government received 600 million rials in fines for profiteering, mostly from shopkeepers of the bazar. In the same year, 20,000 shopkeepers and traders were imprisoned and fined. Files on bazar businessmen pertaining to taxes, fines and anti-profiteering had been compiled in the municipalities and had become a major preoccupation for the courts. In 1978 new regulations were drawn up for taxing the bazar guild. The 1977 tax rates were announced to be the base (retroactively) for the five preceding years. The same rates were to become the basis for taxation in the following five years. Retroactive and high taxation led to protests by the bazar guilds against 'arbitrary' regulations. (Bashiriyeh, 1984: 103).

This brings us to 1978, the year of a series of uprisings, including Black Friday, and the one in which the fortunes of the Pahlavi dynasty began to waver seriously. The revolution was already underway, and the 'Messiah' had just established himself at Neauphle-le Château, a neighbourhood of Paris.

Before ending our discussion of *Hypothesis 3*, we should specify that the economic and political peripherization of the Bazar was, especially under the Pahlavi regime, accentuated by articulations of a cultural order which the Shah's modernizing policies had brought about. In the examination of *Hypothesis 2*, we pointed out the diverse aspects of Bazar culture, indicating that this culture was in fact the culture of the people. This being so, the Shah's undertakings, with the disrupting of facts, were nonetheless unable to eradicate this popular traditional culture. While the Pahlavi policies had in fact caused some disruption, the Bazar culture had not been subdued or peripherized. On the contrary, the effect had instead reduced the Pahlavi culture, which had become dominated and peripherized by traditionalism. In this respect the Islamic revolution may be considered the historical juncture where this mini-culture was eclipsed by the fury of the traditionalist tornado.

Hypothesis 4

The integration of the Bazar into the political and economic system of the country totally changed its violent behaviour vis-à-vis the state.

The system which was established after the Islamic Revolution in Iran was essentially a *triangular system*, with three different but complementary spaces. The political space is occupied by the Ulama under the aegis of Ayatollah Khomeini. The military space is controlled by the Pasdaran (Revolutionary Guards), and finally the economic space is dominated by the people of the Bazar. The spaces are not closed domains. Interaction among them is frequent and their relations are dynamic, i.e. they are both cooperative and conflicting. Thus each space is able to influence the other two and undergo their influence in return. But the essence of power remains ecclesiastical, and Khomeini plays the indispensable role of arbitrator and regulator of this system as a whole.

Practically speaking, the integration of the Bazar into the revolutionary system began during the process of the Islamic Revolution. At the political level, the Bazar's support of Khomeini's project has been wholehearted and unreserved. However, its most conspicuous and perhaps most vital contribution has been financial. Without it, Khomeini would have had difficulty covering the (financial) costs of the revolution and organizing his innumerable support committees which spread like mushrooms during 1978. Of course the Bazar was not the only source of funds. Millions of Iranians outside the traditional circle of the Bazar, caught up in the revolutionary fervour, gave their financial support to the revolution as well. Nonetheless, the Bazar has remained the principal source as well as the principal administrator of funds.[40]

After the triumph of the revolution and the establishment of the Islamic Republic, the Bazar hastened to become part of the new regime. Its integration took place at every level: economic, political, military and cultural. But integration of the Bazar within the Islamic regime does not mean that the state is under the exclusive control of the Bazar. Naturally, the logic of the state goes beyond the specific logic of the Bazar, just as it overrides the logic of other influential groups. In other words, the Islamic state is not the political instrument of the Bazar but represents the space where Bazar interests meet and collaborate with the interests of other groups. This means that the integration of the Bazar into the new regime over which it exercises some influence, was not accomplished without conflict. The Bazar was compelled to struggle to put through its own interests and obtain new advantages. The struggle of the Bazar is not in itself a novelty. We have seen that the Bazar has regularly struggled against a succession of regimes before the Islamic Revolution. Nonetheless, there is a difference of scale between this struggle before and after the revolution. During the preceding period, the Bazar struggle was *outside* the state system, but since the revolution it has taken place *within*. The logic of this interactive struggle requires that the Bazar's conduct and its excessive appetite for accumulating wealth is criticized from time to time by certain high officials of the regime as well as some parliamentary deputies. But experience clearly demonstrates that the regime is unable to take measures that affect the vital interests of the Bazaris. And this is essential — in the final analysis, the rest is only part of the ordinary interplay and ups and downs of political life. We therefore agree with Wolfgang Lautenschlager (a pseudonym) when he says:

What should not be surprising, but what has been overlooked or under-emphasized by most analysts, is the extent to which the Islamic Republic has tailored its economic policies to meet the interest of the bazar merchants. The merchants, a key social group for the Islamic revolution as for many social movements in Iran in the last century, have reason to be pleased with the Islamic Republic's economic policy. ... While merchants have reason to be troubled by developments such as the anti-price-gouging campaign and the nationalization of foreign trade, on the whole the bazar had done well under the Islamic Republic. (Lautenschlager, 1986: 50)

But Lautenschlager also argues that the spectacular advance of the Bazar took place to the detriment of the industrial and manufacturing sector. This thesis has been vigorously criticized by Sohrab Behdad (1988) who says that:

It is, no doubt, too simplistic to consider the economic policies of the [Islamic Republic] merchant pleasing, even though the Islamic movement in Iran has been nurtured and financed by bazar merchants. The imperatives of ruling a capitalist state necessitate formation of class alliances between the [Islamic Republic] and the industrialists, in spite of the original merchant mentality of the regime's leaders.

Though this is so, Behdad does not deny the huge benefits to the Bazar derived from the post-revolutionary situation. On the contrary, not only have the Bazaris been able to accelerate and reinforce their hold on traditional sectors, they are now in the process of expanding into the industrial sectors. Precisely because 'the Islamic Republic has provided them with the opportunity they longed for, and they certainly are taking advantage of it. Some have already made advances in extending their activity into the industrial sector' (Behdad, 1988: 15). Consequently, the economic predominance of the Bazar under the Islamic Republic is an undisputed and established fact. What we must do now is analyze the mechanisms of the assimilation of the Bazar into the regime and the way it has made use of its position to achieve its own ends. The following will help us explore this question:

First, the original objective of the Bazar, which is first and foremost an economic entity of a commercial nature, was to obtain control over the principal networks of trade and distribution. Under the Shah, as we have seen earlier, the most fertile of these networks (non-petroleum) was in the hands of groups outside the traditional circle of the Bazar. The fall of the Shah, accompanied by the flight of the big export-import lords left a vacuum. This vacuum was filled by either the state or the private sector or a combination of the two. As regards the state monopoly over foreign trade (excluding oil and arms, which were already held by the state), there were in fact some efforts at 'nationalization' which in the Iranian political vocabulary actually signify 'statization'. These efforts met with forceful resistance from Bazari quarters as well as from their protectors within the Shi'a ecclesiastical hierarchy. As a result, the project of placing foreign trade under the state has remained a project without prospects. But leaving the totality of the trade and distribution networks in the hands of the private sector was not considered a viable solution either because of the reservations, vividly expressed, of the upholders of the 'statist' tendency — a tendency which is present both within the government and the parliament as well as among certain eminent members of the clergy. A third alternative remains, i.e. an intermediary solution which for all practical purposes has been adopted, and is operating now in the Islamic Republic. The upshot is that in reality the system which existed at the time of the Shah has been reinstalled. The structures have remained intact. Change has taken place at the *actor* and not the *structure* level. With the state continuing to exist, the Bazaris after the revolution moved into the places occupied by the non-Bazaris (e.g. industrial and petro-bourgeoisie, Shah family) during the time of the Shah.

Effective control of commercial networks requires an adequate financial system, and in fact the Bazaris wasted no time establishing such a system. About three months after the revolution, the first Islamic bank was founded. A perusal of the list of founders of this bank is interesting. Some 52 of the 60 founding members are from the Bazar (*bazargan*); eight represent the following professions: two white collar workers, one lawyer, one factory owner, one broker and two ayatollahs. These two ayatollahs, whose names are at the head of the list, are the celebrated and influential Ayatollah Beheshti (killed in 1981) and Ayatollah Ardabili, Beheshti's successor as head of the judiciary power.

To give some idea of the importance and influence of the Bazar and its allies within the new regime, it is sufficient to mention that the Islamic bank was the only bank which, by order of Khomeini himself, was exempted from the decree on nationalization of the banks proposed by the provisional government of Mehdi Bazargan and adopted by the revolutionary council.[41]

To camouflage its identity as a bank, the Islamic bank changed its name to the Islamic Economic Organization (*Sazman-e Egtesadi-e Eslami*). Two years after the foundation of this institution, a deputy, calling attention in parliament to the exorbitant profits of the private sector, quoted as an example those at the Islamic Economic Organization who, for example, imported industrial fibers at the price of 65 rials per kilo and sold them at 1,800 rials per kilo.[42] The revolution thus gave an unprecedented boost to the activities of the private sector.

According to the Minister of Trade, 90 percent of commercial activities in 1983 were controlled by the private sector.[43] Furthermore, according to official Iranian statistics, the share of the private sector in imports was 65 percent, 69 percent and 58 percent, respectively, in the first three post-revolutionary years. In the last three years of the Shah's reign, these figures were 49 percent, 46 percent and 55 percent, respectively.[44] There was a similar substantial increase in the volume of current accounts of the private sector in the banks. In 1983, this figure was 3.5 times larger than in 1979, the year of the Revolution.[45]

While it may be true that the state imports a portion of merchandise and foodstuffs, the circulation and distribution of imported goods is in practical terms one of the most abundant sources of profit for the private sector. In other words, the state is in charge of import, but the Bazar and especially the groups of Bazaris closest to the circles of power receive the profits. The mechanism of this transfer is simple. Stocks imported by the state are re-purchased by the different 'Islamic' corporations who then re-sell this merchandise to consumers (at a higher price) either directly or through retailers. Also, some of the merchandise is stocked by corporations for purposes of speculation. The result is higher prices and accentuation of inflationary tendencies.

Second, in addition to the import-export business and the networks of commodity distribution, the Bazar also became the great beneficiary of bank credits during the post-revolutionary period (and moreover at a preferential rate) and above all, of state allocations the official purpose of which was to encourage the export of non-petroleum or non-oil products. One law requires the government to 'provide the necessary means to encourage and guide the non-state sector (the corporations and the private sector)...'[46] This law was put into effect immediately, giving rise to huge allocations of credit by the state to the private sector.

Some idea of their scale can be gained from comments by Rafsanjani, former Speaker of Parliament, who in enumerating the positive economic effects of the Revolution was pleased to declare that the size of credits allocated to the private sector during the financial year 1983-1984 was ten times greater than the largest amount that the Shah regime had allocated to the same sector during its time.[47] This pace has continued and privileged circles in the Bazar continue to profit from the exceptional abundance of the financial facilities offered by the state and banks.

Third, some of the Bazar's speculative and lucrative activities take place in the parallel markets, which are quite flourishing. We say *parallel markets* rather than *black markets*, because they are authorized, at least de facto. The parallel markets are essentially a privileged space for exchange of goods which are practically not found on the free market. Veritable operations of purchase and sale of foreign goods also take place on the parallel markets. The goods for exchange are generally those which the Bazaris have already purchased from the state but then stocked instead of placing them on the regular market.[48] The parallel markets are exclusively speculative markets in which the purchase and sale of goods are of a more fictional nature with the sole aim of jacking up prices further to be able to reap the maximum profits. Thus, within the space of a single day, the same article passes through several

hands, returning to the initial seller at the end of the day. The latter
will then resell it the next day at an even higher price. The same
procedure takes place in the foreign exchange market.[49] Geo-
graphically, the parallel markets are within the Bazar in the narrow
sense (*hujra, sérails* and shops) or the transactions take place around
the buildings of the Bazar. In the latter case, circles form at specific
places according to the type of merchandise or item. There is a
market for medical instruments, a market for dollars, and further
on, people negotiate for construction materials and over to the side
the deutschmark is being traded.

Fourth, the control of the Foundation for the Deprived (*Bonyard-
e Mostaz'afan*). This foundation is one of the richest institutions in
the country. It is the product of the holdings of the former Pahlavi
Foundation and the movable goods and real estate confiscated or
expropriated after the Revolution. It thus disposes over literally
fabulous resources: more than 460 corporations (industry and
construction), factories, mines, hotels, cinemas, vast stocks of
automobiles, farm land, domestic construction (150,000 dwellings
including châteaux and luxurious private homes) and foreign
construction (for example, six stories of a building on 5th Avenue
in New York), a large amount of gold and precious metals. And
this list is far from exhaustive.

Since the Revolution, the Bazaris have also gained a foothold
within the administration in addition to their hold on the resources
of the Foundation for the Deprived (FD) — taking advantage, of
course, of their very close ties with the new masters. Thus, some
Bazari personages were appointed to the position of general
director of the FD.[50] The Bazar's hold on the administration of these
vast resources was accompanied by Bazaris' purchases of certain
movable objects (especially gold, silver, jewels, luxury automobiles,
antiques and precious works of art, etc.) at ridiculous prices.[51] But
the FD is only one example. There are other foundations of the
same type which are for all practical purposes controlled by people
from the Bazar, for example the Foundation of the Prophecy
(*Bonyad-e Nobowwat*) and the Martyr Foundation (*Bonyad-e Shahid*).

Fifth, the Bazar's representation in Parliament, in the Government and in the Pasdaran: Under the Pahlavi regime, the Bazar was totally absent from all the instances of power. The Bazar was represented only in the first legislature which was established after the installation of the constitutional monarchy in 1906, and later in the 17th legislature (under Mosaddeq). It is necessary to draw a distinction between the Bazaris as such and persons who are descendants of Bazaris, but pursue other occupations and professions than those proper to the Bazar. Under the Pahlavis, the professional Bazaris had been practically eliminated from the circles of power, although former Bazaris who had severed their relations with the Bazar to become part of the Pahlavi system had access to the Parliament and Government.[52] In effect, one of the great novelties of the Islamic Revolution was that it enabled professional Bazaris to enter Parliament, to assume ministerial responsibilities and thus to participate in the elaboration and implementation of political decisions.

Unfortunately, the two volumes which the Islamic Assembly have published on its deputies are very vague and incomplete as regards the real professions of the members of Parliament. For example, only four of the 339 deputies in the first post-revolutionary legislature declared trade as their profession in the period before the Revolution. One of these is also a renowned priest (the celebrated Shaykh Sadeq Khalkhali, the first Attorney General of the revolutionary courts), two others had trade as a secondary profession, and another two had occupations similar to Bazar occupations (bookseller and tailor). The remainder, i.e. the majority of the deputies fall into three principal professional categories: propagandists (*moballeghin*), officials (*karmandan*) and finally those engaged in research and study (*tahsil*). The truth is different; among these three categories, there are people who were directly engaged in commerce or had occupations close to commerce. For example, Hashemi Rafsanjani, former President of the Republic and the current Chaiman of the Expediency Council, had a flourishing business (essentially in construction) before the

Revolution. In any case, according to the information of the Islamic
Assembly, professional Bazaris are in a clear minority in the two
successive legislatures. But this invites the following question: how
is it possible that the Bazaris, despite their insignificant representation in the Assembly, are nonetheless capable of undermining
all endeavours which in one manner or other might limit their field
of activities or affect their vital interests? The answer to this
question must unquestionably be sought in the bonds of alliance
which have long linked the Ulama and the Bazaris. These bonds
were reinforced after the Revolution so that now the Bazar
constitutes the only social base of the regime. The regime can
therefore not dispense with this vital support without which it
would risk losing its most reliable bastion.

As regards Bazari participation in the government for the first
time in history, they have been able to assume ministerial positions
in the post-revolutionary period. The available data is not sufficient
to determine the exact number of professional Bazaris and fully-
fledged Bazaris in government positions, but all evidence points to
the fact that Bazaris have been represented in different ministerial
cabinets since 1981. Clearly, the Ministries of Economy and Trade
are the favourite ministries of the Bazaris. Thus, the head of the
Bazaris (Askar Owladi) was Minister of Commerce and Trade for
two crucial years (August 1981 to August 1983). They were crucial
because during this period the economic policies of the Islamic
regime assumed their current form. In addition to the presence of
Bazaris by profession, Bazaris by blood (on the paternal side, or
persons who were linked by close kinship ties with the Bazaris) in
the government is a very common fact. The Minister of Foreign
Affairs (Kamal Kharrazi) is representative of this group.

The effective participation and political influence of the Bazar
in the diverse bodies of political power is reinforced by the
presence of people from the Bazar at the head of the Command and
the Ministry of *Pasdaran* (revolutionary guards). For an idea of the
importance of the political influence of the Bazar under the
Khomeini regime it is sufficient to mention that the Commander-

Isfahan Bazar
Photo: Pernille Bramming

in-Chief of the Pasdaran, Mohsen Rezai (replaced in Summer 1997), and the former Minister of the Pasdaran, Mohsen Rafiq-Doust, come from the traditional Bazar circles. This does not mean that the Pasdaran are the military arm of the Bazar; nonetheless the presence of Bazaris at the head of and within the Pasdaran unquestionably give that indispensable certainty that the revolutionary army will jeopardize neither the vital interests nor the traditional values of the Bazar, at least as long as the present balance of power lasts.

Sixth, the Islamic regime satisfies the Bazar culturally. As we have seen, the Bazar is a traditional and traditionalist social unit. It is traditional in the sense that its fundamental structures (purchase, sale, distribution, etc.) have undergone no substantial transformation. The very idea of modernization is a sacrilege to the Bazaris. The traditionalism of the Bazar flows naturally from its traditional character. It subcribes to traditional values most of which are formed and formulated by the Ulama. Under the Shah, traditional values were irreconcilable with the policy of modernization. The films and programmes on television, the unveiling of women, restriction on polygamy, the proliferation of night clubs, the disruptions in eating habits, apartment living, and many other things were upsetting in traditionalist circles, which regarded all these things with distrust. Some even went to the point of thinking that these things were part of a premeditated diabolic plan, that everything had been decided by the Americans for the purpose of destroying Islam. Thus traditionalist circles perceived the Islamic Revolution as a salvation and as a return to pure sources and healthy morality.

Since the revolution is Islamic, it must necessarily cleanse the country of symbols that come from the corrupt West. Wearing a tie, the symbol of a Muslim's subjugation by the West, was practically prohibited, and wearing the chador, the symbol of female chastity, became obligatory. Likewise, the beard, symbol of religiosity and respectability, became universal. The Islamic Republic has established a lifestyle which in fact corresponds nicely to the rhythms, the values and the tastes of the Bazaris. They no longer feel frustrated by what they had formerly considered cultural rape. Quite contrary, since the Revolution, the culture of the Bazar has become dominant, if through the use of force. The spread of the culture of the Bazar has meant that the Bazaris for the first time in history are able to live in harmony with the surrounding society. This in itself is a major source of satisfaction for the people of the Bazar and another reason for them to support the Islamic regime.

Conclusion

Our examination of the four hypotheses which served as a basis for our discussion and analysis leads us to the following comments:

1) The authoritarianism of the three regimes — tribal, imperial and Imâmite — which have been successively installed in Iran, was the original and principal source of violence. Consequently, the violent actions initiated by Bazari circles and in general by Shi'a Islamists against the state, against its allies and its agents, must be seen as mandatory reactions with the purpose of neutralizing the violence of the state.

Nonetheless, since the outbreak of the Revolution, followed by the installation of the Islamic Republic, Bazar violence, which hitherto had always been against the state, would be henceforth incorporated into state violence. Hence we can say when the Bazar rallied around the Islamic regime, it contributed to reinforcing and intensifying state violence in all its forms (repression, terrorism and war).

2) If the Bazar has been able to remain continually in opposition and in a state of civil disobedience (with the exception of brief periods), and if it has conducted violent actions against the regimes in power without itself being crushed under the weight of the repression of which it was the object, survival, and beyond that the maintenance of its dynamism and continuation of its acts of opposition and violence, derives directly from its exceptional social

homogeneity. This homogeneity has served as its protective cover and shielded it from the destructive effects of fragmentation and dislocation. Its alliance with the Ulama has incontestably strengthened the firmness of its position and increased its capacity for resistance.

3) We noted that the special importance of the Bazar was accentuated by the absence of other social groups with at least the same degree of homogeneity and the same social and political consciousness.

4) The economic peripherization of the Bazar undeniably left its mark on its political behaviour. What this means is that the Bazar's opposition to the government, and getting it to renounce its violent acts against the government, was achieved by satisfying the Bazaris' economic interests. This postulate is confirmed by two facts: The first is the movement for nationalization of the oil industry which ended with the establishment of the Mosaddeq government. Through its protectionist policies, it succeeded in moderating, if not eliminating, at least temporarily the Bazar's traditional hostility to the government. The second fact, by far the most important and no less significant, is the attitude adopted by the Bazar towards the post-revolutionary Islamic regime. A detailed study of this period is beyond the framework of our present undertaking, but there is enough data to assert that the Bazar's support of the Khomeini regime has been essentially motivated by the numerable economic and financial advantages which this regime has generously afforded the Bazar. Consequently, it seems evident enough that in the past the economic factor headed the list of factors which put the Bazar into opposition and drove it to violence.

We can therefore argue that the thesis of a collective psychology based on the sequence of deprivation — frustration — violence must be modified on at least two essential points to be applicable to the case of the Bazar in Iran. The first point is the factor of social homogeneity; the second is the determining nature of the economic factor. With a few modifications, we will arrive at the result that no social group (marginalized) necessarily resorts to violence. All things being equal, only the most homogeneous social group can resort to violence of a historical scale, i.e. a violent change and transformation. This was the case of the Bazar in Iran. Only such a group has the necessary capabilities to pay the price of its acts and submit to the consequences. Thus, the violence of the Bazar as a social and political phenomenon may be explained essentially in terms of socio-economic contradictions, and secondarily in terms of a religious, psychological and cultural order. The sequence of events which we have just mentioned as well as the unleashing of Shi'a violence in the general context of Iranian society leads us to the following general theoretical proposition: *the peripherization of the most homogeneous social group is a necessary condition for that group to unleash an aggressiveness of historical scope.*

5) We have not compared the Bazar with similar groups in other societies in our study. Nonetheless, it seems to us that such comparisons yield some enriching perspectives. In particular the petit-bourgeois groups that supported Nazism in Germany, Francoism in Spain, and Poujadism in France could also be compared with the Bazar.

Blasphemy and Discourtesy

Your blasphemy, Salman, can't be forgiven.
Salman Rushdie, *The Satanic Verses*: 374.

Le blasphème des grands esprits est plus agréable à Dieu
que le prière intéressée de l'homme vulgaire.
Ernest Renan

The death sentence against Rushdie was 'justified' by reason of blasphemy. The term *blasphemy*, which comes from the Greek *blasphemia*, signifies a 'malicious statement' which in the Hebrew/Christian vocabulary is translated as an offense against divinity. Blasphemy is also a term that has been used at different times with varying and, often, not very precise meanings. Moral theologians regard blasphemy as a sin; St. Thomas Aquinas described it as a 'sin against faith. Originally, blasphemy was the term used to translate the Hebrew words *heref, giddef* and *niez* (that is, Isaiah 37:6, where the servants of the King of Assyria denied the Lord's power to save Israel). Today theologians define *blasphemy* as 'the act of claiming for oneself the powers and rights of God'; whereas in the narrower and more precise sense, the word expresses 'any contemptuous or profane act, utterance, or writing against God'.

Now that we have looked at the respective positions of the three great monolithic religions on the subject of blasphemy, as well as the views of the Sunnite and Shi'a schools, let us now examine how and to what extent *The Satanic Verses* have touched on the foundations, the symbols, and the personages which Muslims consider sacred.

The Judeo-Christian Position

In Judaism only God can be blasphemed. According to Talmudic law, the penalty for blasphemy is death by stoning (Lev. 24:15; Joshua 10:33). However this is only applicable where the blasphemer has offended against the name of God: *tetragrammaton* YHVH. Among other legal restrictions (Sotah 56a), it is necessary for two witnesses to say that they had warned the blasphemer of the transgression before it was committed. Thus, if any punishment was applied at all, excommunication was the most common.

Christianity defines blasphemy in a much broader context, considering both offenses against God and those against the divine character of Jesus' miracles as blasphemous. These offenses must be accompanied by a mocking and derisive spirit. Otherwise, the offense is simply heresy. Blasphemy against God, *injuriosa in Deum locutio*, may be *immediate* when God is directly affected, or *mediated*, when the offense first touches a sacred thing or person specially united with God, that is, an offense against the Holy Virgin or the saints in Heaven redounds ultimately on God himself. Blasphemy is considered *direct* when it aims to offend God and *indirect* if it is the product of an attack of impatience or anger. Often, blasphemy and heresy were considered identical. Nonetheless, there are differences. Whereas 'heresy consists in holding a belief contrary to the orthodox one, blasphemy imports the idea of irreverence and profanity'. Thus, according to the *Encyclopedia Britannica*, it is not blasphemous to deny the existence of God or to question the established tenets of the Christian faith unless this is done in a mocking and derisive spirit.

Christianity draws a distinction between blasphemy against the Son of Man and blasphemy against the Holy Spirit. Blasphemy in the first case consists in uttering offensive statements against Jesus as a *man*, for example, if he ate and drank as all other men when he sat at the table of innkeepers, treating him as a gourmand, a drinker, a friend of publicans and sinners (Matthew 11:19). Blasphemy against the Holy Spirit and, hence, against Jesus' *divine nature* was irremediable and unpardonable. In the words of Jesus himself, 'All sin and all blasphemy will be remitted to men, but blasphemy against the holy spirit will not' (Matthew 12:31).

According to older ecclesiastical legislation, severe penalties were imposed on blasphemers. Blasphemous laymen were initially fined and then exiled if there was a relapse; ordinary people, unable to pay the fine, were first condemned to a day of public penance at the doors of the church, and then to a beating; finally they had their tongue pierced and were sent to the slave ships. The clergy were first deprived of the revenues from their benefices, then their benefices themselves and their dignities, and finally sentenced to exile. Clergy who had no benefits were fined for their first offense or bodily punishment, then imprisoned, then degraded, and finally sent in exile. Justinian I decreed the death sentence for the sin of blasphemy against God (Levy, 1993: 50).

The question of heresy and blasphemy has been extensively discussed by the Christian theologians and Christian philosohers. St. Augustine (354-430), argued that heretics should be punished for their own good. St. Thomas Aquinas (1225-74) argued that the heretic's crime was worse that the forger's: 'it is , indeed, far more serious to pervert the faith which ensures the life of the soul than to counterfeit money which is only necessary for our temporal needs' (quoted in Remer, 1996: 225). Erasmus (1469-1536) who is one of the precursor of Christian humanism, permit the prince to use capital punishment against heretics only 'in the most necessray cases' (quoted by Remer, 1996: 85).

The Muslim Position

Whereas in Christianity blasphemy consists, strictly, in an act of derision and *lèse majesté* against God, in Islam there is no exact term to translate blasphemy. The Koranic term 'statement of impiety or infidelity' (*kalimât al-kufr*) is the closest thing that exists (Sura IX, verse 75/74).

Like Jesus, Mohammad was also sometimes the object of derision and insult from his detractors, who accused him of being a magician, a poet, a forger, or simply possessed. Muslim historiography reports that companions of the Prophet killed two poets who in their satirical compositions had ridiculed Mohammad.

These events aside, the Koran's attitude towards blasphemy is, strange as it might seem in the present context, on the whole relatively moderate. For example, the Koran challenges its detractors to compose more beautiful verses if they are capable, as in Sura LII and continued in Sura LXIX:

Sura LI   (30) Or do they say, 'He is a poet for whom
                 we await Fate's uncertainty?' Say:
                 'Await! I shall be awaiting with you'.

                 Or do their intellects bid them do this?
                 Or are they an insolent people?
                 Or do they say, 'He has invented it?'
                 Nay, but they do not believe.
                 Then let them bring a discourse like it,
                 if they speak truly.

Sura LXIX (40) No! I swear by that you see
                 and by that that you do not see,
                 It is the speech of a noble Messenger
                 it is not the speech of a poet
                 (little do you believe)
                 nor the speech of a soothsayer
                 (little do you remember)
                 A sending down from the Lord of Being:

      (50) Surely it is a reminder to the God-fearing;
                 but We know that some of you will cry lies.
                 Surely it is a sorrow to the unbelievers;
                 yet indeed it is the truth of certainty.

                 Then magnify the Name of thy Lord, the Almighty.

Further, the Koran in some places is very tolerant of non-believers when it says: 'Abuse not those to whom they pray, apart from

Allah, or they will abuse Allah in revenge without knowledge'
(Sura VI, verse 108).

Thus, the Koran does not have a rigorous position towards this
form of blasphemy; it is not even considered blasphemy. According
to the Koran, true blasphemy consists in apostasy (*ridda*) and
infidelity (*kufr*). Of the two, apostasy is the closest to blasphemy.
For the apostate is someone who abandons Islam after having
accepted it. Insults towards Islam, infidelity, is also, in the vast
majority of cases, regarded as blasphemy. The lines between these
two sins are not unbridgeable. Quite the contrary. However, despite
its severity vis-à-vis apostasy, the Koran decrees no concrete
punishment at all on the apostate. The Koran continually places the
chastisement of the apostate in the hands of God. It says,
'Apostates will be the hosts of fire where they will be immortal'; or
'They will have a cruel torment and they will have no succor; or
'He who denies Allah after [having had] faith in him ... those
whose breasts have opened to impiety, on these shall fall the wrath
of Allah and a terrible torment' (Sura XIV, verse 108/109). Sometimes even the Koran minimizes the act of apostasy, stating, for
example, that 'those who will be infidels, [who] will turn from the
path of Allah, and separate from the apostle after the leadership
has been manifested to them, those will cause no damage to Allah
who will render their action vain' (Sura XLVII, verse 34/32). And
more specifically, those who have uttered 'words of impiety' and
have been 'infidels' after having been Muslims, are invited in a
mediating tone by the Koran to return from their error for 'that will
be good for them ...' (Sura IX, verse 75/74).

The Koran decrees no concrete punishment. The silence is of
capital importance. Islam normally provides two categories of
punishments: *hudûd* and *ta'zirât*. The first are fixed and decreed
explicitly in the Koran for acts like theft and adultery. The second
are discretionary, the magnitude and form of which are left to the
decision of the Imam. In principle, apostasy belongs in the second
category. However, Muslim legal experts have included it among
the acts belonging to the first category.

The Sunni Attitude

After the death of Mohammad, his immediate successor (Abu Bakr) very quickly embarked upon punitive military expeditions against movements of apostasy (which at that time were spreading) and 'false prophets' (one of whom was a woman). However, the discretionary character within Muslim law opened several avenues of action and with the formation of the four Sunnite legal schools (*Hanafi, Mâliki, Shâfi'i* and *Hanbali*), and then the *Ja'fari* school (Shi'a), the question of blasphemy, in particular in relation to heresy and apostasy, was diversely interpreted.

For Abu Hanifa (8th century), founder of the Hanafite school, blasphemous acts towards God and the prophets are acts of infidelity (*kufr*), and for Mâlik ibn Anas (8th century) they are squarely equated to apostasy (*ridda*). The Shâfi'i school (named after its founder Al-Shâfi'i, d. 820) — especially under the eminent Iranian theologian Al-Ghazâli (12th century) — argues that it is impossible to accuse someone of infidelity if he prays towards Mecca and utters the confession of Muslim faith (*shahâda*). In contrast, the Hanbali school (named after Ibn Hanbal, d. 820), as interpreted by Ibn Taymiyya (d. 855), condemned to death anyone who committed any of the following: association with gods other than Allah, doubting one of the attributes of Allah, an act of hostility towards the Prophet, or questioning the sincerity of the companions (*shahâda*) of the Prophet or the companions of the companions (*tâbi'in*) or the companions of the latter (*atbâ*) (Ibn Taymiyya, 1965: vol. 4, 606).

Before resorting to capital punishment for blasphemy, a number of other punitive measures can be applied such as withdrawal of legal rights, dissolvement of marriage, confiscation of possessions, and annulment of all rights of inheritance.

Repentance (*tawba*), a question which has been amply discussed by Muslim legal experts, is not always accepted among the Sunni. A minority accepts repentance and accords grace to the repentant, but the majority is against grace because it is believed that the executed repentant will benefit from his repentance in the other world! (Ibn Taymiyya, 1965: vol. 5, 110). Not only is a clear position on blasphemy impossible to define, but also there is no centralized body within Sunni Islam to administer any decisions or actions based upon such a decision.

The Shi'a Attitude

The Shi'a leadership has traditionally condemned the apostate to death (Hilli, 1981: vol. 4, 1893), so on this point there is no difference between the Shi'a and the Sunnite school. Still, the Shi'a school draws a distinction between the native Muslim (*fitri*) and the converted Muslim (*melli*) in the case of apostasy. In the first case, i.e. when a person born to Islam commits an act of apostasy, he must be executed even if he repents. Judgment is entrusted only to the *Imâm* and his delegates. Are others authorized to kill the apostate on their own initiative? Shi'a legal experts disagree on this question. Some, like Shahid the First, for example, are in favour of execution of the apostate by any person who is able to do so. This opinion is not shared by the large majority of Shi'a legal experts. They believe that only the competent authorities are authorized to execute the apostate. And, if some other person should execute him without prior authority from the *Imâm*, this individual shall be punished in turn by the *Imâm*. The punishment of such a person, however, is largely symbolic (Hilli, ibid.).

A converted Muslim who commits apostasy will also be sentenced to death, but with the reservation that he must be accorded a period of reflection, which is set for three days according to some, while, according to others, it is the *Imâm* who will decide. At the end of this period, the apostate shall have the choice between repentance, i.e. saving his life, or confirmation of his apostasy, i.e., death.

In the case of Salman Rushdie, Khomeini, a qualified expert on Shi'a law, explicitly authorizes every Muslim to execute Rushdie, theoretically investing any Muslim with the powers of the *Imâm* in this particular case. In his *Risâla* entitled 'Explication of Questions'

(*Tawzih al-Masâ'il*), Ayatollah Khomeini declares that any Muslim who denies the existence of God, doubts the prophecy of his emissary, or does not recognize the obligatory nature of religious duties such as prayer, pilgrimage to Mecca, paying alms, etc., is an apostate (Khomeini, no date: 495). Moreover, the specifically Shi'a character comes into the picture here; he judges anyone who insults one of the twelve *Imâms* or commits acts of hostility towards them to be impure and infidel (ibid: 23).

The Shi'a provisions concerning the civil consequences (marriage, inheritance, possessions, etc.) of apostasy are by and large identical with those of the Sunnites. Shi'a law, however, tends to be more indulgent towards female apostasy. The apostate is not executed even if she is born a Muslim. She is imprisoned and beaten five times a day during regular prayers! The number of blows is determined by the *Imâm* (Hilli: 1894).

Although there is a considerable convergence in opinion between Sunnism and Shi'asm on matters of law, i.e., blasphemy, apostasy, and heresy, we must remember their different historical experiences. Sunnism, profiting from favourable historical conditions, was able to erect a state organization in the form of the Caliphate, and ruled under this title for centuries. Shi'asm, that is Imâmism, never had an equivalent organization. A few local dynasties (the Buyides, the Hamdanides, and some Ilkhâns; the Sarbdârân and the Sâdât — see Mozaffari, 1998: part 2, ch. 3) of negligible importance claimed Imâmism. But these were ephemeral and their fields of action were very limited. The reign of the great Safavid dynasty (16th century) was the only period in which serious attempts were undertaken to assimilate the Shi'a canonical system into a state legal system. These attempts were never successful because the Shi'a canonical apparatus continued by and large to function independent of and parallel to that of the state. Even though most of the Safavid kings were Shi'a, Shi'a was not power. This is the point of view of the Shi'a ecclesiastical authorities (like Khomeini), and also that of the Shi'a intellectuals such as Ali Shari'ati (d. 1977). Under Qajar (1779-1925), the jurisdiction of the state and the canonical jurisdiction suffered even more from ambiguity and confusion (on Qajar, see Lambton, 1987). One example is the case of a very influential Shi'a priest from the early 19th century, named Mohammad Baqir Shafti, who had seventy persons (Tunkâbuni, no date: 144) executed on his own initiative (in some cases by his own hand). The lack of genuine trials must be seen in the light of the limited practical experience of Shi'a priests and their fear of persecution on the part of the state. The case of Kasravi, mentioned above, is a recent example of this. By contrast, in Sunnism, judgment by trial has been an ongoing experience as exemplified by the trial of al-Hallâj or the trial of 'Ayn al-Quzât (d. 1131). The establishment of the Islamic Republic in Iran is in fact the first Imâmite experience of political power and state organization. Nonetheless, it is astonishing that Shi'a priests continued to practice in the same way, that is, without any form of trial, even if at present, according to their own statements, they have established the first 'authentic' Islamic power and the first Shi'a state in the entire history of Islam.

Blasphemy and Secular Law

For centuries, blasphemy was included (as a crime) in the civil legislation of various countries. Louis xii, in the ordnance of March 9, 1510, and later confirmed by Louis xiv on September 9, 1651, decreed punishments from simple fines to cutting out the tongue. In Scotland, blasphemy was subject to the death sentence until the 18th century. In England, in 1553, during the reign of Elizabeth, the Protestant codification of ecclesiastic legislation devoted a special section to blasphemy. The last executions for criminal blasphemy were carried out in 1612, when two anti-Trinitarians were executed. In 1648, the English parliament adopted a law against blasphemy. William Penn, also accused of anti-Trinitarianism, was the last prisoner of this kind after the Restoration.

The most significant event was the Taylor affair in 1676. John Taylor, a farmer, blasphemed publicly against religion and Christ by saying 'Religion is a cheat: Christ is a bastard'. The Taylor affair created a precedence through the decision of Judge Matthew Hale who handled the case. Judge Hale proclaimed the authority of civil courts in matters of blasphemy. His argument was based on the fact that Christianity was an integral part of the constitution, and hence the state had the duty to prevent a separation of religion and the state. Although the waning of the Reformation saw the general end of blasphemy cases, the subject continued to be considered the state's affair in England because of this legal precedence. Consequently, the last blasphemy judgment and conviction from a British court is from 1977. British law protects only Christianity against blasphemy.

A similar situation exists in the US, where individual states have been able to punish blasphemy since the New York affair of 1811. However, in 1938, a Massachusetts state court, dealing with a case of blasphemy, rejected the charge of criminal blasphemy on the principle of freedom of conscience and the fact that Christianity was not part of American law. This acquittal was to a large extent due to the efforts of men such as John Adams and Thomas Jefferson, who in 1825 had squarely underlined the contradiction between blasphemy and freedom of expression as guaranteed in the Federal Constitution. This refusal to apply the old anti-blasphemy law was also upheld in the most recent case of blasphemy in the United States (1977), when a Massachusetts court acquitted the defendant.

In France, there is no punishment for blasphemy since the penal code came into effect on September 25, 1791. The lack of such punishment had motivated the Paris Court to reject a Muslim request to banish *The Satanic Verses* (July 22, 1989). But, on April 11, 1995, a Paris Court decided to ban some passages of the Bible (translated from Spanish by Fathers Bernard and Louis Hurault) suspected of being 'anti-Jewish'. Further, Charles Pasqua, French Minister of Home Affairs, banned the publication of the book *Licit and illicit in Islam* written by an Egyptian theologian (Yussef Qaradhawi), because it was considered against the 'Laws of the

Republic' of France. A few days later, the same minister, under the pressure of public opinion, annulled his own decision. And the incriminated book went free (May 2, 1995).

In Denmark, however, the penal code's paragraph 140 affirms that 'anyone who should publicly do violence to legally recognized beliefs or publicly mock the worship of God will be punished by imprisonment or by a fine if there are attenuating circumstances. Only the Procurator General (of the Kingdom) has the power to initiate a criminal procedure'. In 1938, a Danish court handed down a conviction for anti-Semitic propaganda, and in 1971, the court prosecuted the author of a song entitled *The Eye* but subsequently acquitted him of the blasphemy charges. The most celebrated case was that of the Danish artist and writer Jens Jørgen Thorsen who had obtained financial support from the state to make a film on the life of Jesus based on a manuscript written by Thorsen himself. The announcement of the film production aroused Christian circles in Denmark and elsewhere, and, faced with an intense protest movement supported by the Vatican, the Social Democratic government withdrew its financial involvement and the production was stopped. It was not until 1989 that the Danish courts adjudged the government decision as being wrong, without however acknowledging any obligation on the part of the state to restore the sums it had initially undertaken to invest in the film.

In Spain, in 1997, a professor at the University of Complutense in Madrid published a book on psychology in which he declared that Muslims are 'violent'; Oriental people, 'slow and clumsy'; black people have a 'primitive mentality, inferior to whites'; and that women are 'weak, unstable, smart with quite sophisticated manners in their hatred'. Confronted with protests, especially from women's associations, he withdrew his book from the market, because he feared a trial (*Le Monde*, January 9, 1997: front page). Almost the same thing happened to Milos Forman, a film instructor who was sued in a Paris Court for offending the person of Jesus Christ in the poster advertising the film *The Last Temptation of Christ*. He also withdrew the litigious poster from distribution (*Le*

Monde, February 26, 1997: 34). In fact, trials and lawsuits are not exclusive to matters related to blasphemy and religious sensitivities: individual and personal cases regarding honor, integrity, legacy and reputation of common people or celebrities are daily occurrences in the courts, not only in the West but in all countries. An example of 'secular' offenses and complaints was the dispute over a book (*Le Grand Secret*) written by Dr. Gubler, the personal doctor of the late French President, François Mitterrand. In this book, doctor Gubler revealed that Mitterrand's cancer started in 1981 at the beginning of Mitterrand's first term as president and not in 1992 as the public had been told. Mitterrand's family went to courts to have Dr. Gubler's book stopped. On January 28, 1996, the Paris Court ordered a withdrawal of the book from the market, arguing that this book was an 'intrusion on the privacy of President François Mitterrand's family'.

Further, on Friday, February 27, 1998 Roger Garaudy, 84 years old, was fined 120,000 francs ($20,000) by a French court for contesting crimes against humanity in a book that called into question whether 6 million Jews died in the Nazi Holocaust. In his 1996 book, *The Founding Myths of Israeli Politics*, Garaudy questioned the figure of 6 million as the number of Jews killed by the Nazis in World War II and denounced the 'Shoah business'. Garaudy was convicted on the charge of contesting crimes against humanity,which carried a maximum 300,000 francs ($50,000) fine and one year in jail.

To sum up, civil courts in several Western countries such as the United States, England, and Denmark, are empowered to deal with litigation concerning blasphemy, although this power remains largely unexercised. By contrast, the Vatican vacillates between a more moderate attitude, as with its inaction against Scorsese's film *The Last Temptation of Christ*, and a more forceful attitude, as in its excommunication of Monseigneur Lefevbre.

Islam has never had an institutionalized or a centralized religious authority (except under Mohammad and to some extent under his four immediate successors) equivalent to that of the

Catholic Church. Questions relating to blasphemy, heresy and apostasy have therefore been questions of interpretation by diverse and numerous religious and political bodies. A case in point is the spectacular gesture of President Bourguiba in the early 1960s. In the midst of the month of Ramadan he drank a glass of fruit juice on Tunisian television, declaring essentially that 'when one is applying all his efforts to economic reconstruction, it is the same as being at war, and hence one can dispense with fasting'. Such an interpretation on the part of a state authority with regard to a religious duty, and moreover one decreed by the Koran, when it was followed by Bourguiba's act (public breaking of the fast) provoked a wave of protest throughout the Muslim world. According to Muslim theological schools of diverse allegiances, an act of this sort is subject to the punishment provided for apostasy. Nonetheless, precisely because no supreme Muslim authority existed, no trial was instituted against the Tunisian president, and no one even dreamed that he might be excommunicated. This confusion reigns in the Muslim world every time it is confronted with a grave problem which in some way touches on the very foundations of Islam. In the absence of a supreme religious authority in Islam, Khomeini's action assumed great proportions and significance. Indeed, while he was alive, he was the only Muslim religious leader who was simultaneously a political head of state. Profiting from this unique situation, he was always taking positions on all the problems concerning the entire Muslim community. The death sentence against Rushdie is the last and perhaps the most celebrated act of judgment rendered by Khomeini. However, as demonstrated in Sura II, Khomeini as Leader no longer had the competence which he had as *Mufti* (before he seized power), to deliver a fatwa, especially not in political matters. Neither the Prophet nor the 12 Imâms, or any Caliph in all of Islam (14 centuries), delivered a *fatwa* while they were in office. How could Khomeini, whose legitimacy is based on precisely the Koran, on the Prophet and the Imâms' traditions, be the only ruler to have this competence? As we saw previously, the great *faqih* Al-Ghazâli excluded the ruler from the category of people who are qualified to deliver a *fatwa*. Ghazâli's opinion is in complete accordance with the whole Islamic history and tradition. It also sounds logical and reasonable, because the ruler — even in the Islamic tradition — cannot be the judge of his own actions.

Rushdie's Discourtesy

The question of courtesy or discourtesy in the matter of freedom of expression is ultimately related to a broader question which is about the limits to freedom of speech. Is freedom of speech totally and absolutely free, or is it bounded by formal or self-imposed limitations? This question has no unanimously accepted answer. There are different answers depending on which approach is taken. The four following approaches are the most representative:

The first is the *religious approach* which is highly restrictive and imposes its own rules and restrictions on freedom of speech. In reality, the 'word' or 'speech' belongs to God, and the word is free only if it respects God's scriptural rules and serves God's will. As we saw earlier in this chapter, any attempt to offend the holy scriptures are in principle considered blasphemous and are consequently subject to punishment. The terrifying inquisition system in the Middle Ages — with its burning of books and human beings — is in fact a religious reaction to what the same religion considers blasphemy.

With the beginning of the Enlightenment and the emergence of *philosophers*, especially anti-clerical authors like Voltaire and Diderot, the religious approach was weakened, at least in Europe. With the French revolution of 1789, the debate on freedom of expression began, effectively leading to the birth of the *legalist approach*, the dominant tendency among the French revolutionaries. The leader of this tendency was Abbey de Sieyès who advocated controlled freedom of the press that ended whenever the '*droits d'autrui*' were violated (G. Gersmann, 1993: 203). Other revolutionaries, like Robespierre and Carra, advocated total freedom and *'liberté indefinie de la presse pour tous les ouvrages, quiconque de litterature, de science, de politique, de finance, de droit naturel, de droit public et de législation civile et criminelle'* (quoted by Gersmann, ibid.). Ironically, Robespierre, who was once an ardent advocate of absolute freedom of press and speech, installed the *Régime de Terreur* once he gained power, and got the Convention to adopt the Law of March 29, 1793 which was a weapon against any unwanted publicist or author. Any journalist could be jailed and dragged before the *Tribunal Revolutionnaire* while his articles were burned on the funeral pyre, as in the old days of the Bourbon monarchy (ibid: 210). Nowadays, the legalist approach is dominant; every country has legislation that determines the rules and the limits of this kind of freedom. Some countries, obviously the illiberal ones, have an arsenal of severe and dissuasive laws and regulations intended to repress all freedoms, especially freedom of speech and press which are the most visible of all liberties. In contrast, the liberal, the democratic and pluralistic, societies have a more flexible and soft legislation on this matter. The third approach is the *ethical approach*. There are no limits to freedom of speech, except those dictated by ethics and decency. But morality and decency are not absolute — they are subject to taste and interpretations. However, in addition to the public opinion which can punish moral abuse quite severely (in some cases driving the abuser to suicide (hara-kiri), the liberal societies have a number of associations and organizations that represent different professions. These associations and organizations undertake the task of investigation and the 'punishment' before a case reaches the courts. For instance, the press has its own ethical committee, the medical corps has the medical ethics committee, car salesmen also have theirs, and so on and so forth. The fourth and the last approach is what we could call the *paparazzi approach*. There are no rules, no privacy, no limits, no respect for anybody or anything. Everything can (must) be said the way the writer likes to express it. From this angle, the writers see themselves as a unique and exclusive group, exempted from any legal limits and any self-imposed, moral rules. Therefore, the 'offense' is

not only contradictory to decency, it is in fact judged as a 'necessity'. This is roughly Salman Rushdie's ultimate position when he says that:

What is freedom of expression without the freedom to offend, it ceases to exist, without the freedom to challenge, even to satirize all orthodoxies, including religious orthodoxies, it ceases to exist. (Interview in *The Sunday Independent*, February 4, 1990)

This standpoint contains three different elements which are not necessarily related. The first is the *freedom to offend*, the second is the *freedom to challenge* and, the third is the *freedom to satirize*. If 'offense' means 'insulting' and 'injuring' the beliefs, symbols and deep feelings of a specific group of people, it is hard to understand that this kind of behaviour has anything to do with freedom at all. It is rather the *violation* of freedom itself. Saying, for instance, that the wives of Mohammad, Prophet of Islam, were whores or that Abraham was a bastard — as Rushdie has written in *The Satanic Verses* — are examples of offense. Where is the 'challenge,' where is the 'satire'? It is obviously nothing more than an unnecessary provocation, without a clear purpose of provocation or even objective on the part of the author. Authors such as Nobel Laureate Naguib Mahfouz, himself a victim of Islamic fundamentalism and fanaticism, implicitly distinguishes between the *'freedom of challenge'* and the *'freedom of insulting'*. Moreover, Mahfouz has accused Ayatollah Khomeini of 'intellectual terrorism.' He felt that *The Satanic Verses* 'do not merit a reaction' because this book is not an 'intellectual work; and Mr. Rushdie is not an intellectual. A person who writes a book like this does not think, he is merely seeking consciously to insult and to injure. Thus he does not merit a response because one responds to thought with thought, and what we have before us here is not thought.' (*Le Monde*, March 9, 1989).

Consequently, *The Satanic Verses* is not an intellectual work. It does not properly challenge Islamic belief. There is no argumentation, no reasoning, only *satire*. Not simple satire, but insults and offensive satire, which Mahfouz refuses to answer because he simply does not regard it (or Rushdie) as a critical-intellectual work with which one can establish a dialogue. In his defense, Rushdie argues that:

To say that a work of fiction is basically a work of fact in disguise [whose aim] is to distort facts is wrong. The real purpose of fiction is not to distort facts but to explore human nature, to explore ideas on which the human race rests itself. (Interview before the death sentence. Published in *Far Eastern Economic Review*, March 2, 1989)

Without being an expert on literature, one might understand the word 'fiction' as something not real and emanating from the pure imagination of the author. If this understanding is correct, one may say that Rushdie failed in his *art romanesque*. All persons and places that are supposed to be 'fiction' are easily identifiable. They are not fiction, they are real. Even a Muslim child knows who Ayesha is, who Abraham is, who Salman (Parsi) is, where Mecca is (a brothel in Rushdie's imagination), and so on and so forth. Rushdie, who went through a painful post-publication process of the *Satanic Verses*, constantly and understandably changed his attitude. At the beginning of the protests in England and elsewhere, but before Khomeini's 'fatwa', he adopted a gentle and open attitude, demonstrating his understanding of, and sadness about, Muslim reactions. However, immediately after the fatwa, he radicalized his position, expressing his regret by saying:

Frankly I wish I had written a more critical book. A religion that claims it is able to behave like this, religious leaders who are able to behave like this, and then say that this is a religion.

After reviewing the above approaches and knowing Rushdie's position toward the critics, and especially his reaction to Khomeini's 'fatwa', we move on to the study of Rushdie's distortion of the universe of Islam.

Rushdie and the Universe of Islam

The universe of Islam is made up of a certain number of concepts, persons, signs, and symbols which all together form a circle around the One, that is, Allah, whose unity (*tawhid*) cannot be doubted. The absolute and inalterable character of this dogma is so evident that it requires no discussion. The second principle is the prophecy of Mohammad (*nabuwwat*), seen as the last of the true prophets. These two principles go indissolubly hand in hand, and their explicit acceptance (*shahâda*) is indispensable.

Beyond these concepts, angels, presided over by the Archangel Gabriel, occupy a separate place. The ex-Archangel, Satan (*Shaytân /Iblis*), who was banished from the kingdom of angels after refusing to prostrate himself before Adam, plays the role of provocateur and troublemaker among the sons of Adam. Next comes the sphere of the prophets, like the patriarch Abraham, Noah, Moses and Jesus, and all these prophets are venerated as an integral part of Muslim faith. The companions, the wives, and generally the family of Mohammad occupy a respectable place and must also be venerated.

All these elements, and obviously the Koran, constitute the sacred part of the Islamic universe, which also includes a profane sphere where men are arranged in a determinate hierarchic order, including the following categories:

* The Sincere Believers (*Mu'minûn*),
* The Formal Believers (*Muslimûn*),
* The People of the Book (*Ahl al-Kitâb*), that is, the Jews, the Christians, and the Zoroastrians,
* The Hypocrites (*Munafiqûn*),
* Non-believers (*Kuffâr*),
* The Polytheists (*Mushrikûn*), and finally
* The Apostates (*Murtaddûn*).

These are the constituents of the Universe of Islam. Now let us see what part of this edifice was supposedly affected by Salman Rushdie's blasphemy.

It is not our purpose here to undertake a literary criticism of Rushdie's book. This would require skills we do not have. Our undertaking is much more modest, namely to put ourselves in the place of a believing and practicing Muslim, who believes in the veracity and authenticity of the Islamic edifice with all that it entails. In other words, one whose everyday life is paced and ordered by the dogmas which in his eyes are invariable and eternal. With regard to the Rushdie Affair, the violence began with the man in the street. The intervention of religious authorities and of Khomeini — despite the weight they carried and the noise they produced — came only after the wrath accompanying the revolt of the ordinary Muslim. This is by no means a mere detail. It is a significant and considerable event.

First, the novel's central theme may be the distress and woes of exile, the hardship and humiliations felt by most immigrants in their adopted countries, in this case England. It nonetheless bears a title which by all appearances has nothing to do with this supposedly central theme. By choosing such a provocative title as *The Satanic Verses*, Rushdie, whether deliberately or not, added considerable fuel to the suspicion that he really meant *The Koranic Verses*. It is also quite possible that in his choice of title, Rushdie was unconsciously guided by a fascination with the shock value of the title. This kind of literary device is certainly common among writers, and, in Rushdie's particular usage, is a sin among Muslims. If Rushdie's real intention was to shock his audience, and in particular Muslims, he certainly achieved his objective.

And also, it is ultimately irrelevant whether the Universe of Islam is true or false. What is above all important is the Muslim *perception* of this universe, and of the idea of this edifice which every Muslim fashions for himself. In fact, at this level (i.e. the level of the ordinary Muslim), *The Satanic Verses* contains a number of elements which have been perceived by millions of Muslims as deliberately injurious and humiliating.

The shock of the title apart, Rushdie does not hold back on 'playing' with all of Islam's most sacrosanct principles. Within the book's reinterpretation, the concept of divine unity (*tawhid*) is greatly compromised. Mohammad, an entertaining gigolo and businessman, haggles with the polytheistic leaders of *Jâhilliya* (literally, the City of Ignorance), associating Allah with the three goddesses of the City (Lat, Uzza and Manat), in exchange for a seat in its council (Rushdie, 1988: ch. 'Mahound'), thereby degrading the cornerstone of the Islamic edifice, *tawhid*, to a negotiable and even saleable commodity.

Prophesy, the second fundamental principle of Islam, also suffers insults at Rushdie's hand. Thus, the patriarch Abraham is a 'bastard' (ibid: 95), Moses is a 'grocer' (ibid: 378), and Mohammad is a businessman transformed into a Mahound, the synonym of the devil (ibid: 93). Moreover, he is a gigolo (in relation to his first marriage with Khadija) and a pimp, whose wives are 'the whores of the curtain' (ibid: 381). Among his wives, Ayesha, the daughter of Abu Bakr (the companion, and later the immediate successor of the Prophet) occupies a place of choice in both the great brothel of Mecca and in Rushdie's novel (he dedicates an entire chapter to her). Ayesha, the youngest of Mohammad's wives, and the only one who was a virgin at the time of her marriage, is not only Mohammad's favourite. She seems — considering the space Rushdie devotes to her — also to be the favourite of the author of *The Satanic Verses*. He turns to her again in another chapter entitled 'Return to *Jâhilliya*.' In this chapter, Ayesha is faced with a double who curiously bears the same name. The resemblance between these two Ayeshas is striking in all respects. The double, a girl of fifteen, works in the brothel of the 'Curtain'. She is by far the favorite of most clients, but also the most expensive. The brothel of the Curtain is administered by a good old whore called Sawda (the Negress), whose marriage with Mahound took place the same day as Mahound's marriage with Ayesha (ibid: 381-82).

Nor are the Companions of the Prophet spared Rushdie's deri-

sive and airy comments. Among them, Salman Rushdie entertains
a certain respect for Salman the Persian. Did homonymity have
anything to do with it? In any event, Salman the Persian is presented as the most educated (implicitly the most civilized) of all the
Companions (ibid: 365). He is the most esteemed strategist and the
most listened-to counsellor. But his qualities do not prevent him
from being a regular client of the brothels (ibid: 374) and a client of
Ayesha (ibid: 385). Salman also likes to drink wine (ibid: 388). The
other Companions do not enjoy the same considerations. Osman,
the third successor of he Prophet, is a 'clown' (ibid: 236) and Bilal,
the first spokesman *Mu'azzin* of Islam is a 'great black' whose voice
is the 'Voice of American Confidence' (ibid: 211).

As for Satan, the archangel formerly banished and rejected, he
regains his rank and prestige in the *Verses*, which are, moreover,
dedicated to him. On top of that, Satan (Chamcha) suddenly notices
during his fall from heaven that he is accompanied by his former
colleague the Archangel Gabriel.

Finally the Koran, the sacred and divine text, whose verses in
the eyes of Muslims have descended word for word from heaven,
is quite simply falsified. Falsified by Salman the Persian who,
feeling tired of sitting at his master's feet and continually noting
down the revealed verses, one day decided to falsify the words
dictated to him by the Prophet, just to get some diversion. Where
Mohammad said Christians, Salman wrote down Jews, and so forth
(ibid: 387).

And there you see, oh Muslims! The divine unity so viable to
you was established only as a consequence of the dealings of your
Prophet with the Polytheists, the prophets whom you respect were
bastards, businessmen, panderers, the Companions of your Prophet
were only a gang of ordinary people, Mohammad's wives whores
at a brothel, Satan is as respectable as Gabriel, and finally your
sacred and venerated book is a falsified text.

In conclusion, the religious approach that condemns and
punishes all art perceived as 'anti-religious' is not compatible with
freedom of expression which is in itself a result of centuries of

struggle precisely against censorship and arbitrary restrictions. This is definitively not the way to treat a writer in our time. Any attempt to return to the Middle Ages and the Inquisition is an attempt to 'enslave' the mind again. The legal approach appears more adequate in Rushdie's case, although Khomeini condemned Rushdie without a trial. On the other hand, when Muslim groups in Europe tried to bring it to justice, the European courts declared themselves incompetent. Therefore, the final choice should be between the paparazzian and the ethical approaches. Obviously, Rushdie chose a paparazzian approach by producing a porno-graphical work, at least perceived as such by convinced Muslims. At the same time, he is aware that he deeply hurt the feelings of his ex-coreligionists. The *Satanic Verses* shall be regarded as a 'dis-courteous book' and the author as a person who deliberately ignores the elementary rules of courtesy, which means toleration and decency. In a sense, this work of Rushdie's is in contradiction to the general Western/European rules, based on respect for legality, honor and integrity of individual persons or groups of individuals. The 'punishment' for this kind of discourtesy or 'offense', as Rushdie himself described it, is certainly not death nor prison. Discourtesy shall be answered by courtesy if possible, otherwise it shall be ignored and Rushdie's 'apology' accepted:

As the author of *The Satanic Verses* I recognize that Muslims in many parts of the world are genuinely distressed by the publication of my novel. I profoundly regret the distress that publication has occasioned to the sincere followers of Islam. Living as we do in a world of many faiths this experience has served to remind us that we must all be conscious of the sensibilities of others. (February 18, 1989, reproduced in Appignanesi: 120)

International Reactions

In this chapter, we will first examine systematically the reactions following Khomeini's *fatwa*. Second, we will refer to certain pre-fatwa reactions produced especially among the Muslim masses. The international reactions were manifold and diverse, and they can be classified as follows: those issuing from worldwide or regional inter-governmental organizations (IGO), those originating from individual states, and finally those issuing from world public opinion.

The most lively and most important reactions at the IGO level were clearly those of the Common Market countries which we have just discussed. At the same level, the position of the Organization of the Islamic Conference (OIC) is particularly interesting.

The OIC embraces 46 Muslim countries and it is important to notice how this unique Islamic organization reacted. The 18th session of the Conference of Ministers of Foreign Affairs took place at Ryad on March 13, 1989, that is, in the midst of the crisis of the Rushdie Affair. Iran was represented not by its Foreign Affairs Minister but by a clergyman named Ali Taskhiri, Vice-Director of Islamic Affairs in the Ministry of Orientation (Information). The Conference did not approve of Khomeini's death sentence, despite the insistence of the Iranian delegate, who was supported by the Libyan delegate. Still, the OIC gave satisfaction to Khomeini as regards the substance of the affair. *The Satanic Verses* was judged blasphemous. 'This publication', said the final declaration, 'transgresses all norms of civility and decency and is a deliberate attempt to malign Islam and the venerated Islamic personality', and the declaration referred to the author as an *apostate*. However, the OIC contemplated absolutely no action; it simply deplored the publication of this book.

At the European level, the Rushdie Affair created one of the most complicated interactions between today's European Union (the former European Economic Community) and the Iranian government which are still hanging without a definitive solution. Khomeini's fatwa was a challenge to the European countries and especially Great Britain, leaving them with three alternatives: 1) no reaction; 2) adopt a conciliatory tone towards Iran by prohibiting the publication and distribution of *The Satanic Verses* on their territories; or 3) adopt a critical attitude towards Iran and express their irritation with Khomeini's *fatwa*. Actually, the two first alternatives were not true alternatives in the sense that it was absolutely unthinkable that European countries should not respond to such a direct challenge. Nor would European public opinion have permitted a nonchalant and evasive attitude. If the European governments had succumbed to passivity, it would have been immediately interpreted as a blatant sign of weakness that would have brought about an major, irrecoverable loss of prestige. The Europeans could not prohibit the publishing of *The Satanic Verses* to please Khomeini; such a measure would have been technically impossible, and the pressure of public opinion would have been irresistible. Furthermore, Ayatollah Khomeini had hardly showed himself to be a reliable political leader on whom one could count, and with whom one could negotiate. Finally, what Khomeini was demanding was much more and far more dramatic than simple prohibition of the incriminated book. Consequently, by a process of elimination, only the third alternative was, rationally speaking, left for the Europeans, namely, to condemn Khomeini's *fatwa* openly and clearly, and set about dealing with future relations between Europe and Iran.

The declaration of the twelve Ministers of Foreign Affairs who met on February 20, 1989, in Brussels was a kind of *resistance*. The most concrete act of this resistance was certainly the recall of ambassadors and heads of EEC delegations in Tehran. Thus, we have on the one hand the challenge and on the other the resistance which inevitably ends in *confrontation*. The confrontation was gravity. Not only did the Iranians reply very swiftly to the declaration of the twelve by recalling all their ambassadors from the EU countries. With their Lebanese and Palestinian allies they also made some serious threats to the lives of Western hostages in Lebanon, while serving notice that they were contemplating the resumption of their terrorist activities in the West — and all this without even mentioning the danger of Rushdie's execution.

How did this Irano-European confrontation end? There was no war, and in a sense, there was neither capitulation nor compromise. Simultaneously, it was uncertain whether the confrontation would continue. Alternatively, it may be perceived as still going on since the death threat against Rushdie has not been eliminated. Quite on the contrary, it has even been confirmed by Khomeini's heirs. Furthermore, diplomatic relations between Iran and Great Britain were suspended. Even so, the intensity of the confrontation between Iran and the EU has undeniably declined considerably to the point that we can ask if it is still a confrontation. The diplomatic tension between the two parties in question only lasted one month. On March 20, 1989, the same Ministers of the Twelve, meeting again in Brussels, decided unilaterally to return their ambassadors to Tehran.

This decision, which was motivated essentially by economic reasons, might in a sense be interpreted as the end of the confrontation, especially as the Iranian authorities also went back on their previous decision and sent all of their ambassadors back to the capitals of the Common Market countries as well. The European initiative to reassign their ambassadors to Tehran could be interpreted as a kind of capitulation, a camouflaged or diplomatic capitulation. This was in any case the interpretation Tehran chose. The Iranian Minister of Foreign Affairs, Ali Akbar Velayati, voiced the opinion on March 21 that the decision taken the previous day in Brussels underscored the 'strength of Islam'. While insisting on the 'very important' character of the *fatwa*, the

Minister added that the 'strong support' given by Muslims to Khomeini's *fatwa* had forced the EEC to 'return to realism'. Some Western papers, such as *Le Monde*, were astonished, if not indignant, over the European about-face, saying that the March 20 decision 'seems at least premature'. In a bitter and ironic tone, *Le Monde's* editorial noted that 'the virtuous indignation of political leaders stops where reasons of state begin' (*Le Monde*, March 22, 1989).

To understand this indignation, we must recall that in their first declaration on February 20, the twelve had clearly motivated their condemnation of Khomeini's sentence by invoking first and foremost two fundamental principles. The first was *freedom of expression* and the second a set of principles deriving from *international law*. In addition, the twelve made normalization of relations with Iran contingent on Iran's renunciation of 'the use and the threat of using violence'. But Iran had not given any signal that it intended to renounce violence as an instrument of its foreign policy, much less renounce the assassination of Salman Rushdie. Quite the contrary, Iranian authorities were quick to reaffirm the 'validity' of their leader's *fatwa*, immediately after the decision of the twelve to return their ambassadors. The only point on which the governments of the Common Market countries remained firm was the principle of freedom of thought and expression. On the other hand, the Iranians, while retaining and confirming their threat of death against Rushdie, have not acted in any way to carry out this threat, especially as they also decided to send back their ambassadors to Common Market countries, although with the exception of Great Britain.

In 1991, because of the Gulf War and its aftermath, the Rushdie Affair was almost being neglected. After the end of the war and particularly after the liberation of the last Western hostages in Lebanon, Rushdie, whose case was no longer connected with the fate of the hostages, began to mobilize Western public opinion, hoping that Western governments would put more pressure on Iran to obtain the Tehran government's guarantee that they were no longer planning or sending people to kill Rushdie. A new phase began at the end of 1992, when the European Council (EEC) held its regular meeting in Edinburgh (11-12 December 1992). The Council issued a Declaration that intitiated a new policy toward Iran; a policy which is now known as *Critical Dialogue*. The declaration stipulated as follows:

Given Iran's importance in the region, the European Council reaffirms its belief that a dialogue should be maintained with the Iranian Government. This should be a critical dialogue which reflects concern about Iranian behaviour and calls for improvement in a number of areas, particularly human rights; the death sentence, pronounced to be a Fatwa, of Ayatollah Khomeini against the author Salman Rushdie, which is contrary to international law; and terrorism. [sic] Improvement in these areas will be important in determining the extent to which closer relations and confidence can be developed.

After the Edinburgh Declaration, the EEC/EU established a semi-institutionalized arrangement with Iran on the basis of periodical meetings. The most formal is the famous *Troika* which meets with the Iranian representatives, especially at the beginning of a new EEC/EU presidency.

Several Western leaders met with Rushdie in public to show their sympathy for him, for example the British Prime Minister, John Major (on May 11, 1993), US President Bill Clinton (on November 25, 1993), and representatives of the EU Council of Ministers (on November 28, 1994). Parallel to these meetings, the EU countries will: 1) pursue their fully normal relations with Iran in economic, political and cultural areas; 2) at the same time, they will try to obtain from Tehran an official statement that the Iranian government will not do anything to implement the death threat to Rushdie. In February 1995, things began to move in a positive direction, when Iranian Vice Minister of Foreign Affairs Mahmoud Vaezi declared in Copenhagen the non-intention of his government to kill Rushdie. On April 19, 1995, the EU had formally pressed for the Iranian government's confirmation of the 'Copenhagen Declaration'. The EU specified that the Iranian official declaration was a condition for improved economic, political and cultural ties with Iran. The fateful date for handing this document to the EU troika, France, Germany and Spain, was set for June 22 in Paris. But after the EU-Iranian meeting, both European and Iranian spokesmen reported that Tehran had said it would not submit a written response on the subject (*Le Monde*, March 22, 1989).

The situation remained unchanged until April 10, 1997, when the Berlin Court delivered its judgement on the 'Mykonos assassination'. Following this judgement, the Iranian high authorities had planned, organized and ordered the assassination of exiled Iranians. Consequently, Germany called its ambassador back from Tehran, followed rapidly by the 14 other European ambassadors. However, at the moment (February 1998), diplomatic relations between EU and Iran are re-established.

The reactions of the UN were more subtle and even more cautious. The Nepalese President of the Security Council thought that it was not opportune for the Council to take up the Rushdie Affair (March 2, 1989). The next day, Javier Perez de Cuellar, Secretary General of the UN, who at this moment was visiting India, declared that:

We must respect all religions. At the same time we must respect the freedom of expression. We must have these two precepts in mind when we take up this question. It is also necessary to understand the concerns of the Islamic country and the entire world.

Aside from general considerations, the real reasons which dictated caution to the UN had to do with the peace negotiations between Iran and Iraq under the auspices of the Secretary General. The UN simply felt that it must not isolate Iran.

At the *state* level, there were many diverse reactions to Khomeini's *fatwa* and the events that it provoked. The United States condemned without reservation Khomeini's declaration, judging it to be 'deeply offensive to the norms of civilized behaviour ... and Tehran would be held accountable [for its actions]' (*Time Magazine*,

March 6, 1989). The Soviet Union refrained from any unequivocal statement. We should recall that it was precisely at this time that relations between the USSR and Iran were entering into a new and quite positive stage. On February 26, Shevardnadze had visited Tehran and, in an exceptional if not unique gesture, Ayatollah Khomeini gave him an audience. The two countries declared themselves prepared to establish 'strong relations'. This explains the rather 'pro-Iranian' attitude of the Soviet authorities on the Rushdie matter. The Kremlin curiously tried to render the Iranian government innocent by drawing an artificial and quite bizarre distinction between the Iranian government and its leader in the person of Khomeini. The Soviet press agency TASS wrote:

perhaps the Imâm Khomeini, the supreme religious authority in Iran had no other choice if he was to follow the teachings of the Koran than to denounce a person who had insulted Islam. This denunciation was nothing more in the end than the position of a religious leader. The government had not condemned Rushdie to death... (March 1,1989)

On March 3, the Soviets, encouraged by the new era in their relations with Tehran, declared themselves prepared to offer their good offices 'to attempt to defuse the tension between Iran and the Western countries'. For, according to Shevardnadze, the Rushdie Affair 'has become a conflagration that must be extinguished'.

The reactions of other non-Muslim states were quite diverse, but in most cases they condemned Khomeini's act. Brazil and Australia condemned the call to murder, but David Lange, Prime Minister of New Zealand, announced that his country could not join the protest movement against Iran because of the importance of New Zealand beef exports to this country.

The case of Japan is significant. Initially, the Japanese government promised the British government its support for the declaration of the Twelve. But a few days later, after a meeting between Sosuke Uno, Japanese Minister of Foreign Affairs, and the advisor of the President of the Islamic Republic, Japan reneged on its promise by saying that 'proper consideration should have been given to the Islamic people [by Rushdie]' and he should not have written what he did.

As for the Vatican, the Holy See, through its official daily, the *Osservatore Romano*, criticized the ingredient of 'irreverence and blasphemy' in Rushdie's book. The Vatican expressed its 'solidarity with those who had felt injured in their dignity as believers' adding nonetheless that Muslims should 'abandon attitudes of hate which offend God and the principles of morality', and finally underscoring that the 'sacred character of the religious conscience cannot prevail over the sacred character of the life of others'.

We must not forget that most Muslims had condemned the book without demanding a legal prosecution of the author, much less his death. Khomeini's Iran was in effect alone in condemning him to death in absentia.

Generally speaking, Western *public opinion*, largely mobilized by the media, took a position *en bloc* which can be qualified as clearly pro-Rushdie and anti-Khomeini. It would not be wrong to say that anti-Islamic sentiments made it easier to take such clear position. The pro-Rushdie reaction came from Western writers and their diverse associations. Several hundred writers from different countries signed petitions to demonstrate their 'total solidarity with Salman Rushdie and his editors'. In New York City, the Authors' Guild, the PEN American Centre, and the Writers' Guild of America (East) fired off letters of protest to the bookstore chains, 'for caving in to censorship by terrorism'. Similarly, in London, demonstrations were organized by writers, and in France, 114 writers demonstrated for Rushdie. An International Committee for the Defense of Salman Rushdie and his Publishers was established in London, and more than 700 writers appealed to 'international opinion to support the right of everyone to express his ideas and beliefs on the basis of mutual tolerance, without censure, intolerance, or violence'. One word sums up the attitude of international writers: *corporatism*. It must be said that the vast majority of them acted in this spirit motivated above all by the defense of one of their own whose life had been seriously threatened. Indeed,

very few chose a more balanced and objective attitude, namely that
of finding a way to accommodate the conflict between freedom of
expression and the respect of religious sentiments. Curiously, this
question was not even posed. Only a few rare writers such as John
Le Carré or orientalists such as the late Jacques Berque, who had
profound knowledge of Islam, attempted to see both sides of the
coin. For Le Carré, 'absolute free speech is not a God-given right in
any country. It is curtailed by prejudice, by perceptions of morality
and by perceptions of decency. Nobody has a God-given right to
insult a great religion and be published with impunity' (*The
Guardian*, January 15, 1990).

As for Western political leaders and officials, generally
speaking, those on the left squarely assumed the unconditional
defense of Rushdie, whereas the others opted for a more subdued
attitude, condemning both Khomeini and Rushdie. For example,
Neil Kinnock, leader of the British Labour Party, declared that his
party fully supported the firmest international action in favour of
Rushdie, while the Conservative British Prime Minister strongly
criticized the author of *The Satanic Verses*, and Geoffrey Howe, the
Secretary of Foreign Affairs, clearly expressed his government's
disapproval of the book. 'We don't agree with his views', he said,
'we can understand why it can be criticized, and it goes without
saying that we are not in sympathy with the book or in support of
it' (*The Guardian*, March 3, 1989). France had the same split between
left and right where the communists and socialists supported
Rushdie whereas Jacques Chirac, head of the RPR (Gaullists),
severely condemned Khomeini's call, but declared that it had 'no
respect for him nor for people who use blasphemy to make money,
as did that opportunist called Scorsese, the author of a movie *The
Last Temptation of Christ*. When the irrational is set into motion, one
must not be surprised how things go' (*Le Monde*, March 2, 1989).

Muslims, however, did not wait for Khomeini's call to react.
Several months before, the Muslim minority in England (one and
a half million distributed among 382 mosques), the majority of
whom are Indo-Pakistani, demonstrated in early October, that is,

Burning The Satanic Verses *in Bradford*
Photo: Sygma/Derek Hudson/IFOT

only a few days after the September 26 publication of the book. The protest movements spread and became almost an everyday affair. On January 14, Muslims from Bradford in Yorkshire burned copies of *The Satanic Verses*. Following these events, Muslims in other countries organized impressive demonstrations. Under the pressure of Muslim minorities, India and then South Africa quickly decided to prohibit Rushdie's book (on October 5 and November 24, 1988, respectively). The month of February was bloody. On February 12, Pakistani police fired on demonstrators in Islamabad. Six persons were killed. The next day one demonstrator was killed in Kashmir. According to some sources, it seems that Ayatollah Khomeini decided to make his celebrated *fatwa* public on February 14 after having seen the scenes of these demonstrations on television. Muslim protest movements took a new, quite dramatic, turn after Khomeini's call. As the supreme religious authority, he established the assassination of Rushdie and his 'conscious' publishers as a religious duty. There was no lack of volunteers to carry out this mission. Numerous Iranians and Lebanese (including Iran's Ambassador to the Vatican) volunteered to kill Rushdie. Others, such as Ahmed Jibril, leader of the Popular Front for the Liberation of the Palestine General Command, said that '[w]e in the PFLP-GC will confront this new conspiracy [against Islam] and work to execute the legal action against Rushdie' (*The Guardian*, March 6, 1989). The Lebanese Shi'a Asad Berro was the author of a 'suicidal' bombing action against an Israeli military convoy and was killed in the operation. He wrote in his will that he 'would have loved to have carried out the death sentence against the hypocritical agent Rushdie, and thereby obey the order of the Imam Khomeini ...' (*Le Monde*, August 13-14, 1989). Similarly, a few days before the suicidal operation, London police discovered the body of a Moroccan who allegedly had come to England to kill Rushdie (BBC, May 5, 1989). And, according to a survey carried out by the Harris Institute in October 1989, one in four Muslims residing in England wanted Rushdie dead.

Just mentioning all the protest movements and all the Muslim reactions to the Rushdie Affair would make quite a long list. These reactions were varied and diverse, but may, nonetheless, with some simplification be divided into two categories: those who allied themselves with Western intellectuals and those who took a more nuanced attitude, even sometimes to the point of criticizing the general Western position. These two tendencies nonetheless had one thing in common: *all* Muslim intellectuals who spoke out beyond the Iranian borders condemned the call to murder. This also applies to the Muslim religious authorities with the exception of the Lebanese Shi'as who followed Khomeini on all points. The two categories of intellectuals diverged on one essential point, namely, what attitude to adopt on Rushdie's book.

Whereas the 'Westernized' intellectuals approved of *The Satanic Verses* by putting their signature on various petitions in the name of freedom of expression, the other larger group, including persons otherwise known for their lay views, criticized Rushdie's book while condemning Khomeini's call. Here are a few examples:

Dr. Shabbir Akhtar, member of Bradford's Council for Mosques, thought that *'The Satanic Verses* is blasphemous ... [and] anyone who fails to be offended by Rushdie's book *ipso facto* ceases to be a Muslim ... [but] defending it at all costs is as unjustified as threats to its author's life' (*The Guardian*, February 27, 1989).

Abolhassan Bani Sadr, former president of the Islamic Republic of Iran, said that he was shocked 'that a writer could bring up after fourteen centuries the sexual relations of a man respected by a billion people'. At the same time, he thought that 'Ayatollah Khomeini's declaration has nothing religious about it' (*Le Nouvel Observateur*, February 23-March 1, 1989).

This second group of Muslim intellectuals included those who criticized the general Western attitude on the Rushdie Affair. This criticism took place on two levels: the intellectual and the political level. Mohammed Arkoun, professor at Sorbonne, represents the *intellectual* tendency, while Ali Muzrui, Professor of Political Science at the University of Michigan, represents the *political* one. For Arkoun, it would be wrong to:

react merely by invoking Voltaire, Rousseau, the rights of man, freedom of the artist and writer; that is merely referring to well-known themes and conquests of the spirit that are precious to all men, but you cannot demand that all cultures follow the trajectory traced out for two centuries by France and Europe. To take up this discourse would be to require other cultures to encapsulate themselves in the exclusively Western model of historical development and intellectual and artistic realization. It would be to repeat the colonial discourse which legitimated the domination over other peoples and cultures by exporting the civilization developed in Europe.

One interesting political criticism of the West, and of Great Britain in particular, was found in Muzrui's speech on March 1 at Cornell University. He first took up the question of freedom of expression in Western societies:

In Britain, elaborate efforts have been made by the government to discourage journalists interviewing so-called Northern Ireland terrorists. The British have a category of censorship concerning Northern Ireland... The Thatcher administration [stopped] the publication of the book by Peter Wright called *Spy Catcher*... And who is demanding that this book not be published? Not Ayatollah Khomeini, but Maggie in London.

Muzrui then took up the question of *treason* and said that:

The Western world understands the concept of treason to the state. The Western world even understands capital punishment for treason against the state. The Western world sometimes, even with people fighting for their country but within the Western empire, may have been executed... Now in Islam there is a concept which can be translated as treason not to the state but to the Ummah, to the religious community and to the faith... Salman Rushdie has been viewed by some as being a traitor in that sense... In English law... treason still includes violating the King's consorts sexually... The US law on treason defines treason more narrowly in terms of war and military defense. But in the Rosenbergs' case in the 1950s... it does include this defense of the political system against the rival system of communism. So, instead of religion in the old sense you have a secular style of ideological preference for which the United States is armed to defend even at the expense of the human species.

And last, Muzrui attacks the great Western powers for also carrying out summary executions. Only that when they do it:

... it becomes a part of a covert operation, not a radio announcement. The CIA or MI5 may take the initiative; the Israelis may fly all the way to Tunis and kill somebody in his bedroom; and then they deny it. Just deny it... Is the Ayatollah just opening a whole new tactic? It is not more immoral the day it was done, it is just bad taste. He announces it on the radio instead of sending his spy to do it for him.

Even so Muzrui rejects Khomeini's call:

The Ayatollah is still wrong in the death sentence. When all is said and done Islam began with the act of reading; read, from the very beginning. And it tells the Prophet [...] that reading is how God teaches.

In conclusion, we may say that the fatwa has been a shock to everybody, even Khomeini's own entourage. In general, reactions to this fatwa have been characterized by prudence and some understanding, even by Rushdie himself who apologized for the way his book has offended Muslim's beliefs and feelings. At this stage, Western writers — some of them predictably — supported Rushdie and resolutely condemned the fatwa. On the other hand, Muslim intellectuals, with few exceptions, also condemned the fatwa but at the same time criticized the lack of Western comprehension of Muslim religion and Western hypocrisy.

Islam and Freedom of Expression

I cannot convince myself that there is anyone so wise, so universally comprehensive in his judgment, that he can be trusted with the power to tell others: You shall not express yourself thus, you shall not describe your own experiences; or depict the fantasies which your mind has created; or laugh at what others have set up as respectable; or question old beliefs; or contradict the dogmas of the church, or our society, our economic system, and our political orthodoxy. (Jake Zeitlin, *Library Journal*, June 1, 1965)

Everyone shall have the right to express his opinion freely in such manner *as would not* (emphasis added) be contrary to the principles of the Shari'ah. (*The Cairo Declaration of Human Rights in Islam*, article 22, § a.)

Since the beginning of the Rushdie Affair, public attention has largely been focused on freedom of speech. The reason of this particular interest for freedom of speech can be explained by the fact that precisely this form of freedom seems more tangible than others. Freedom of speech is in a way a thermometer which indicates the temperature of the environment. If the environment is of such a nature that people at large do not have freedom of speech, the thermometer automatically indicates the lack of all other forms for freedom. Nevertheless, freedom of speech is only one of a multitude of freedoms. Freedom in its multiple dimension, forms and aspects is generally dubbed *freedom of expression*. Freedom of expression embraces, *inter alia* freedom of figurative art in its different forms, freedom of visual and cinematographic art, freedom of musical (instrumental and vocal) art, freedom of painting, freedom of clothing, and so on.

Recognizing 'freedom of expression' is necessary in order to respect it. The question is, does Islam recognize freedom of expression at all? Is Islam familiar with this concept? Our answer is that Islam as any other religion, at least any other monotheist religion, is unfamiliar with freedom of expression for individuals. Freedom of expression belongs exclusively and completely to God. He is the unique Creator of everything and the unique Legislator. Therefore, human freedom of expression cannot be viewed, within the Islamic universe, as *essential and independent*. Only God's expression is essential. Humans must relate and subordinate their freedom to God's will. Consequently, human freedom of expression is only *aleatory and secondary*. The issue is not the legal *limitation* of freedom which is a normal rule in every social life. The real issue is that freedom of expression as such has no place in the religious universe. Therefore, the question about the limitation or criticism of limitation seems quite irrelevant. Moreover, religions in general and the three main monotheist religions (Judaism, Christianity and Islam) in particular, did not promote freedom of speech or democracy. Nor did they ever pretend to have such objectives in mind. It is too much to ask them to fulfil something that has never been on their programme. The main purpose of religion is obviously *salvation*, not freedom nor democracy. In the religious perspective, one could be a slave and be saved, without creating incompatibility between *salavation* and *slavery*. Furthermore, religion is based exclusively on *belief* and on the *sacred*. Belief, per definition, cannot be criticized; otherwise it is not belief. Likewise, a sacred personage or symbol cannot be criticized either. Any attempt at criticism will be interpreted as an offense. Since freedom of expression without free criticism is an illusion, the religious environment is not exactly conducive to freedom of expression. Even in Ancient Greece, Socrates was accused of doing unjust things, of not believing in the gods which the *city* believed in.

If we agree on the existence of a direct relation between freedom of expression and a religious environment, we have to admit that freedom of expression can flourish only in a non-religious environment. It does not really mean that the environment must be hostile to religion. Religion as one variant of expression is tolerated with the same respect as all other human expressions.

However, religion must not be politically dominant. Arguing for the pre-existence of a secular context does not mean that every secular regime automatically ensures freedom, or that freedom will necessarily be respected. There must be some other conditions for it. The first condition is that secularism itself does not turn into a new religion or a dogma. Creating secular sacred symbols, personalities, ideas and sacred rituals in a way that leads to evacuation of all others (secular or non-secular) is not *per se* different from religion. The second and equally important condition is the effective presence of democracy in a secular society. The best example of a non-democratic secular system is the communist regimes. The communists closed the doors not only to all criticism, they strangely misinterpreted secularism. Instead of leaving room for religious expression, they combated religion itself.

Returning to Islam, we can say that Islam as a religion is unfamiliar with the freedom of criticism and the consequence of this which is the freedom of expression. Why? There are many reasons. Before discussing this question, we have to define Islam in a neutral way. Is Islam only the Koran? Or is Islam composed of the Koran and the *Sunna* (Description of Prophet's behaviour)? What about the innumerable interpretations of both the Koran and *Sunna*? And Islam's history? Our aim here is not really to open a discussion about the *right* and the *wrong* Islam. We must only find a way, without going into too much detail, of describing some principal and significant trends which characterize Islam. From this point of view, Islam consists of a Book, the Koran, and a history of fourteen centuries. In connection with freedom of expression, we will examine the Koran's attitude towards freedom of expression and the state of this freedom throughout Islam's history.

We argue that freedom of expression is not recognized by the Koran, and the proof is in the Koran itself. The Koran explicitly states that it represents the *last word*, and Mohammad is the *last prophet*. Such a statement does not leave any room for discussion. Because, if something is the last word, all other opinions are already disqualified and may be subject to repression.

Despite this objection, we can say in favour of the Koran that it is important that Mohammad delivered a *book* as his miracle. With Moses, the miracle was the transformation of a stick to a snake, and Jesus' miracle was to cure the sick. We have to admit that Islam, having a book, seems more intellectual than other religions. It is also true that two chapters in the Koran are titled *The Pen* (Sura LXVIII) and *The Poets* (Sura XXVI), which indicates the Koran's positive attitude towards intellectual works. The problem is that the contents of these two chapters have very little to do with their respective titles — they directly criticize non-believing poets. *The Pen* Sura begins with the following verse:

By the Pen, and what they inscribe, thou art not,
by the blessing of the Lord, a man possessed.

In other words, Allah swears on the pen that Mohammad is not mad! This is the only thing about the pen that exists in this Sura. The Sura on *The Poets* does not really deal with poetry. Only in the last verse, the Koran attacks poets in general except those who believe in Islam:

Shall I tell you on whom the Satan come down?
They come down on every guilty
They give ear, but most of them are liars.
And the poets — the perverts follow them.

These sentences evidently have nothing to do with freedom of expression. Yet, the positive thing is that the Koran explicitly recognizes the pen and the poets.

One could also argue that the Koran recommends dialogue. We would go even further by admitting that the whole Koranic tone follows an arguing style. It argues that the sun and the moon as well as the sky and the earth are God's creation. It argues also that knowledge is better than ignorance, and so on and so forth. In reality, the Koran does not search dialogue; its aim is to convince the non-believers. Sometimes by words, sometimes by force. Because, according to the Koran, there is only one truth: the Koranic truth. How can one argue with something that is convinced that it is the truth itself?

Second, it is a fact that during the long history of Islam, freedom of expression has been an unknown concept. This history, like Christianity in the Middle Ages, is tarnished by repression, torture, banishment, executions, and destruction. The powerful caliphs, emirs, sultans, shaykhs, khâns and ayatollahs have never allowed freedom of expression in the entire history of all the different dynasties. However, in relation to a more open intellectual and scientific forum, there are two periods that represent the glorious epochs of Islam, 1) Al-Ma'mûn and the 'House of Wisdom', and 2) Andalusia and the Cosmopolitan Culture.

Al-Ma'mûn and the 'House of Wisdom'

The first period was in the 9th century and coincided with the zenith of the Islamic empire under the Abbasids. It was really under Caliph Al-Ma'mûn (813-833) whose 'intellectual curiosity was far-reaching, and his works are collections of rare and interesting knowledge concerning the human and natural world: countries, animals, the oddness of human beings' (Hourani, 1991: 52). Al-Ma'mûn was the first Islamic ruler who created an official forum for free debates for intellectuals and scientists. This forum was called the 'House of Wisdom' (*Bayt al-Hikma*).

Al-Ma'mûn opened his court to all kinds of intellectual tendencies, also to those philosophers and moralists whose ideas were banished by the orthodox Ulama. His personal preference was undoubtedly rationalism and especially the *Mu'tazili* movement which at that time was the dominant school of thought in both Basra and Baghdad. There is evidence that prominent *mu'tazili* figures like Bishr ibn al-Mu'tamir and Thumâma ben Ashras had free access to the Caliph's court. Some other *mu'tazili* (like Bishr al-Marisi) played the role of mentor for Al-Ma'mun. Josef Van Ess, who has studied Mu'tazilism intensely, thinks that it is very plausible that Al-Ma'mun's inclination for rationalism stems from the period of his residence in Khorasan, where Hellenism was dominant from the epoch of Alexander the Great. Furthermore, it is also possible that Al-Ma'mûn created the 'House of Wisdom' under Hellenistic inspiration, the *Academy* (Van Ess 1984: 86/[27]).

Hellenism survived a few centuries more in Islamic life, producing a group of philosophers, moralists and writers like Al-Khârazmi (780-850), Al-Râzi (865-923/932), Al-Fârâbi (872-950), who tried to reconcile Hellenism with Islam, Avicenna (980-1037), and Averroes (1126-98) who still shine in the memory of Muslims. They disappeared gradually and gave way to the Dogmatics and Theologians. Jurists like Al-Ghazâli and Ibn Taymiyya belong to this group.

In short, this epoch was characterized by two trends. The Islamic empire reached its peak of power, conquest, and prosperity. The Abbasid empire represented at that time the most powerful state in the world. The second predominant trend was deep infiltration of Hellenistic ideas and cosmology which contributed to an opening of dialogue and exchange of arguments. After the end of this period, the Islamic intellectual vitality changed place, moving slowly from Baghdad, Basra, Damascus and Cairo to Southern Spain to Andalusia, which represents the second Islamic intellectual, glorious epoch.

Andalusia and the Cosmopolitan Culture

Andalusia evokes to Muslims a splendid epoch, intellectually and scientifically. Politically, however, the Muslim situation at that particular time was almost chaotic and full of confusion.

In political terms, Andalusia was in clear opposition to Al-Ma'mûn's epoch. At this time, the central authority in Baghdad began to weaken and faced new and serious challenges. Consequently, some relatively small dynasties began to establish themselves as autonomous or independent in different parts of the immense Abbasid empire. One of them was founded in Southern Spain by some Umayyad 'princes' who had escaped from the Abbasids' yoke. The Andalusian adventure, in the best meaning of the word, began with the Cordoba Caliphate (929-1031) and continued for three centuries. This Caliphate was a successor of an Emirate which was established by the emigrants who came to North Africa and then to Southern Spain because of the Abbasid repression. During these centuries, there was great political and religious tolerance in this area. A necessary condition for close collaboration between the scientists of different races, religious and political opinions. Juan Vernet's (Vernet, 1978/1985) great book on *La cultura hispnoàrab en Oriente y Occidente* and the two volumes edited by Salma Khadra Jayyusi, entitled *The Legacy of Muslim Spain* (1994) perfectly describe the rise and fall of the Andulasian epoch. All disciplines of arts, music, botany, mathematics, medicine, astrology, astronomy, physics, chemistry, and many other branches were represented at that time in Andalusia. The extraordinary vitality of culture and science in this period was so great and of such variety that it is difficult to choose specific examples.

The Andalusian experience accomplished at least two main objectives: Firstly, it created a cosmopolitan forum for different scholars of different disciplines. This extraordinary task could not have been accomplished without creating a hospitable environment. The result was overwhelming and greatly benefitted Europe. As Margarita Lópes Gómez put it:

The flood of translations centred around the preferred fields of mathematics and science. It is to Islamic culture that we owe our knowledge of numbers, including the zero, of Indian origin but transmitted by a Muslim from Persia named al-Khwârizmî,and Muslims also developed geometry, demonstrated the position and movements of the planets and made many other scientific and medical discoveries, such as the discovery of the minor circulation of the blood, in the 13th century, by the Arab doctor Ibn-al-Nafîs. (In Jayyusi, 1994: 1060)

Second, and actually the result of the first, is the transfer of Hellenistic knowledge to medieval Europe. This transfer was undoubtedly crucial to the beginning of the Renaissance in Europe. Montesquieu affirms that 'there were the Mahometans (Moors of Spain)
who transmitted sciences to Occident; since then, they have never
wished to take benefit of what they had given us' (Montesquieu,
1949: 1569).

The glorious epoch of rationalism and Hellenism reached its
end when *dogmatism and juridism* again became dominant in Islam.
Montesquieu believes that the destruction of the Caliphate led to
the destruction of sciences for Mahometans (ibid). In fact, al-
Ghazâli (1058-1111) was perhaps the first, or at least the most
reputed, theologian who introduced Islam to dogmatism. Later, in
the 14th century, Ibn Khaldun (1332-1406) tried to re-introduce
rationalism in Islamic culture by founding the sociological school
and his famous *Prologomen (Al-Muqaddama)*. Unfortunately, he was
too late because the people of Islam were already in a deep crisis
which finally led them to several centuries of decadence.

The Ma'mûnian and the Andalusian examples showed that free
dialogue and exchange of views and experiences were possible in
two different contexts. When the central authority of the Islamic
empire was strong enough and sure of itself, like the Abbasids
under Al-Ma'mûn, it could afford and neutralize any subversive
attempt. But when the central authority was disintegrated into
different, small emirates, sultanates and caliphates in Andalusia, the
opposite was the case.

The question which could be raised now is why the Islamic
world today, which is deprived of a central authority and has
disintegrated into different states, cannot reproduce something
similar to the Andalusian experience. The answer may be found in
the particular political difference between Islam today and Islam in
Spain.

We have to remember that despite the fact that the Andalusian
political system was relatively weak, it was not under any external
domination or colonized. The Muslim world of today has liberated

itself quite recently from colonialism and it still living under powerful external domination.

Aristotle or Plato?

Now, a question will presumably emerge in connection with the impact of Hellenism on Islamic political features. We know that Muslim philosophers (*falâsafa*) were familiar with Hellenism long before the Westenerns. So how to explain that in the West, Hellenism led to secularization and democratization, but it did not have the same effect on Muslims? The answer to this question should be found in some particularities of (Islamic) Hellenism and (Western) Hellenism. The fact is that we are dealing with two different Hellenistic schools: *Aristotelian and Platonic*. While the former represents the primordial inspiring source for Western societies, the Islamic world — also at the zenith of the Hellenistic epoch under Ma'mun and in Andalusia — preferred the latter. The essential difference of political matters between these two schools concerns the existence or non-existence of a Law and an Ideal model which is absolutely superior to any man-made law. Aristotle established two different categories of laws: *particular* and *general*. 'By particular laws I mean those established by each people in reference to themselves, which is again divided into written and unwritten; by general laws I mean those based upon nature' (Aristotle, *Art of Rhetoric*: I, 13.3) The first category of laws corresponds precisely to what John Rawls nowadays calls *practical reason* (Rawls, 1993: xx). Aristotle emphasized that '[r]eligion should be part of a city, but it should not be part of government' (Aristotle, *Politics*: 1299a 19, 1322b 18-19). The Aristotelian position on this matter would later be used as the foundation of the Western political system. It has inspired the French Revolution of 1789 and above all the *Declaration of the Rights of Man and Citizens*. In this Declaration, 'the rights of *Man*' refers directly to the second category of Aristotelian right (the *natural* right) while the 'right of *Citizens*' clearly indicates the presence of the first category (the *particular* right).

Thomas Paine (1737-1809) is among the thinkers of the Enlightenment who reformulated these two different laws by saying that:

Natural rights are those which always appertain to man in right of his existence. Of this kind are all the intellectual rights, or rights of the mind, and also all those rights of acting as an individual for his own comfort and happiness, which are not injurious to the rights of others. Civil rights are those which appertain to man in right of his being a member of society. Every civil rights has for its foundation some natural right pre-existing in the individual, but to which his individual power is not, in all cases, sufficiently competent. Of this kind are all those which relate to security and protection. (Paine, 1987: 43)

Obviously, in Aristotelian thinking there is a law [the natural], but no ideal model, exterior and superior to the law (in society). But the law in society is decided only by mankind. Because the law is nothing but the expression of the will of the components of society, and the political order does not obey any other law except the law emanating from the competing and complementary social relations. In contrast to this approach, the Platonic model is constructed on *Nomos* which is superior and exterior to all other laws. Therefore, society must strictly follow *Nomos* and move in the direction of the *Ideal City*, if society intends to reach happiness and salvation. The Islamic model is quite close to the Platonic. There is a law expressed in the Koran. It is divine and has been designed and decided by God and has been communicated to mankind through the Messenger. The Koranic law is *The Law* above all other laws and must be implemented in human societies. As the result of perfect implementation of the Law, the perfect society model will emerge (the *Umma*) as it did when it was established under the Messenger himself in Medina. Therefore, Muslim philosophers like Fârâbi, Averroes and Avicenna were more comfortable with Platonian than with Aristotelian philosophy.

The existence of a 'perfect city' and a perfect ruler ('philosophers' for Plato and 'prophet' for the Muslims) has attracted Muslim interest in Plato. Another decisive difference between

Muslims and Aristotelian thinking resides in the statute that each accords to the *reason*. While the Aristotelians believe in the autonomy of the reason (*primordial*), the Muslims see in the reason merely as an instrument which must lead the believers to fulfil the Divine Law (*instrumental*).

Islam and Reformation

In the beginning of this chapter, we indicated that freedom of expression cannot exist without two conditions: secularism and democracy. Here, we are dealing with secularism, the question being: is Islam compatible with secularism? We use 'secularism' and 'secularization' interchangeably. According to Daniel Bell, secularization means 'disengagement of religion from political life, and the sundering of religion from aesthetics, so that art need no longer bend to moral norms but can follow its own impulses' whatever they may lead to. 'In short, it is the shrinkage of institutional authority over the spheres of public life, the retreat to a private world where religions have authority only over their followers, and not over any other section of the polity or society' (Bell, 1977: 426-27). The same idea has been formulated by Paul Valadier, but with more precision and accuracy. For him, secularism (*laïcité* in French) is the existence of 'a public space neutral, open and guaranteed by the legitimate government with the purpose of assuring a pacific co-existence, in as much as this was possible, of different intellectual and spiritual components of civil society and the nation' (*Le Monde diplomatique*, June 1989). If we could draw the most significant elements from these two definitions of secularism, there would be two closely associated elements: first, the idea of *privatization of religion*, and second, the idea of the existence of a *consensual neutral space*. Are these two elements compatible with Islam? In this connection, our point is that Islam cannot be secularized internally, because nobody can secularize a religion. It is a contradiction in terms. Secularization is essentially based on the individual human being, the universe of

Islam is totally based on Allah, and a human being is only Allah's Slave (*'Abd Allah*). While religion is 'unsecularizable,' it can, however, be reformed.

The impossibility of secularization is not characteristic of Islam alone; neither Judaism nor Christianity, as such, have ever been, or can be, secularized. Furthermore, while Islam is a religion, secularization is a profane process. Islam is God's product and is self-sufficient. Secularization is a product of humankind and, like all other human creations, it will always remain unfinished. Islam is a *holistic* concept and construction; secularization is a *disintegrative* process, based on separation and individualization.

Secularization does not challenge the essence of religion but merely opposes the holistic and totalitarian dimension of religion. Another point is that in monotheist religions, the *unity* is the *value*, even the supreme value (unity of God, unity of human beings and God, unity of religion and state, and so on and so forth). On the contrary, in secular thinking, *separation* (religion and politics, private and public, art and belief, etc.) represents the value. It makes an enormous difference both at the philosophical and practical levels. In Islam, the *Umma*, the Community, comes before the individual. In a secular Western model, *principium individuationis* (John Locke) has priority. Further, in the Islamic heritage there is no tradition comparable to the Western theory of natural rights in the sense of individual entitlements of an individual vis-à-vis a community, and of their institutional enforcement (Tibbi, 1994: 4-5). The only law that Islam recognizes is the 'Divine Right'. Consequently, the real question is not whether Islam can be secularized, which is an absurd question. We must examine the Islam's *reaction* to the secularization of a *society* in which Islam represents the majority of the population. In other terms, will Islam tolerate being merely a private matter? There are at least three different elements inherent to Islam which prevent both its 'privatization' and its neutral attitude towards secularization of society. The first obstacle is found in the main character of Islam as a political religion. Islam was born as a political design to a group of people in Mecca. Contrary to primitive Christianity which has not created a state, Islam has created a state, the Medina state (Mozaffari, 1987: ch. 2). Mohammad himself was not only a Prophet, he was at the same time and equally a statesman, head of state, commander-in-chief of the army, and the supreme judge. His immediate followers were also both spiritual and political leaders; according to history, they were actually more political than spiritual. How can a Muslim forget these indisputable facts and believe that Islam is neutral toward politics. Here, we only talk about the historical facts, but it is not at all difficult to find several direct references to politics at all levels in the Koran. The only way to make Islam apolitical may be to ignore the real history of Islam under Mohammad and his successors, by taking refuge in mysticism. This is the reason that Max Weber in this classification of religions into three categories calls mysticism a *world-fleeing* religious approach. The two other Weberian types are *Two-worldly* and *This-worldly*. While Christianity would be an ideal type for the former, Islam is undoubtedly the best representative of the former. Therefore, it appears that the so-called Islamic fundamentalists in fact have a point here, saying that 'Islam is politics, and politics is Islam'. This substantial and determinant difference between Christianity and Islam on the matter of religion and politic reciprocal relations attracted Alexis de Tocqueville's attention when he pertinently formulated it as follows:

Mohammed brought down from Heaven, and put into the Koran not only religious doctrines, but political maxims, civil and criminal laws, and theories of science. The Gospels, on the contrary, speak only of general relations of men to God and to each other, beyond which it inculcates and imposes no point of faith. That alone, among a thousand reasons, is sufficient to show that Islam can never predominate for long in a cultivated and democratic age, while Christianity is destined to retain its sway in these as in all other periods. (Tocqueville, 1990: vol. II, 23)

The second obstacle is that for Muslims, the Koran is in itself a *sacred text*. The Bible and the Old Testament are also sacred, but the significant difference is that while these two sacred books are not semantically God's word, the Koran is *God's word*. Consequently, the Koran is immutable not only because it is sacred, but also and especially because it is Allah's word, word by word. Therefore, the Koran will potentially always be against any attempt at transforming a sacred society into a secular one. Faced with such an unchangeable and sacred text, there will be no room for freedom of expression.

The third obstacle is that Islam has no central religious authority in the form of an organized and recognized Church and priesthood, which both Judaism and Catholicism have. When the European renaissance started, the Europeans could easily point to the Church as an adversary. The Church was physically visible with the Pope as its head. Calvin and Luther could criticize the Church, because the Church was physically there. Where is the Islamic equivalent of the Catholic Church? Where is the Muslim Pope? Nowhere. Islam is a diffuse religion. Theoretically, the relations between Allah and believers are direct, without any intermediary. Since Islam is diffuse, the separation of religion and state becomes extremely difficult, because it is hard to draw the line between these two. One can separate them from each other, but only on paper. Turkey's lay Constitutions are in this case the best example. But nobody will succeed, unless the diffusion and confusion in the mind of Muslims have been clarified. A person must clarify in his mind what is religious and what is political before proceeding with the separation. Because we must know with precision what is the subject of separation. As long as unity dominates the minds of people and the intellectual and mental separation between, for example, aesthetics and belief, remains a perverse process, freedom cannot be realized in society. As Bassem Tibbi wrote: 'Freedom is a secular project' (Tibbi, 1995: 80-92).

It is also highly noticeable that the concept of *freedom* as such does not exist in Islamic tradition and culture. Instead, the concept of justice (*'adl / 'adâla*) is the keyword in Islam. For example, the

Shi'as believe in five fundamental principles (Unity of God, True prophecy of Mohammad, Doomsday, Imamate and *Justice*), while the Sunnis believe only in the first three principles. But nothing on *freedom*, which is after all a new notion for Muslims.

The constitutional revolution in Iran in the beginning of the 20th century was a revolution for *justice* not for freedom. The revolutionaries wanted to establish a *House of Justice* ('*Adâlat Khâneh*) which later turned into the Iranian parliament (*Majliss*). The emblematic inscription on the old Majliss' portal in a sense illustrated the essential message of the constitutionalist movement. It consisted of two words: '*Adl-e Mozaffar* (Justice of Mozaffar [al-din Shah], who authorized the establishment of the House of Justice. Actually, everything indicates that the Muslims borrowed the notion of freedom from the West. They often used it to demand liberation from foreign domination (*hurriya* in Arabic and *âzâdi* in Persian) and not in the common sense of liberty and freedom of man inside the society. As examples of someone achieving 'freedom' from external domination, one can mention the Algerian Front de la Libération Nationale (FLN) or Palestine Liberation Organization (PLO).

Here we have to add that the Muslim and the democratic — pluralistic concepts of *justice* are quite different. In John Rawls' jargon, the democratic — pluralistic society is dubbed as 'well-ordered'. In Muslim societies, justice means roughly 'avoidance of excess of *in*justice'. It is a question of negative justice as opposed to positive justice. Furthermore, justice is not organically connected to liberty. In Islamic political vision and perception, justice and liberty represent two different concepts, and 'justice' always gets priority in the sense that it has been mentioned. God is just, so the Prince must also be just in respecting the Law of God and applying it to everybody without any discrimination. The problem which we will discuss later is that the Law of God — codified in the Koran and in *shari'a* — is in itself discriminatory. But among Muslims, the Prince must observe the rule of equality and equity. One can also say that in Islam, the notion of justice, especially in its political version, represents equitable relations between the Prince on one side, and Muslim believers on the other. The origin of justice in Islam stems from the Law of God. God had once and for ever formulated the rules of justice; the task of man is application of God's will. Things are indeed different in a well-ordered society. Justice in such a society is based on two principles which are absolutely inseparable. The simultaneous presence of both principles is a *sine qua non* condition for attesting the presence and realization of justice. These two principles are:

a) Each person has an equal right to a fully adequate scheme of equal and basic liberties.

b) Social and economic inequalities must satisfy two conditions. First, they must be attached to offices and positions open to all under conditions of equal opportunity; and second, they must be to the greatest benefit of the least advantaged members of society (Rawls, 1993: 291).

We are not going into long interpretation of Rawls' definition of justice. Rawls himself has done it eloquently in *A Theory of Justice* (1971) and in its newer version, *Political Liberalism* (1993). Thus two remarks on Rawls' definition of justice will elucidate the differences between his definition and the Islamic definition. First, the concept of justice in its social interpretation is closely connected to the notion of 'equal basic liberties' which obviously means that justice without 'liberties for all' is not conceivable. Second, it is not God who decides on the substance and shape of justice, but the citizens themselves. Reinterpreting Jean-Jacques Rousseau's *'contrat social'* and *'intérêt général,'* Rawls invented the *original position*. The building process of this construction goes on behind 'the veil of ignorance' which means that the parties do not know the social position, or the conception of the good, or the realized abilities and psychological propensities, and other things, of the persons they represent (Rawls, 1993: 305). The parties 'must agree to certain principles of justice on a short list of alternatives given by the tradition of moral and political philosophy' (ibid). As mentioned before, justice in Islam is the work of God, so it is authoritarian, inalterable and eternal. In the democratic-pluralistic model, justice is mankind's work. Its authority is based only on the decision of free men and women. It is inalterable insofar as it is not subject to contest in its foundation. It means that this justice as a concept, as well as a guideline, is not eternal. These two differences make up a substantial distinction between Islam (or Medina model) on the one hand and the 'well-ordered society's' position in matters of justice and liberties on the other.

While 'secularization' stands as the *necessary* condition for freedom of expression, democracy represents the *sufficient* condition. By democracy we mean a pluralist and participative regime which allows peaceful transmission of power from one group of citizens to another. Rawls takes at least one step further in deepening the sense of democracy when he writes that '[a] modern democratic society is characterized not simply by pluralism of comprehensive religious, philosophical, and moral doctrines but by a pluralism of incompatible yet reasonable comprehensive doctrines' (Rawls 1993: xvi). Democracy in this sense is only a system, an instrument which is itself a product and consequence of a specific state of mind and an intellectual position. In this connection, the Muslims attitude towards democracy is divided into two main directions. The Moderate and the Radical or Fundamentalist. The partisans of the Moderates claim that Islam is compatible with democracy. They argue that Islam, already from its beginning, possesses some institutions and some procedures of a democratic character. In this respect, the *Shurâ* and *Bay'at* are often used as examples. The *Shurâ* which has been recommended by the Koran and has been used by the Prophet himself, is a 'consultative body' which assisted the Leader in decision making. Its members were not elected and its opinions were not executory. Equivalent institutions existed in China, India, Persia, and even in Mongolia, where the *quriltai*, the assembly of Mongol-Tartar nobles and clan chiefs, gathered to elect a new *khân*. This kind of institution, however, has nothing to do with democracy, in essence or form. The *bay'a* means 'the act by which a certain number of persons recognize the authority of another person'. This is also alien from democracy in which the recognition of authority is decided by free election, and not only by co-optation, designation, or seizing power by force, which has happened so often in Islamic history. Thus, the tension between Islam and democracy is not only institutional, but predominantly philosophical. Democracy is based on citizens' rights, which is unknown in Islam. The only right which exists is God's right. How is it possible to conciliate these two rights with each other, especially when they contradict each other?

The so-called Fundamentalists are closer to both Islam as 'value' and Islam as 'fact'. None of them have ever claimed that Islam is compatible with democracy. On the contrary, they think that Islam is a unique system of government which is superior to all other systems, including democracy. In his book on *Islamic Government*, Khomeini explicitly rejects any democratic idea when he writes that '[t]he Islamic government is subject to the Law of Islam, which comes from neither the people nor its representatives, but directly from God and his divine will' (Khomeini, 1971: 53-54). In a Shi'a context, Khomeini believes the concept of *velâyat-e faqih* (the governance of Shi'a *juris consultus*). This concept was later elaborated and revised by Khomeini himself and took the form of *velâyat-e mutlaqah-e faqih* (absolute governance of the Shi'a *juris consultus*). In Algeria, Ali Ben Hadj, one of the prominent leaders of the Front Islamique du Salut (FIS) has repeatedly declared that 'democracy is *kufr* (infidelity)' (Interview in *Horizon*, February 23, 1989). In Sudan, Hassan al-Turâbi, the leading theoretician of Islamism believes that the denotations of *shura* and democracy are similar, but their connotations are dissimilar. 'They denote public participation in the making of political affairs; democracy connotes, however, the ultimate sovereignty of the people, *shura*, the ultimate sovereignty of God' (Moussali, 1994: 57). The above three examples, which are not the only ones, show that at least the leading fundamentalists are quite consistent, presenting a comprehensive mental picture, which in fact corresponds very well with the Medina Model at the time of the Prophet.

In our discussion on secularization, we rejected the possibility of secularization of Islam as well as all other monotheist religions. At the same time, we leave open the option for reformation of religion. Reformation means crudely proceeding to a new inter-pretation of religious scriptures and behaviour. In other words, once a religion stands before a completely new and unprecedented situation, it reacts to the challenge by renewing itself in a such way that its *adaptation* becomes possible. In this sense, reformation, like revolution, is not an everyday event. It happens quite rarely and always under, and because of, exceptional circumstances. Refor-mation is religion's answer to a *rupture*. Rupture takes place in society as well as in people's minds; a process which is occurring outside of religion's body. The religious body, as well as all other social components, are required to take a stand vis-à-vis the rupture. The most successful and maybe unique religious reform in history is the Christian Reformation, which was enterprised essentially by Luther (1483-1546) and Calvin (1509-64). The Christian Reformation was a religious reaction to the huge and unprecedented economic, political, and mental storm which crossed Europe during a specific period. Europe would come out from the darkness of the middle ages with or without Luther and Calvin. Calvinism and Lutheranism made possible the survival of Christianity in modern Europe as an integrated part of European culture. The emergence of capitalism, the formation of civil society, and the foundation of state-nation inevitably led to the separation of Church and State, resulting in the separation of the sacred from the political. The Renaissance and Enlightenment radically trans-formed the role of religion in society. It removed God from public life and managed to 'privatize' God, although the privatization did not really mean the 'death of God'. The Renaissance and Enlighten-ment were successful Promethean devices, employed by people who wanted to take charge of their own fate. Probably nobody has caught and defined the essence of this movement better than Immanuel Kant. In his words :

Enlightenment is man's release from the self-incurred tutelage. Tutelage is man's inability to make use of his understanding without direction from another. Self-incurred is this tutelage when its cause lies not in the lack of reason but in the lack of resolution and courage to use it without direction from another. *Sapere aude* 'Have courage to use your own reason' — that is the motto of enlightenment. (Kant, 1983: 3)

Calvinism and Protestantism for their part contributed largely but maybe not consciously to this transformation. Christianity before the Reformation was an authoritative, salvationist, and expansionist religion. Luther and Calvin were as dogmatic and intolerant as the Roman Church but still contributed to the division of Christianity. This 'inevitably means the appearance within the same society of a rival authoritative and salvationist religion, different in some ways from the original religion from which it split off, but having for a certain period of time many of the same features' (Rawls, 1993: xxiii). Faced with the new situation, Catholicism had no other choice but to submit itself to the time's exigencies. In Muslim societies, however, the idea of abstraction from God has not even started yet. With a few exceptions, Muslims keep trying to interpret God, to 'add' God to the destiny of humankind, to attach God to Socialism, Marxism, Liberalism, Arabism, or whatever. By attaching God to everything, without any abstraction, they accumulate instead of separating and selecting. This may involve almost everything: new and old, private and public, religion and state, the city and the countryside, the chador and Yves Saint-Laurent, Allah Akbar, and Michael Jackson. Perhaps it is possible to have some or all of these things at the same time if a decision has been made to keep them separate from each other, both mentally and intellectually. But the Muslims, at least on an intellectual level, will not, or dare not, eliminate anything. They want to have a little bit of everything. Therefore, the Muslims have not even started the necessary intellectual process of separation, classification, and selection. No choice, no peace of mind. No choice, no clarity, and no progress. Returning to Christianity, we can admit that the success of modernizing Christianity is due to multiple factors. Three of them are, in our view, of overwhelming significance. The two favourable factors which are inherent in Christianity are the concepts of *Duality* and *Trinity*. The third one is the *Rupture*. Christianity as a 'two-worldly' religion is mild monotheism. The borders between God on the one hand and Caesar on the other have been fixed from the beginning. Therefore, the idea of separation of Church and State is not alien to Christianity. Moreover, the invention of the concept of *duality* was, at that time, an attempt at adaptation from the first Christians, St. Paul being the most prominent.

While the concept of *duality* has facilitated acceptance of political separation, the concept of *the Holy Trinity* emphasized this incorporation into *Montesquian-Lay Trinity* dividing political power into three different and equal bodies: legislative, executive and judicial.

The most decisive factor which activated the Reformation movement remains, however, the *deep rupture* that took place in European societies and which finally led to a 'new birth', the Renaissance. It was this rupture that pushed Christianity towards its own renovation.

Now, let us place Islam in its own temporal space with the purpose of assessing its capability for adaptation. In contrast to Christianity, Islam as rigid monotheism, vigorously rejected any idea of duality and *à fortiori* the concept of trinity. Not only does the Koran reject these concepts, it vehemently opposes them. As we have discussed before, the keyword in Islam is neither 'separation' nor 'association,' there is *unity* at all levels, theological as well as social. So, on this front, we cannot expect anything positive from the Islamic sacred scripture. The lack of more flexible concepts in Islam makes it extremely difficult for those Muslims who intend to reform Islam and adapt it to modern times. The next issue is the existence of a rupture within Muslim societies. Is there any rupture which is calling Islam to challenge it? By rupture we mean a deep substantial change which regenerates a new vision of the world, human beings, thoughts, the arts, nature, and so on. It is a fact that nowadays a lot of things are going on in Muslim societies. A considerable part of international news actually deals with events connected to Islam, Muslims, and events related to Muslim societies. These societies have witnessed decolonization, revolutions, coups d'état, violence, terrorism and war. One could ask if the magnitude and intensity of violence alone is enough to test the production of a deep and qualitative transformation within these societies. Or maybe these events, despite their tragic character and intensity, are less significant in historic perspectives than one would actually believe.

In other words, what kind of mental, intellectual, societal, and political transformation took place under the pressure of these events? Evidently, some regimes changed from monarchy to republic (Egypt, Iraq, Yemen, Iran) as a result of revolutions or coups d'état. There are surely more cars in the streets of Cairo, Tehran and Jeddah now than 30 years ago. New and impressive buildings were erected in different Muslim cities. Almost everyone watches television and has a radio. But how big is the rupture in all this instrumental novelty? Very little or non-existent. In reality, Muslim societies look like a night club with lots of noise and not much light. When you look inside them, you see that the view of the world, the perception of human rights, freedom of expression, the fate of women, art, literature, music, and a lot of other important elements which are indicative of a rupture are *essentially* the same as they were before.

The lack, or at least the weakness, of civil society is evident, democracy is still absent, and capitalism as a coherent and rational economic system is lacking, because of weak production sectors. This means that the Muslim societies — despite some appearance — are not facing a rupture; they are continuing to live as they always did. In the absence of a rupture, a number of people, outside and inside these societies, are desperately asking for Islam's reformation, but this is too much to expect from Islam which is not facing any internal challenge. As a result, it is quite unrealistic to ask and wait for Islamic reformation. Since the idea of the future and the vision of the world generally remains unchanged, they look *back* to the Medina Model which again and again becomes the mirror for the future. To look back is not really specific to the fundamentalists, those who want a modern Islam do the same. Therefore the reform *(islâh)* in:

an Islamic context should be distinguished from reformism within Christian churches. Islamic reformists did not — and do not— claim that Islam in itself needs any reform, but the various misunderstandings and misinterpretations have come to distort some of the original texts, introducing some harmful practices. Islamic reformism is thus a movement aimed at returning Islam to its original message, with a theological emphasis on unity. (Abukhalil, 1995, *'Islâh'*)

Generally, Muslims want to change the world (or dominate it) in such way that the world will fit into Islam. The Christian reformists adapted Christianity to the new world. This make a huge difference.

The above discussion points out that as long as Muslim societies do not face a real rupture, there will be no reason and no motivation for Islamic reform. In prolongation of this discussion, we have to notice that the essence of European *Renaissance* was a rupture or breaking-away from religion as a model for social and political life. At the same time, the Renaissance was also a ricorsi aiming to return to pre-Christian and especially to ancient time, the antique Greece. The *model* was the Athenian City-State. Yet, the Athenian democratic model was *not* perceived in Europe as sublime or ideal, but merely as a starting point. In contrast, the Islamic 'Renaissance/*nahda*,' both in its 'reformist' and its 'fundamentalist' versions, proclaims and demands the return to ancient time, but with the important difference that the Muslim return to ancient time is not the result of a rupture from religion. On the contrary, Islam is looking to strengthen and reinforce religion. It is a return to religion and absolutely not a rupture. The Medina Model, in the religious sense, is indeed not perceived as the 'starting point', but as the 'destination', because in the Muslim mind, this model is in itself a perfect and a sublime model which illustrates the most supreme phase of achievement that humanity can ever reach. In this sense, we have before us two diametrically opposite visions of history, the fate of humankind and the finality of life. On the one hand, the so-called Western model, which is free from any pre-fabricated idea of perfection, is also free from any memory of a perfect model. On the other hand, the Islamic vision, which is inspired by the conviction that Islam has already produced *the* perfect model, and that the ultimate objective of humanity consists in regenerating the same model. In other words, one vision is to *create*, slowly and progressively, a better model (the Western model), while the other vision is to *imitate* the old, 'perfect' model (the Islamic model). Therefore, it is hard to say that Muslims have any real reformation project at all.

Modernity is Challenging Islam

In the above discussion, we have argued that the challenge to Islam is not *endogenous* and that the mental and societal rupture is either very week or absent. In the following, we will argue that Islam is facing a challenge and it must take a stand vis-à-vis a rupture which is *exogenous*. To begin with, let us briefly repeat that the Christian reformation was totally autonomous and dictated by internal dynamics in European societies at the time. At that time — Renaissance and Reform — these societies had not been challenged by any exogenous model. It was the first time in history that such things happened. This is not the case with Islam, and for that matter not the case for all non-Western societies in our time. All other models have positioned themselves vis-à-vis an already existing model which is Western. Nobody can ignore this model which aspires and claims to be universal. The political, military, and economic domination by the West is so impressive that it influences everyone and every other model. The Model is there, and it is successful. Other models (i.e. Marxist, Islamist) are also there, but they are far from successful. Precisely because of its success, some scholars (Francis Fukayama) think that we have reached 'The End of History'. It means that any other model can rival the Western model successfully. Successfully or not, this point is not within the scope of this discussion. The point is that there exists a single, successful model: The Western Model. In this perspective, the situation is diametrically in opposition to Samuel Huntington's presumption that Islam challenges or will challenge the West in the future. In reality, the West is challenging Islam intellectually. The Western challenge to Islam became evident at least from the second half of the 19th century. A review of the works of those who, in Muslim eyes, are perceived as the great thinkers and great reformers outlines this challenge clearly. The West is constantly and explicitly present in the works of all these writers. Let us mention a few of the most influential representatives. Sayyed Jamal al-Afghani (1838-97) concludes that:

the Europeans have now put their hands on every part of the world ... In reality this usurpation, aggression, and conquest have not come from the French or the English. Rather it is science that everywhere manifests its greatness and power. (See Donohue and Esposito, 1982: 17)

Mohammad Abduh (1849-1905), the leading Egyptian *Mufti*, takes an interesting position in attributing the success of the West to Islam. He writes:

It was the nations of Europe [who] began to throw off their bondage and reform their condition, re-ordering the affairs of their life in a manner akin to the message of Islam. (ibid: 27)

Hassan al-Banna (1906-49), founding father of the Muslim Brotherhood, believes that:

European civilization consisted of atheism, immorality, individual and class selfishness, and usury... To compound the harmful effects of European culture, most Muslims misunderstood their own religion. (Commins, 1994: 133)

Concerning Ayatollah Khomeini's views about the West, there is really no need to quote him. The West is omnipresent in his discourse and in his actions. The West is the Great Satan, the West is Anti-Islam, the West is corrupt, and so on. But one thing is completely clear: Khomeini had to take a position on the West, and only the West. All other targets (the Shah, Iraq, and internal opposition) were fully marginalized in relation to the West.

Khomeini's revolution was against the West, his hostage-taking in Iran, in Lebanon, and all other violent actions were all against the West. It is worth mentioning that the Muslim anti-Western attitude contains two principal aspects: political and intellectual. Politically, the Muslim discourse is not very different from other discourses in Latin American, African and Asian countrites that have been subject to Western colonialism and domination. However, Islamist (and Islamic) discourse has the particularity that it claims to be *intellectually* superior to the Western culture. All Muslims agree on this point, because all Muslims have already accepted once and for all the Prophet's statement that 'Islam is superior to all, and nothing will be superior to Islam'. This sentence probably contains the frustration and tenacity of Muslims who are not ready to consider the possibility that another culture, religion, or whatever, could be superior, or at least equal, to Islam. At the same time, it is obvious to them in their daily life as well as at all other levels (political, cultural, scientific) that Islam is not superior to all other religions, cultures and social models. Such evidence naturally gives all Muslims headaches and frustration.

Now, if we continue our analysis, we will find that intellectually, Muslims fear not so much the West, but the pillar concept and idea on which the whole Western culture and thought system is based: *modernity*. Modernity and not *modernization* alone. Modernization is a process as well as it is a set of instruments. It is technical, not intellectual. On the contrary, modernity is an intellectual concept, an intellectual approach and position based on criticism, even *criticism of criticism*. In fact, both secularization and democracy are born of modernity. Modernity was also the origin of rupture in Europe at the time of Renaissance. Confusion between these two concepts — modernity and modernization — has already produced many catastrophes. Among intellectuals in Muslim societies, and in some Western circles dealing with the study of development, the dominant tendency is that modernization alone will result in a kind of modernity which creates secular conditions and a secular society. Aeroplanes, railways, IBM, Coca-Cola, and Channel No. 5, do not and cannot create modernity; none of these are able to change the mentality or way of thinking. It is precisely the reason why the Fundamentalists are not at all reluctant themselves to extensively and ostentatiously use modern equipment with the proclaimed intention of demonstrating that Islam is not against science and technology. The only danger that they are afraid and aware of is *communication*. Communication can change ideas and behaviour by opening new horizons. Their fear of the impact of CNN, Internet and the telefax is evident. Desperately, they try to limit — as much as they can — the onslaught of free communication. In Iran, the Fundamentalist Islamist government and parliament declared it illegal to watch foreign television shows. This decision provoked protests in the population, and the government had to give up and cancel the bill concerning satellite TV.

With this background, it is fair to say that in the future, this kind of modernization, which is closely related with communication and exchange of ideas, will challenge the Fundamentalists more intensively. The fear of free communication and free information is in reality the fear of modernity as intellectual criticism. The Fundamentalists are not so much against the 'technical' criticism consisting of, for example, high prices, high inflation rates, or even criticism of the flourishing corruption. Their fear is of the intellectual and basic criticism, the kind of criticism that will question Islam itself, or at least their interpretation of Islam. Modernity has no meaning without basic criticism. In a democratic, pluralist society, anyone can freely contest even the bases of democracy. Because democracy, despite its importance as a form of government, is not the essence of modernity: The spirit of criticism is. Democracy will not survive without political and intellectual criticism. Islam's survival depends on a non-critical spirit. Believing is being unable to tolerate criticism.

Modernity is also directly related to two conditions which are both essential for the realization of modernity. The first is *freedom* of human beings and the second is *differentiation*. The first condition refers to what Charles Taylor formulates as follows: 'The modern subject is self-defining, where on previous views the subject is defined in relation to the cosmic order' (Taylor, 1991: 6). The second condition is connected with the 'process of societal and cultural differentiation and pluralization propelled by and revolving around a series of developmental logic or dynamics which may be located within each of the differentiating spheres' (Rundell, 1987: 2).

To sum up, I have tried in this chapter to demonstrate that freedom of speech is not a goal of religion. The primordial goal of religion is *salvation*, not democratization; therefore, it seems inadequate to ask any religion to provide something that is not a part of its project or of its mission. Religions can coexist within a society which is allocated the freedom of speech for everybody and every confession, if religion abandons its hegemonic ambitions to restore its order by excluding all others. We saw also that while Christianity survived the Renaissance and the movements of the Enlightenment, it was partly because of Reformation and partly by necessity. It had no choice. While, in order to progress, the European renaissance returned to ancient Greek philosophy, the various Muslim tendencies are looking to the Medina model as the perfect and ultimate construction. In this sense, the return to the formative period of Islam is not a point of departure, it is simply a final stage of perfection. Nevertheless, there were some periods in the history of Islam when toleration was relatively high, with dynamic and flourishing intellectual debates, i.e., under Al-Ma'mûn and during the Andalusian epoch. Then, slowly the intervening periods of stagnation began, later followed by Western domination and colonization.

Lastly, I would argue that it is not really Islam which is challenging the West; on the contrary, the idea of modernity (not modernization) is challenging Islam.

Glossary

'adâlat	justice
âdil	just
Ahl al-Kitâb	People of the Book
'Allâma	highly savant
amir	ruler
amr	order
ârâ	opinion
Ayatollah	sign of Allah
Ayatollah Ozma	Great Ayatollah
Bayt al-Hikma	House of Wisdom
dâkhil	internal
Dâr al-Harb	Anti-Islam Universe
Dâr al-Islam	Universe of Islam
Erâdeh-e azali	Primal Will
farmân	order
forû'	subsidiary principles
Ghaybat al-Kubra	Great Occultation
halal	licit
haqq-e nezârat	powers of supervision
haram	illicit
hijir	Islamic calendar
Hizb al-Shaytân	Party of Satan
Hujjat ul-Islam	Proof of Islam
hukm	order
hukma al-quadâ	judiciary verdict
ijâza	authorization
ijmâ'	consensus
intizâr	waiting
islâh	reform
istiftâ	asking for a *fatwa*
Jâhilliya	City of Ignorance
khârij	external
kitmân	dissimulation
khûn	blood

Kuffâr	Non-Believers
kufr	infidelity
ma'mur	executive of orders
maktab-e khûn va shahâdat	doctrine of blood and martyr-dom
maktab-e shahâdat	cult of martyrdom
Marja'-e Taqlid	Source of Emulation
Marj'a Koll-e Taqlid	Supreme Source of Emulation
melli	nationalist
mirzâ	script
mu'âd	doomsday
muddarris	teacher in Islamic law
mufti	fatwa-giver
mujtahid	doctor of theology
mulâzim	one who is assiduous, constant in attendance
mullâ	literal
Mu'minûn	Sincere Believers
Munafiqûn	Hypocrites
Murtaddûn	Apostates
Mushrikûn	Polytheists
Muslimûn	Formal Believers
mustafti	fatwa caller
nubuwwat	prophecy of Mohammad
payâm	message
qâdi	judge
qânûn	law or act of law
qiyâs	analogy
ra'y	opinion
Rahbar-e Enqelâb	Leader of Revolution
Râshidûn	Rightly Guided Vicars
ridda	apostasy
sahn	public lecturing
shahâda	martyrdom
shar'	law or act of law
shari'a	Islamic law
sunna	the Prophet's verbal expression besides his practical expression
tabrik	felicitations
tama'nina	inner peace

taqiyya	dissimulation of political/ religious opinion
taqlid	following
tawhid	unity of God
tchupân	shepherd
Velâyat-e Faqih	Governance of Jurisconsult
Velâyat-e motlaqa-ye Faqih	*Absolute* Governance of Jurisconsult
zendeh bâd!	long live!

Notes

1. During 1986-88, France, and especially Paris, witnessed several serious terrorist actions against innocent people in the streets. Many were killed or injured as victims of these actions. It became clear that the Iranian authorities (especially one employee of the Iranian embassy named Gorji) were behind these actions. The French government with the Interior Minister Charles Pasqua, as the central figure, successfully negotiated an agreement with the Tehran government. One part of the agreement was to hush up the accusations against Gorji, the presumed *chief of activities* at the Iranian embassy in Paris. Despite the evidence of his involvement in planning the terrorist actions, Gorji was safely returned to Iran.

2. Ayatollah Khomeini banned the practice of *taqiyya* in a telegram he sent to his peers in Tehran. 'The practice of *taqiyya*', he proclaimed, 'is henceforth unlawful, and enunciation of the verities is obligatory. So be it!' I should point out that Khomeini is the only Ayatollah so far to have banned the practice of *taqiyya*. The text of the telegram, presented by S.H. Rowhâni in his book, gives no date, but the most plausible date is late March 1963. Cf. Seyyed Hamid Rowhâni, *Nehzat-e Emâm Khomeini*, the first volume of which was published before the Revolution. This volume makes no mention of the place and date of publication. The copy in our possession has an inscription by Rowhâni (to someone other than the author of these lines) dated Paris, December 8, 1978, vol. 1, pp. 372-73.

3. For their part, the Fadâ'iyân-e published their programme entitled 'Guide to the Verities', *Ketâb-e Râhnamây-e Haqâyeq* in 1950. This guide is in no way a political discourse, but a series of practical measures which an ideal Islamic state should carry out. A summary of this Guide (in French) is found in an article by Yann Richard (see note 6). For the English version cf. Adele K. Ferdows, 'Religion and Iranian Nationalism: The Study of the Fadayan-e Islam'. PhD thesis, Indiana University, 1967.

4. On the Ulama in general, and the 1906 Constitution, cf., M. Mozaffari, *Pouvoir Shî'ite: Théorie et Evolution*, Paris: L'Harmattan, 1998.

5. Khomeini's reserve on this point could be explained by the fact that at the time he did not himself occupy an important position in the Shi'a hierarchy; or perhaps he did not consider this a propitious moment for calling directly for Ulama power.

6. Yann, Richard, 'L'organisation des Fadâ'iyân-e Eslâm' in Olivier Carré and Paul Dumont (eds.), *Radicalismes islamiques*, Paris, l'Harmattan, 1985, p. 74. Cf. also Farhad Kazemi, 'The Fadâ'iyan-e Islam: fanaticism, Politics and Terror, in Said Amir Arjomand (ed.), *From Nationalism to Revolutionary Islam*. New York: State University of New York Press, 1984.

7. Ibid. p. 25.

8. Jomhuri Eslâmi (Journal de), January 16, 1985.

9. This *fatwa* was delivered by Ayatollah Amini, residing in Iraq.

10. From this date onward, very close relations developed between the Palestinians and the Shi'a Islamists, even to the point of political and military cooperation. Thus, in the 1960s, groups of young Islamists, including the son of Ayatollah Montazeri (the designated successor of Khomeini) trained in Palestinian camps. From his exile in Iraq, Khomeini in turn authorized the payment of a portion of the religious taxes (*zakât*) as well as charitable donations (*sadaqât*) to the Palestinians. It is interesting that in the original version of this *fatwa* (in Persian) Khomeini does not use the term 'Palestinian,' but prefers the expression '*mudâfi'in*' (defenders). In the Arab version, the term used is *mudâfi'in-e bayzatal Eslâm* (defenders of the cause of Islam). Cf. Rowhâni, op. cit. (Tehran 1986), vol. 2, pp. 387-91 and 886 (Documents, nos. 156 and 157).

11. It should be added that some Ulama were themselves owners of large landed properties. According to available statistics, in 1946 there were three times more clerical families in the province of Isfahan owning such properties than families of other social strata. Cf. Shahrokh Akhavi, *Religion and Politics in Contemporary Iran*, New York: State University of New York, 1980, pp. 96-97.

12. After Burujerdi's death, a group of experts got together to decide who would fill the vacancy of the *marja-iyyat-e kol*. This group, consisting mainly of pro-Khomeini people (including Mehdi Bazargan, Ayatollah Motahhari, and Ayatollah Beheshti), proposed the establishment of a collegial presidency instead of an individual presidency, which prior to Burujerdi's death had been the usual form of leadership of the Imâmite community. Actually, by resorting to this strategem, the team of experts was trying to prevent, or at least to delay any Ayatollah but Khomeini from achieving the dignity of the *marja-iyyat-e kol*.

13. That is why the Shah, in his telegrams and overtures, chose to favour Ayatollah Mohsen Hakîm, who was a native and resident of Iraq.
14. Women's right to vote was finally established on June 1, 1964, i.e. one year after the June 5 insurrection.
15. The five other principles were nationalization of timber resources, sale of shares in state enterprises, profit sharing with workers, reform of the electoral law, and finally establishment of the Army of Knowledge.
16. Rowhâni, *op. cit.*, vol. 1, p. 348.
17. *'Ashurâ* is the day commemorating the assassination of Husayn, the third Shi'a Imâm at Karbalâ on October 10, 680.
18. The text of Khomeini's speech is reproduced in Rowhâni, *op. cit.*, vol. 1, pp. 716-26.
19. Seyyed Javâd Madani, *Târikh-e Siyâsiy-e Moâser-e Iran*, Tehran, 1984, p. 101.
20. There is as yet no precise information on the composition of this committee. All that is known is that Mehdi 'Araqi and Habibollah 'Askar Owlâdi (bazar merchants) are among its members. Both later played an important political role in the post-revolutionary period.
21. The Ayatollahs Motahari, Beheshti, Anvâri and Mowlâ'i were among the members of this Council. Cf. Madani, *op. cit.*, p. 101, note 2.
22. The *fatwa* authorizing Mansour's assassination was delivered by Ayatollah Milâni, resident of Mashhad. Cf. Madani, *op. cit.*, p. 103, note 2.
23. The four persons executed were Mohammad Bokhârâ'i, Sâdeq Amâni, Reza Harandi, and Mortaza Nik-Nejâd. Six other persons (Mehdi 'Arâqi, Hâshem Amâni, Habibollah 'Askar, Owlâdi (the future Minister of Commerce and candidate for the Presidency of the Islamic Republic), 'Abbâs Modarresi Fard, Abolfazi Heydar, and Mohammad taqi Kalafchi, were sentenced to life imprisonment. Cf. Rowhâni, *op. cit.*, vol. 1, p. 817.
24. On relations between Sa'idi and Khomeini, as well as on SAVAK's secret reports on Sa'idi, see Rowhâni, *op. cit.*, vol. 2, pp. 963-87, and Madani, *op. cit.*, p. 218, note 2.
25. Madani (*op. cit.*, p. 224) mentions the existence of several other minor Islamist groups, namely *Ummat-e Vâhedah, Towhid, Falaq, Fallâh, Badr, Mowaheddin, Saff* and *Msourun*. Madani is silent on the nature of the activities of these groups.
26. On the *Mojahedi-e Khalq*, see e.g., Mozaffari, *Authority in Islam: From Muhammad to Khomeini*, New York: M.E. Sharpe, Inc., 1987, pp. 86-92.
27. This fire was initially attributed to SAVAK. It must be said that such a hypothesis seems most unlikely. At the time, the Shah was in the midst of a veritable crisis and thus had no interest in stirring up the

hatred of the populace against his regime, and even less to have hundreds of people burned to death inside a cinema. Furthermore, the Shah knew that he had cancer and had for all practical purposes assumed a defensive, if not passive, attitude with regard to the events of summer 1978. His foreign visitors 'were surprised by the extraordinary passive and introspective behaviour of the sovereign who seemed to have withdrawn into himself.' Michael Ledeen and William Lewis, *Débacle: l'échec américain en Iran*. Paris: Michel Albin. 1981, p. 142. Consequently, the only group that could objectively have benefitted from the extraordinary impact this criminal tragedy had on the world and Iranian public opinion was incontestibly the Islamists. The Abol-Hasan Bani Sadr's periodical *Enqelab-e Eslâmi* (in exile) published a dossier demonstrating that the Islamists were to blame for this fire. The author does not have access to this dossier.

28. The following leaders all came from Bazari backgrounds: Sa'id Mohsen, Hanif-Nejad, Badi' Zadegan for the *Mojahidin* and the brothers Ahmadzadeh and Pouyan for the *Cherikha*.

29. Regarding the Qajar, see Ann K.S. Lambton entitled *Qajar Persia*, London: I.B. Tauris, 1987.

30. In addition to the Précis (Rasâ'il, singl. Risâla) which each doctor (*mujtahid*) must furnish to his disciples and which contains a number of rules regulating the diverse aspects of daily life including trade, Shi'a business law is based on two fundamental collections, namely *Sharâyi' ul-Eslâm* (Law of Islam) by Mohaqqiq Hilli (13th century) and Sheykh Ansari (19th century) entitled *Kitab ul-Makâsib* (Book of Professions).

31. The major work containing popular ethical rules of Shi'asm is *Holliyat ul-Muttaqin* (Embellishment of the virtures) and was written in the 16th century by Mohammad Bâqir Majlesi. This book contains practically everything which is relevant to the morality of a good Shi'a. After the Islamic Revolution, this book was published according to oral accounts in hundreds of thousands of copies, moreover in a country where illiteracy is still a social evil.

32. One of the best known businessmen in the Tehran Bazar (Hâj Mohammad Shânachi) admitted that for many years he avoided paying taxes and revenues to the state. He gave religious reasons to justify his refusal to pay. Interview in Paris in February 1987.

33. In 1975, the rural Iranian population was about 18.5 million (about 55% of the country's total population). The rural population was spread over 66,000 villages. About 14 million of this population lived in 18,000 villages with more than 250 inhabitants. The rest, i.e., 4.5 million, lived in the 48,000 villages with a population below 250

inhabitants. Moreover, only 16 million hectares of land (8% of the area of the country) are arable, and almost half of this is not worked (Afshar, 1985: 60).

34. There are specific examples where certain well-known businessmen have in fact acquired official positions. Thus, in the 1880s, Mirza Mohammad Rahim Khân, son of Mohammad Ja'far Nazim ul-Tujjâr, was appointed Treasurer of the local government. Mashhad Malek ul-Tujjâr became the official representative of the governorship of Khorasan. Hâj Mohammad Ali Raïs ul-Tujjâr had the position of personal adviser to the influential Shaykh de Mohammara (presently Khorramshahar). In the southern provinces, Moïn ul-Tujjâr played an important role in the administration of the governorship of Lark, Hingam, Minab, Khamir and Hormoz. At Boushir, Malek ul-Tujjâr was the governor of the harbours of the Persian Gulf. In addition, a number of important businessmen were appointed as representatives of the minister of foreign affairs (Floor 1976: 111-12).

35. Reza Shah built 1,394 km of railways using the revenues from supplementary taxes on tea and sugar, two products of mass consumption in Iran.

36. On Ayatollah Kashani, see Yann Richard: 'Ayatollah Kashani: Precursor of the Islamic Republic?' in Nikkie R. Keddie (ed.), *Religion and politics in Iran*. Yale University Press, 1983.

37. Speech given by the Shah in the Holy City of Qom on the eve of the referendum on January 27, 1963. An excerpt from this discourse is found in Rowhani, *Nehzat-e Emâm Khomeini*, t. 1, pp. 263-65.

38. Before the Revolution of 1979, $1 = ca. 70 rials. After the Revolution, $1 = ca. 5000 rials.

39. Among the most prominent representatives of this bourgeoisie are the families Farmanfarmaiyan, Rezai, Khayyami, Sabet Pasal, Lajevardi, Barkhordar, Iravani, Elqanian, Khosrowshahi, Wahhabzadeh, Akhavan, Namazi, Azod, Yazdani, and Arjomand.

40. According to Bani Sadr, to whom Ayatollah Khomeini entrusted his portefeuille as soon as he arrived in Paris, Khomeini 'came to Paris with a few tens of thousands of French francs and left with several million'. Interview at Versailles, June 16, 1988.

41. A detailed list of the names and references of the founders of the Islamic Bank was published by the journal *Keyhan* on Ordibehesht 25, 1358 (spring, 1979).

42. Speech by Ezzatullah Sahabi to parliament on Farvadin 17, 1360 (spring, 1981).

43. *Keyhan*, 20 Ordibehesht 1361 (April 10, 1983).

44. Central Bank of Iran (Statistics) in Bahram Tehrani (1986: 393).

45. Ibid: 399.
46. *Keyhan*, 25 Mordad 1362 (August 16, 1983).
47. *Jomhuri Islami*, September 29, 1984.
48. For example, in the summer of 1988, some 65,000 television sets, 20,000 carpets (industrial), and 20,000 refrigerators were discovered. (Journal *Resalat*, July 19, 1988). Similarly, a business establishment with the name 'de Verdad' officially purchased 3,000 Renaults from the state corporation Saypa and sold them at a price several times higher on the parallel market. Several thousand tons of wheat were also hoarded (illegally) by the private sector and then resold on the same market at unreasonably high prices. Another private company was able, with the help of certain persons in the Pasdaran army, to import spare parts to resell on the parallel markets. Journal *Etellaat*, August 15, 1988.
49. To give an example of the speculative nature of the parallel market, suffice it to point out that while the American dollar had the official exchange rate of 70 rials in July 1988, it was 1,520 rials, i.e., more than 21 times higher on the parallel market!
50. After a transitional period, a Bazari named Khamoushi and another named Karimi Nouri assumed the head of administration of the FD. The FD was then placed under the Prime Minister after a series of scandals involving speculation with foundation resources. But by order of Khomeini, the resources of the FD are kept separate from those of the state. Journal *Resalat*, July 19, 1988.
51. A list of buyers (all from the Bazar) of these goods is found in Bahram Tehrani (1986, chapter 6).
52. Among these former Bazaris who later became partners of the Pahlavis, we will mention the Kashani, the Wahhabzadeh, the Khosrowshahi, the Akhavan, etc.

References

Abrahamian, Ervard 1982. *Iran between Two Revolutions*. Princeton, NJ: Princeton University Press.

Abukhalil, As'ad 1995. Article on *Islâh* in *The Oxford Encyclopedia of the Modern Islamic World*, vol. 2. New York and Oxford: Oxford University Press.

Afshari, Mohammed Reza 1983. 'The Pishivaran and Merchants in Precapitalist Iranian Society'. *International Journal of Middle East Studies*, vol. 15, no. 1, February, 133-55.

American Heritage Dictionary, The.

Appignanesi/Maitland 1989. *The Rushdie File*. London: Fourth Estate.

Arabies, Le Mensuel du Monde Arabe, Paris.

Arendt, Hannah 1969. *On Violence*. London: Penguin.

Aristotle. 1926. *The 'Art' of Rhethoric*, trans. by John Henry Freese, Loeb Classical Library.

Aristotle. 1968. *The Politics*. Trans. by Ernest Barker, Oxford: Clarendon.

Ashraf, Ahmad & Hekmat 1981. 'Merchants and Artisans and the Developmental Processes of Ninetheenth Century Iran', in Abraham L. Udovitch (ed.), *The Islamic Middle-East: 700-1900*. Princeton, NJ: Darwin Press, 725-49.

Barker, Ernest 1968. *The Politics*. Trans. by Ernest Barker, Oxford: Clarendon.

Bashiriyeh, Hossein 1984. *The State and Revolution in Iran*. London: Croom Helm.

Bazargan, Mehdi, et al. 1963. *Marja'iyyat Va Rowhâniyyat*. Tehran: Enteshâr.

Behdad, Sohrab 1988. 'Foreign Exchange Gap. Structural Constraints and the Political Economy of Exchange Rate Determination in Iran'. *International Journal of Middle East Studies*, vol. 20, no. 1, February, 1-21.

Behrooz, Maziar 1991. 'Factionalism in Iran under Khomeini', in *Middle Eastern Studies*, vol. 27, no. 4, October.

Beiner, Ronald and William J. Booth (eds.) 1993. *Kant and Political Philosophy: The Contemporary Legacy*. London: Yale University Press.

Bell, Daniel 1977. 'The return of the sacred? The argument on the future of religion'. *British Journal of Sociology*, vol. 28, no. 4, December.

Calmard, Jean 1995. 'Ayatollah'. *The Oxford Encyclopedia of the Modern Islamic World*, vol. 1. New York & Oxford: Oxford University Press.

Chater, Khalifa 1994. 'A Rereading of Islamic Texts in the Maghreb in the Nineteenth and Early Twentieth Centuries' in John Ruedy (ed.), *Islamic and Secularism in North Africa*. New York: St. Martin's Press.

Commins, David 1994. In Ali Rahnema (ed.), *Pioneers of Islamic Revival*. London: Zed Books.

Corbin, Henri 1963/64. 'Au Pays de l'Imâm Caché' in *Eranos Jahrbuch XXXII*, 31-87.

Dahl, Robert A. 1975. 'Governments and Political Opposition', in Greenstein & Polsby (eds.), *Macropolitical Theory*, vol. 3. Reading, Mass.: Addison-Wesley, 115-61.

Dahrendorf, Ralf 1959. *Class and Class Conflict in Industrial Society*. Stanford, CA: Stanford University Press.

Dallal, Ahmad S. 1995. 'Fatwa : Process and Function' in *The Oxford Encyclopedia of the Modern Islamic World*, vol. 2. New York & Oxford: Oxford University Press, 8-17.

Donohue, John J. & Esposito, John L. 1982. *Islam in Transition*. New York & Oxford: Oxford University Press.

Dictionnaire Théologique Catholique.

Dollard, John (in collaboration with Clellan S. Ford), 1939. *Frustration and Aggression*. New Haven, Conn.: Yale University Press.

Easton, David 1959. *The Political System*. New York: Knopf.

Encyclopedia Britannica.

Faghfoory, Mohammad H. 1987. 'The Ulama-State Relations in Iran: 1921-1924'. *International Journal of Middle East Studies*, vol. 19, no. 1, February, 413-32.

Ferdows, Adele K. 1967. 'Religion and Iranian Nationalism: The Study of the Fadayan-e Islam'. PhD thesis, Indiana University.

Floor, Willem M. 1976. 'The Merchants (tujjâr) in Qâjâr Iran'. *Zeitschrift der Deutschen Morgenländische Gesellschaft*, vol. 126, no. 1, 101-35.

Floor, Willem M. 1984. *Industrialization in Iran: 1900-1941*. Durham: University of Durham.

Fromm, Erich 1973/74. *The Anatomy of Human Destructiveness*. London: Jonathan Cape.

Gersmann, Gudrun.1993, 'Ideal and Reality: The French Revolution and the Debate on the Freedom of the Press', in Schmale, Wolfgang (ed.), *Human Rights And Cultural Diversity*. Goldbach: Keip Publishing, 198-214.

George, Alexander L. 1969. 'The Operational Code: A Neglected Approach to the Study of Political Leaders and Decision-Making'. *International Studies Quarterly*, vol. 13, no. 2, June.

George, Alexander L. & William E. Simons, 1994. *The Limits of Coercive Diplomacy*. Boulder: Westview.

Ghazâli, Abu Hâmid Al. *Kitâb Ihyâ 'ulûm al-dîn*. Cairo: Othmâniyya, 1352*/1933, (4 vols.).

Gilbar, Gad G. 1978. 'Persian Agriculture in the Late Qâjâr Period, 1860-1906'. *Asian and African Studies*, vol. 12, no. 1. March, London, 312-65.

Gilbar, Gad G. 1986. 'The Opening up of Qâjâr Iran: Some Economic and Social Aspects'. *Bulletin of School of Oriental and Africal Studies*, vol. 49, no. 1, 76-89.

Golpayegani, Mohammad Reza 'Ayatollah' 1984. *Tawzih al-Masâ'il*, Qum, Dâr al-Qur'ân.

Greenfield, J. 1906. 'Das Handesrecht, einschliesslich das Obligationen — und Pfandrechtes, das Urkundenrecht, Konkursrecht und das Fremdenrecht von Persien'. *Die Handelsgesetze des Erdballs*, no. 6, 26, Berlin.

Gurr, Ted Robert 1971. *Why Men Rebel*. Princeton N.J.: Princeton University Press.

Hilli, Mohaqqiq 1360*/1981. *Sharâyi' ul-Eslâm*. Tehran: Tehran University Press.

Hourani, Albert 1991. *A History of the Arab Peoples*. London: Faber & Faber.

Huntington, Samuel 1993. 'The Clash of Civilizations'. *Foreign Affairs*, Summer, 22-49.

Ibn Taymiyya 1386*/1965. *Majmû' fatâwi Shaykh ul-Islâm*. Saudi Arabian.

Iran Almanac 1975.

Izutsu, Toshiba 1965, *The Concept of Belief in Islamic Theology*. Yokohama: Yurindo Publishing Co.

Jayyusi, Salma Khadra (ed.) 1994. *The Legacy of Muslim Spain*. E.J. Brill.

Kant, Immanuel 1795. *Zum ewigen Frieden: ein philosophischer Entwurf*. Königsberg.

Kant, Immanuel 1983. 'What is Enlightenment?' in Beck, Lewis White (ed.), *Kant in History*. Indianapolis: Bobbs-Merrill.

Kazemi, Farhad 1984. 'The Fada'iyan-e Islam: fanaticism, Politics and Terror', in Said Amir Arjomand (ed.), *From Nationalism to Revolutionary Islam*. New York: State University of New York Press.

Khadduri, Majid 1966. *The Islamic Law of Nations. Shaybani's Sivar*. Baltimore: John Hopkins University Press.

Khomeini, R. (No date). *Tawzih al-Masâ'il*. (no place).

Khomeini, R. 1943 (?). *Kashf al-Asrâr*. Tehran.

Khomeini, R. 1971. *Hukumat-e Eslâmi* (Islamic Governance), Najaf.

Khomeini, R. 1979. *Pour un gouvernement Islamique*. Trans. by M. Kotobi, B. Simon and Ozra Banisadr, Paris: Fayolle.

Koran, The 1983. Trans. by Arthur J. Arberry, London: Oxford University Press.

Lambton, A.K.S. 1964. 'A Reconsideration of the position of the Marja' Taqlid on the Religious Institution'. *Studia Islamica*, XX, 115-35.

Lambton, A.K.S. 1965. 'The Tobacco Régie: Prelude to Revolution'. *Studia Islamica*, XXII.

Lambton, A.K.S. 1987. *Qajar Persia*. London: I.B. Tauris.

Laoust, Henri 1970. *La Politique de Gazâli*. Paris: Paul Geuthner.

Lautenschlager, Wolfgang 1986. 'The Effects on Overvalued Exchange Rate on the Iranian Economy, 1979-84'. *International Journal of Middle East Studies*, vol. 18, no. 1, February, 31-52.

Ledeen, Michael and William Lewis 1981. *Débacle: l'échec américain en Iran*. Paris: Albin Michel. (Original title, *Debacle: The American Failure in Iran*, New York: Alfred A. Knopf.)

Leits, Nathan 1953. *A Study of Bolshevism*. Illinois: The Free Press.

Levy, Leonard W. 1993. *Blasphemy*. New York: Alfred A. Knopf.

Lewis, Bernard 1985. *The Assassins*. London: Al Saqi.

Linz, Juan J. 1975. 'Totalitarian and Authoritarian Regimes', in Greenstein & Polsby (eds.), *Macropolitical Theory*, vol. 3. Reading, Mass.: Addison-Wesley, 175-353.

Looney, Robert E. 1986. 'Origins of Pre-revolutionary Iran's Development Strategy'. *Middle Eastern Studies*, vol. 22, no. 1, January, 104-19.

MacMillan, John 1994. 'A Kantian Protest Against the Peculiar Discourse of Inter-Liberal State Peace' in *Millennium*, vol. 24, no. 3, 549-62.

Madani, Sayyed Javâd 1984. *Târikh-e Siyâsiy-e Moâser-e Iran*. Tehran.

Maghreb Review, The, vol. 16, nos. 1-2, 109-24.

Marty, Martin E. and R. Scott Appleby, 1991-95. *Fundamentalism*. Chicago & London: University of Chicago Press.

Massignon, Louis and Louis Gardet. *Encyclopedia of Islam*. 101.

Mawardi, Ali Ibn Mohammad ibn Habib 1982. *Al-Ahkâmul Sultâniyya*. Beirut: Dâr ul-Kutubul-'Ilmiyya.

Midlarsky, Manus I. 1975. *On War: Political Violence in the International System*. London: Free Press.

Moin, Baqer. 1994. 'Khomeini's Search for Perfection' in Ali Rahnema (ed.), *Pioneers of Islamic Revival*. London: Zed Books.

Momayezi, Nasser 1986. 'Economic Correlates of Political Violence: The Case of Iran'. *Middle East Journal*, vol. 40, no. 1, 66-81.

Montesquieu 1949. *Oeuvres Complètes*, vol. 1. Paris: Gallimard.

Moussali, Ahmad S. 1994. 'Hasan al-Turabi's Islamist Discourse on democracy and *Shura*'. *Middle Eastern Studies*, vol. 30, no. 1., January.

Mozaffari, Mehdi 1978. *l'IRAN*. Paris: Librarie Générale de Droit et de Jurisprudence.

Mozaffari, Mehdi 1981. *Revolutionen i Iran*. Copenhagen: Danish Institute for International Affairs.

Mozaffari, Mehdi 1984. 'Typologie des Sources des Conflits au Moyen-Orient', in *Tiers-Monde: Diplomatie et Stratégie*. Paris: Economica, 45-74.

Mozaffari, Mehdi 1987. *Authority in Islam: From Mohammad to Khomeini*. New York: M.E. Sharpe, Inc.

Mozaffari, Mehdi 1995. 'Rushdie Affair' in *The Oxford Encyclopedia of the Modern Islamic World*, vol. 3. New York & Oxford: Oxford University Press, 443-45.

Mozaffari, Mehdi 1996. 'Islamism in Algeria and Iran' in A.S. Sidahmed and A. Ehteshami (eds.), *Islamic Fundamentalism*. Boulder: Westview.

Mozaffari, Mehdi 1998. *Pouvoir Shî'ite: Théorie et Evolution*. Paris: L'Harmattan.

Mufid, Abu Nu'mân (no date). *Al-Irshâd*. No place of publication.

New Sharther Oxford Dictionary, The. 1993.

Oberschall, Anthony 1973. *Social Conflict and Social Movements*. Englewood Cliffs, NJ: Prentice-Hall.

Paine, Thomas 1987. *Rights of Man*. New York: Prometheus Books.

Pesaran, M. Hashem. 1985. 'Economic Development and Revolutionary Upheavals', in Halek Afshar, *A Revolution in Turmoil*. London: Macmillan, 15-50

Poulantzas, Nicos 1978. *L'État, le Pouvoir, le Socialisme*. Paris: Presses Universitaires de France.

Qumi, Shaykh Abbas, 1963. *Mafâtih ul-Janân* (Keys of Paradise). Tehran: Elmi.

Rawls, John 1971. *A Theory of Justice*. Cambridge, Mass.: Harvard University Press.

Rawls, John 1993. *Political Liberalism*. New York: Colombia University Press.

Remer, Gary 1996. *Humanism and the Rhetoric of Toleration*. Pennsylvania: Pennsylvania State University Press.

Repp, R.C. 1986. *The Müfti of Istanbul: A Study in the Development of the Ottoman Learned Hierarchy*. London: Ithaca Press.

Richard, Yann 1983. 'Ayatollah Kashani: Precursor of the Islamic Republic?' in Nikkie R. Keddie (ed.), *Religion and politics in Iran*. Yale University Press.

Richard, Yann 1985. 'L'organisation des Fadâ'iyân-e Eslâm' in Olivier Carré and Paul Dumont (eds.), *Radicalismes islamiques*, Paris: l'Harmattan.

Rowhâni, Sayyed Hamid (No year). *Nehzat-e Emâm Khomeini*. (Imam. Khomeini's Movement. No place or publisher given. The first volume of this book was published before the Islamic Revolution and the second volume after the Revolution).

Rundell, John F. 1987. *Origins of Modernity*. Oxford: Polity Press.

Rushdie, Salman 1988. *The Satanic Verses*. London: Viking.

Sahifah-e Nur, 1991-92. Collection of Imâm Khomeini's Guidance Outlines (in Persian), vol. 21. Tehran: Sâzmân-e Madârek-e Farhangui-e Eslâmi.

Shaji'i, Zahra 1966. *Namâyandegân-e Majlisse Shorâye Melli*, (Study of the Members of Parliament). Tehran: Tehran University Press.

Shourie, Arun 1995. *The World of Fatwas*. New Delhi: ASA.

Skocpol, Theda 1979/84. *States & Social Revolutions*. Cambridge: Cambridge University Press.

Taylor, Charles 1991. *Hegel*. Cambridge: Cambridge University Press.

Tibbi, Bassem 1995. 'Security and International Morality: Islam and the

Secular Concept of Human Rights'. Niels Barfoed and Anders Jerichow (eds.) Danish Pen.

Tilly, Charles 1975. 'Revolution and Collective Violence' in F.I. Greenstein and N.W. Polsby (eds.), *Macropolitical Theory*, vol. 3. Reading: Addison-Wesley, 483-555.

Tocqueville, Alexis de 1990. *Democracy in America*. Phillip Bradley (ed.), vol. II, New York: Vintage Classics.

Torrey, Charles C. 1892. *The Commercial-Theological Terms in the Koran*. Leyden: Brill.

Tunkâbuni, Mirza M. (no date). *Qisas ul*-Ulama. Tehran: Elmiyya.

Tyan, Emile 1960. *Histoire de l'Organisation Judiciaire en Pays d'Islam*. Leiden: Brill.

Van Ess, Joseph 1984. *Une lecture à rebours de l'Histoire du Mu'tazilisme*. Paris: Geutner.

Vernet, Juan 1978/85. *Ce que la Culture doit aux Arabes d'Espagne*. French translation. Paris: Sindbad. (Original title, *La Cultura hispanoárabe en Oriente y Occidente*).

Volkan, Vamik D. 1994. *The Need to Have Enemies and Allies*. Northvalw, New Jersey: Janson Aranson.

Walsh, J.R. (1960-). *Encyclopedia of Islam*, new edition, vol. 3, Leiden: Brill, 866-67.

Wilkinson, Paul; Alexander Yonah & David Carlton (eds). 1979. *Terrorism: Theory and Practice*. Boulder: Westview.

Wilkinson, David 1980. *Deadly Quarrels: Lewis F. Richardson and the Statistical Study of Wars*. Berkeley: University of California Press.

Wogler, J. 1989. 'Perspectives on the Foreign Policy System: Psychological Approches', in Michael Clarke & Brian White (eds.), *Understanding Foreign Policy*. England: Edward Elgar.

Wogler, J. 1989. 'Perspectives on the Foreign Policy System: Psychological Approaches', in Michael Clarke & Brian White (eds.), *Understanding Foreign Policy*. England: Edward Elgar.

Zebiri, Katharine P. 1991, 'The Fatwas of Mahmud Shaltut (1893-1963)'.

*   Anno Hejirae

Index